PRUNING
How-To Guide for Gardeners

by Robert L. Stebbins
and Michael MacCaskey

Illustrations by Joan Frain, Roy Jones
and Robert L. Stebbins
Photography by Michael Landis
and William C. Aplin
Additional photography by Derek Fell
and Horticultural Photography

HPBooks

Publishers: Bill and Helen Fisher
Executive Editor: Rick Bailey
Editorial Director: Randy Summerlin
Editor: Larry E. Wood
Art Director: Don Burton
Book Design: Leslie Sinclair

For Horticultural Publishing Inc.

Richard Ray, President
Kathleen S. Parker, Production Editor
Lance Walheim, Associate Editor
Michael Landis, Photographer
William C. Aplin, Photographer
Roy Jones, Illustrator

Acknowledgments

Dan Blair, M.F. Blair Tree Experts, Mountain View, Calif.
Robert Cowden, Horticulturalist, Walnut Creek, Calif.
W. B. Davis, Environmental Horticultural Specialist,
University of California, Cooperative Extension Service,
Davis, Calif.
Bob Evans, Bob's Tree Service, Palo Alto, Calif.
W. Douglas Hamilton, Horticultural Advisor, University of
California, Cooperative Extension Service, Alameda, Calif.
R. W. Harris, Professor, University of California,
Department of Environmental Horticulture, Davis, Calif.
A. M. McCain, Plant Pathologist, University of California,
Cooperative Extension Service, Berkeley, Calif.
Steve's Hardware, St. Helena, Calif.

About the Authors

Robert L. Stebbins is a horticultural specialist with the
Cooperative Extension Service at Oregon State University.
Over the last 20 years he has authored hundreds of
information bulletins and papers on horticultural subjects.
Stebbins is an acknowledged expert on the proper pruning of
plants. He is coauthor of the HPBook, *Western Fruit, Berries
and Nuts: How To Select, Grow and Enjoy.*

Michael MacCaskey has been a horticultural consultant for
the last 10 years. He holds a degree in ornamental
horticulture from California State Polytechnic University,
San Luis Obispo. MacCaskey is author of the HPBook,
Lawns and Ground Covers: How To Select, Grow and Enjoy,
and coauthor of the HPBook, *Roses: How To Select, Grow and
Enjoy.* He has written and contributed to 16 other successful
gardening books.

About the Illustrators

Joan Frain is a professional free-lance botanical illustrator
living in Exton, PA. She was formerly the staff illustrator at
Longwood Gardens in Pennsylvania. Frain has provided
beautifully detailed botanical illustrations for magazines,
books, the Hunt Botanical Library and the Franklin Mint.
She is a member of the Guild of Natural Science Illustrators
and paints watercolors for private collections.

Roy Jones is a professional free-lance designer and illustrator
living in Southern California. His automotive illustrations
have appeared nationally in magazines, books and on
calendars. He has provided horticultural illustrations for
seven other HPBooks.

Published by HPBooks, P.O. Box 5367, Tucson, AZ 85703
602/888-2150

ISBN: 0-89586-188-7
Library of Congress Catalog Card Number: 82-83307
© 1983 Fisher Publishing Inc.
Printed in U.S.A.

CONTENTS

chapter one

The Practice of Pruning

Pruning—Art or Science?

Pruning combines scientific principles of plant structure and growth with an artist's sense of form and texture. Pruning creates attractive, useful plants.

Pruning is an ancient art form, practiced for centuries by both ancient and modern civilizations. It has been developed by gardeners to increase crop yields and create attractive shapes.

For years, gardeners have used their knowledge of how plants grow and respond to outside influences. They combine that knowledge with an artist's eye for pleasing forms. Gardeners have learned that pruning increases production of flowers or fruit and creates pleasing shapes.

Pruning does not involve magic. It does not require a degree in art or *horticulture*. Horticulture is the art or science of growing plants in gardens. Pruning does involve using proven horticultural principles of plant growth and response. It is a simple process with a few basic rules. Observing these rules can help develop an attractive yard or garden. The garden will be filled with plants producing beautiful flowers and fruits.

This beautiful yard requires many hours of hard work to keep plants under control. Semiformal shapes and different textures give variety to the landscape.

Left: Pruning requires manipulating plant growth to make plantings attractive, healthy and productive. This attractive yard contains ornamental trees, shrubs and flowering plants.

This book contains valuable information on how plants grow and respond to pruning. You'll learn how to train ornamental plants and fruit trees to be strong. Strong trees can support a heavy load of fruit. You'll learn how to prune trees and shrubs to create an attractive outdoor environment.

Hundreds of photographs and illustrations show each stage of pruning from start to finish. Step-by-step explanations accompany the photographs and illustrations. You'll learn what tools to use and how to use them properly. The Encyclopedia section starting on page 132 tells how and when to prune hundreds of trees and shrubs.

This book is a pruning guide. Use it to learn the art and science of pruning and to develop practical gardening skills.

It's Your Garden!

The appearance of your garden should reflect your own needs and desires. You select the trees, shrubs and ground covers for your garden. You determine the number of plants, size and planting location.

The health of your plants is your responsibility. The amount of food and water they receive is determined by you. You provide necessary protection from insects, diseases and other natural enemies.

Learn all about the activities in your garden, from planting and early training, to pruning and harvesting. As you learn to control your garden, you'll enjoy it more.

The Purpose of Pruning

CREATIVE PRUNING
The art of pruning can enhance plants in your garden. Trees, shrubs and vines can be beautiful in a natural, unpruned state. If plants grow too large for their space, they shade and crowd out other plants. The garden can begin to look cluttered and small. The landscape becomes unattractive and difficult to maintain. The landscape is no longer art. Pruning can restore order and beauty to a garden, making it an enjoyable place.

As an art form, pruning blends natural and artificial elements into pleasing compositions. Ideally, pruning combines visual appeal and useful functions.

You can create an attractive, interesting garden by pruning trees and shrubs into different sizes and shapes. You can create a visually monotonous landscape by pruning all plants the same size and shape.

The style of pruning used in your garden should reflect the architectural style of your home. This style can be formal or informal.

Formal Styling—Formal pruning style accentuates edges of trees and shrubs. Plants are shaped into

Several different pruning techniques are applied to these plants for various purposes. Most notable here are the beautiful and labor-intensive sheared plants with their geometric formality.

geometric forms, creating a formal atmosphere. Crisp edges, smooth surfaces, regular shapes and uninterrupted lines characterize formal styles. Plantings can be equally spaced and arranged in definite patterns or designs. The formal gardens of England and Italy are excellent examples.

Informal Styling—Pruning that reflects a natural, informal look is emphasized by keeping the natural shapes of the plants. Visual arrangements of plants are varied by using plants of different sizes and textures.

Don't combine contrasting pruning styles in the same landscape. Combining formal and informal pruning styles destroys the unity of composition.

Pruning can improve your landscape by opening new areas to view or the sun. Pruning hedges can develop living screens to block views or provide backgrounds for colorful flower beds.

Pruning usually makes individual plants more attractive, creating accents of color or shape in a garden. This is especially true in plants that depend on large amounts of new growth to produce blooms.

PRACTICAL PRUNING

In addition to styling, pruning has practical application based on proven horticultural methods. Pruning is used to produce trees, shrubs and vines that serve the gardener's needs. Pruning helps supply privacy, shade, straighter timber or more fruit.

Privacy and Protection—Pruning shrubs and hedges can screen unwanted views, reduce noise or create islands of shade or sun. Removing thick undergrowth and brush reduces hazards from brush fires. Pruning tree tops and removing dead limbs prevents injury to people and property from falling limbs.

Production—Proper pruning helps plants produce large, beautiful flowers. Pruning also increases fruit production. Pruning allows the gardener easier access to the ripe fruit for harvesting. Pruned properly, roses and other flowering plants will produce bigger and better flowers for a longer period of time.

Containment—Trees and shrubs may need to be pruned to keep them in their allotted space. Proper pruning keeps tree limbs away from power and utility lines. Root pruning prevents damage to sewer and other underground utility services. Pruning can control invasive, clinging vines and prevent damage to homes or walls. Removing low limbs allows easier access for lawn, garden or flower bed care. Pruning is critically important to grow containerized plants successfully.

Health of Trees and Shrubs—Pruning is vital to plant health. Young trees or shrubs from the nursery will have some roots damaged and lost during transplanting. The top of these plants must be pruned to balance the top limbs with the roots lost during transplanting.

Pruning reduces the effects of drought during periods of low rainfall or low subsoil moisture.

Pruning a tree's interior permits easy penetration of chemical sprays to control insects and diseases. Removal of dead or diseased parts prevents the spread of insects or diseases.

Thinning excess branches can prevent damage from a heavy load of fruit, or ice and snow. Pruning and staking help reduce tree damage in windy locations. Storm-damaged trees and shrubs should be pruned to prevent further damage.

Pruning contributes significantly to overall health of a plant. Pruning is an effective method of removing symptoms of disease and damage to a tree. Pruning is also used to remove causes of the problem if possible. Pruning to keep plants healthy and productive requires knowing how plants grow and respond to pruning.

Careful use of the pruning saw will remove this unwanted branch without damage to the tree.

Summer pruning of these 'Spartan' apples will ensure a plentiful crop of healthy apples.

PRUNING FOR CONTAINMENT

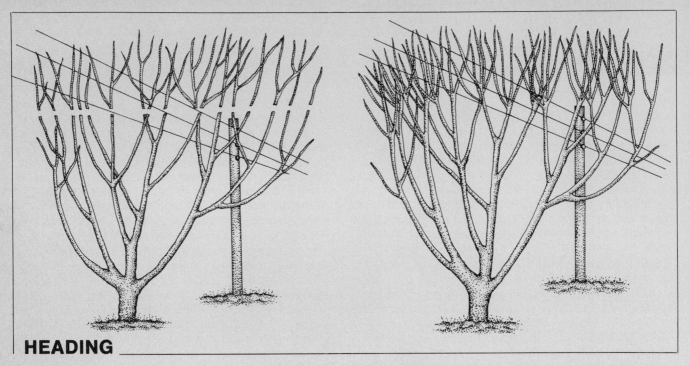

HEADING

Trees are pruned to provide clearance for overhead utility lines. Heading, the removal of all the branches at one level, promotes dense regrowth.

Regrowth after heading results in a tangle of branches even harder to control and can seriously damage overhead utility lines.

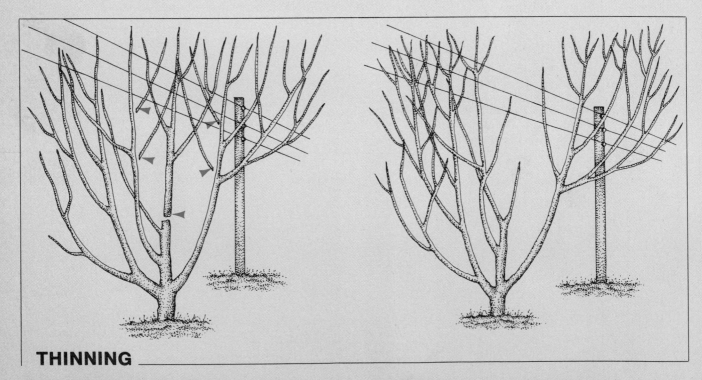

THINNING

Careful selective thinning of uppermost branches creates an easily maintained opening for utility lines.

Regrowth after thinning is controlled and directed away from lines, preventing damage to lines and tree.

Influences on Plant Growth

From the day any plant begins life as a seedling, its growth is influenced by climatic and biological conditions. Climates vary considerably over large and small geographic regions. Differences in climates are determined by amounts of rainfall, sunshine, mountain ranges, longitude and latitude, elevations and bodies of water.

The ability of plants to grow and survive in any particular climate is called *hardiness*. Growth of all plants is influenced by the following conditions:

- Sunlight, Day Length and Temperature.
- Air, Wind, Soil and Water.
- Wildlife and Diseases.
- Genetic Heritage.

Scientists have been studying these influences for centuries. In many cases, their effect on the way some plants function is still not completely understood. Fortunately, the gardener only needs to understand a few basic facts about how plants grow and the influences that affect them.

Sunlight and Day Length—All plants are *phototropic*. This means they respond to light in a positive way. Shrubs, trees and vines all grow toward light.

Sunlight, or solar energy, is essential for plants to live. Leaves are solar collectors. Leaves orient themselves towards the sun. Through a process known as *photosynthesis,* leaves manufacture food for the tree.

Photosynthesis converts energy from the sun into starches and sugars, or food. This food is a basic sugar. When leaves don't receive enough sunlight to manufacture food, they drop from the plant.

Shaded areas of plants tend to become bare of foliage. Shaded parts may fail to bloom, or if they bloom, only a few blooms will set fruit. Pruning helps trees or shrubs arrange foliage to intercept the sunlight.

Day Length, or more correctly the length of night, is the determining factor that tells *deciduous perennial plants* when to develop flowers or drop leaves. Deciduous plants lose all their leaves each year. Perennial plants live from year to year. Studies have produced little knowledge about how day length initiates flowering or leaf-drop. *Evergreen* tropical and subtropical plants are not affected by day length. Evergreen plants don't lose all their leaves each year.

Temperature—Daily and seasonal temperatures have a pronounced effect on plants. Each climate differs in amount and intensity of sunlight, temperature extremes and many other variables. All the factors above have various effects on plants depending upon the season of the year.

Day length and temperature initiate a series of physical and chemical changes in plants each year. These changes are called *acclimation*. The acclimation process helps plants acquire resistance to cold. Acclimation enables plants to survive winter months.

The initial phases of acclimation are started by decreasing day length. Latter phases of acclimation depend on the occurrence of colder temperatures.

Left: The side of a tree that faces a larger tree is dwarfed because the smaller tree is shaded from the sunlight. Center: A tree growing in an open field is more symmetrical because light evenly illuminates all sides. Right: Leaves on plants will always orient themselves toward the dominant light source.

Pruning in late summer can delay acclimation by plants and result in winter-damaged trees and shrubs.

Air and Wind—Atmospheric quality and wind movement have a significant effect on plant growth. If air quality is poor or contains large amounts of pollutants, trees and shrubs may suffer.

Movement of trees by wind stimulates trunks of woody trees to become thicker and more resistant to movement. Constant wind along coastlines produces trees and shrubs that lean away from the wind.

Soil and Water—Water has a profound effect on all plants. Periods of drought can cause trees to lose leaves. The sun can burn exposed limbs and trees can die. Pruning of selected limbs can reduce water requirements. Leaf loss and pruning enables plants to survive periods of drought.

Soil condition is an important influence on plant growth. The texture of the soil can allow roots to grow easily or work harder to anchor plants. Soil quality, or existence of organic matter, nutrients and moisture, is important to trees, shrubs and other plants.

Wildlife and Diseases—Insects, birds and animals are a natural part of a tree's environment. Normal activities of these creatures can both help and damage trees.

Insects or decay fungi may enter wounds caused by deer rubbing against tree trunks. Insects will eat the inside of the tree. Birds, searching for a meal, may eat the insects. Decay fungi can spread inside trees. Decay weakens trees and may leave small cavities. Cavities can provide a nesting place for birds or animals.

Pruning broken branches and repairing damaged bark can prevent entrance of insects or disease. Removing infested parts of trees can prevent spread of insects or disease. Filling cavities closes entrance points for animals and insects.

Genetic Heritage—Every species and variety of plant responds to the environment according to genetic heritage.

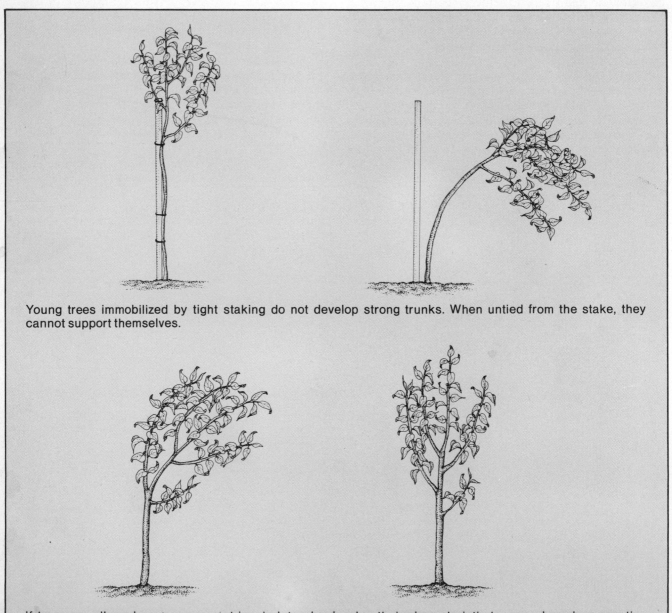

Young trees immobilized by tight staking do not develop strong trunks. When untied from the stake, they cannot support themselves.

If trees are allowed some movement in wind, trunks develop their characteristic taper and produce reactive wood for necessary strength.

This genetic commitment of plants tells them to do many different things. For pruning purposes, genetic programming tells plants to do the following:

- Produce wood for trunks and large limbs.
- Produce and extend shoots with little wood.
- Develop flowers and fruits.

All these commitments can influence plants during different stages of growth. Young trees normally produce lots of wood and shoots. After two or three years, they begin to produce more flowers and small amounts of fruit, while still producing wood. As trees mature, they consistently produce fruit, with little growth of trunk or limbs.

Pruning can sometimes change genetic commitments, but it almost never eliminates these commitments completely.

Growth Habit of a tree refers to the shape in which the tree grows. A tree may grow low to the ground with wide, spreading branches. A tree may be tall and stiff, flexible and willowy, or even weeping. Shape is determined by genetic code.

Growing patterns are controlled to a large extent by the growing shoot tip or leader of plants. The growing shoot tip is sometimes called the *terminal* or *apical bud.* The growing shoot tip plays an important role in the growth of parts of the plant below the tip. In this phenomenon, called *apical dominance,* the growing shoot tip produces a *hormone,* called *auxin.* Auxin is a growth hormone that moves through the tree down toward the earth. Auxin tells shoots to grow up and roots to grow down.

In a way not completely understood by scientists, auxin inhibits or slows growth of most buds formed in *axils* of leaves on the same shoot. The axil is the upper angle formed by a leaf and the branch. Auxin also causes lower shoots to form at wide angles with the main stem or trunk.

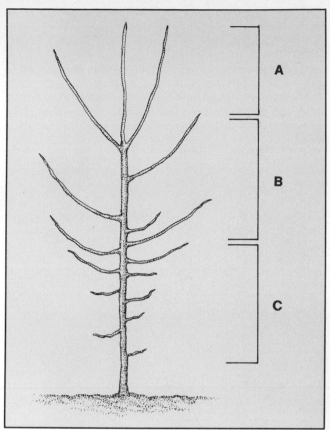

Apical dominance refers to the influence exerted by growing shoot tips on buds and the shoots below them. The hormone that originates in the tips of shoots, section A, migrates toward the ground. The hormone causes shoots in section B to form wide angles with the central axis. Growth of shoots in section C is also suppressed. Knowledge of apical dominance is basic to an understanding of pruning.

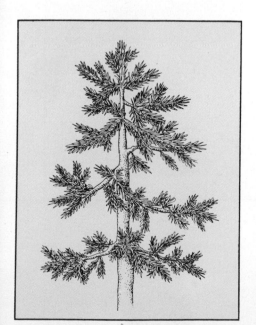

Genetic heritage commits some plants to production of wood.

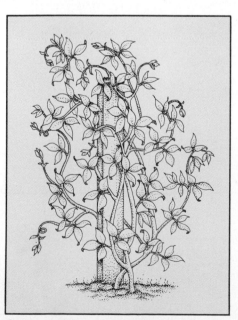

Other plants are committed to the extension of stems with little wood.

Other plants produce more blossoms and seeds than wood and stems.

Removing the growing shoot tip by pruning, or bending a shoot toward a horizontal position, changes the hormone's response and growth pattern of the branch.

Gravitational Pull influences apical dominance in plants. Gravitational pull can also change the direction branches grow because of the weight of leaves or fruit.

Other environmental factors can influence plant growth. Wind caused by passage of automobile traffic can force trees to grow in a different direction. Foreign chemicals may be toxic to young plants, stunting growth.

Flowering Habit refers to age and position of wood that bears flowers. Flowers may appear on current season's growth of wood, on last season's growth or on long-lived spurs several years old. Flowers may also be born *terminally* at the end of growing wood, or *laterally* on the sides of growing wood.

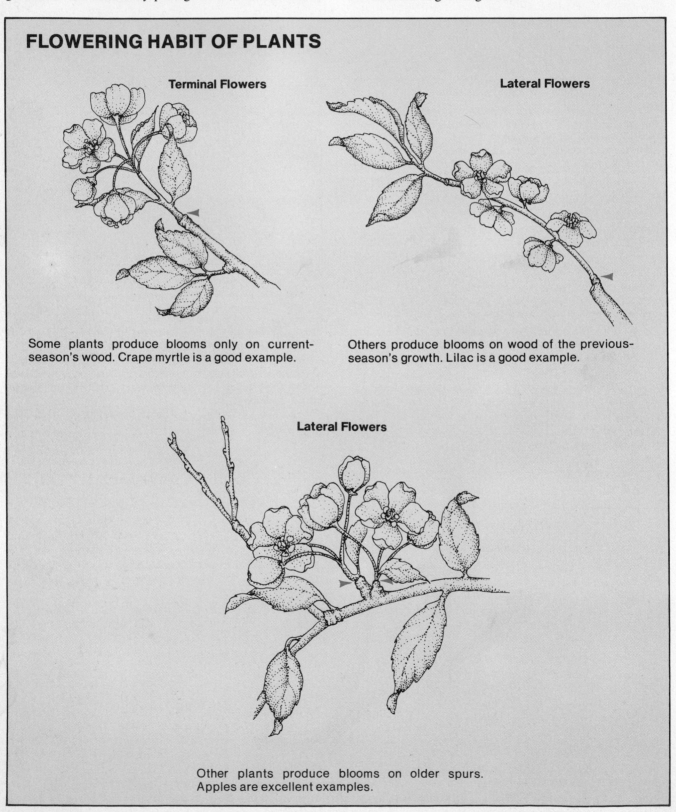

FLOWERING HABIT OF PLANTS

Terminal Flowers

Lateral Flowers

Some plants produce blooms only on current-season's wood. Crape myrtle is a good example.

Others produce blooms on wood of the previous-season's growth. Lilac is a good example.

Lateral Flowers

Other plants produce blooms on older spurs. Apples are excellent examples.

Perennial Plants

For a better understanding of why and how to prune plants, it is important to know the name and function of each plant part. Refer to the illustration on page 14. This illustration provides the basis for information in this section.

PARTS AND FUNCTIONS

All plants contain the following parts:
- Roots
- Trunk or Stem
- Branches, Limbs and Twigs
- Leaves

Roots—They form the basic anchoring system for all plants. Roots hold plants firmly in place in the soil. Roots obtain all essential inorganic nutrients, minerals, and water from soil.

Roots accomplish their tasks through a complex system of *lateral* and *feeder* roots. Roots are covered with tiny *root hairs*. As roots grow, they force their way through soil in search of water and minerals. This strong network of growing roots helps anchor plants to the ground.

Trunk—The trunk or stem provides the main support system of the trees. The internal structure is composed of *xylem, phloem* and *cambium*. The xylem, phloem and cambium form a complex vascular system. This vascular system is made up of conducting cells. These cells transport water, minerals and food throughout trees.

Branches—There are two types of branches in trees: *scaffold* branches and *lateral* branches.

Scaffold branches are large, forming the basic shape of trees and providing support.

Lateral branches are smaller. They tend to fill in the outline of trees. Lateral branches support growing twigs, leaves and fruit.

Twigs—These small structures are commonly called the *growing shoots*. They contain the growing shoot tip or terminal bud. This is sometimes called the *apical bud*. Twigs contain many lateral buds along the side of the twig. Basic materials for development of the leaves and flowers are inside these buds.

Buds—Buds are formed in axils of leaves during the growing season. Buds are covered by layers of protective scales. Basic *primordia,* or partially formed parts of leaves or flowers, are found under these layers of scales.

Buds may contain only leaf primordia, only flower primordia, or a combination of both leaf and flower primordia. Flower buds are usually larger and rounder than leaf buds.

The Flowering Habit of trees refers to age and position of twigs that contain flower buds. Buds may be positioned terminally at the end of twigs or laterally on the side of twigs. Buds can appear on current season's growth, last season's growth or on long-lived spurs.

Leaves—Food for plants is produced by leaves. Leaves are food factories. Leaves collect energy from the sun and change energy into starches and sugars —carbohydrates—for plants. During this food production process, called *photosynthesis,* leaves absorb carbon dioxide and release water and oxygen into the atmosphere.

INTERNAL STRUCTURE AND FUNCTION

It is important to remember that different parts of a tree are interconnected and dependent on each other.

Let's take a closer look at the internal structure of a typical plant and see how it actually works.

Xylem—The innermost part of a tree is called *xylem*. This inner cylinder of wood contains old heartwood and young sapwood. *Heartwood* is the non-living part of the tree. Heartwood provides structural support for the tree. *Sapwood* is the living part of the tree. Sapwood conducts water and mineral nutrients from the roots to all branches and leaves.

The young xylem, or sapwood, is interconnected throughout the tree. If you prune off a small limb, water going to that limb is sent to the remaining limbs. If you cut off a root from one side of a tree, roots from the tree's other side will supply the entire tree with water.

This interconnection allows water to bypass a wound on one side of the trunk. You can supply water to only 25% of a tree's root system without causing any other part of the tree to suffer stress—if enough water is provided. This interconnectedness is one reason why pruning helps prevent stress during drought conditions.

Because heartwood in xylem is not alive, it can't heal itself. Bacteria and wood-rotting fungi can live and thrive in heartwood.

Although an old, hollow-centered tree can be healthy, it usually is not as strong as a young tree. Once old xylem or heartwood has lost the ability to conduct nutrients, its main purpose is to help support the tree. Heartwood also stores food and plant waste.

Large pruning wounds expose heartwood. This exposure can allow entrance of wood-rotting fungi and bacteria. These organisms weaken tree structure. Because spores of wood-rotting fungi are present everywhere, a fresh wound is immediately infected by them. With good training and regular pruning, trees should not need large pruning cuts.

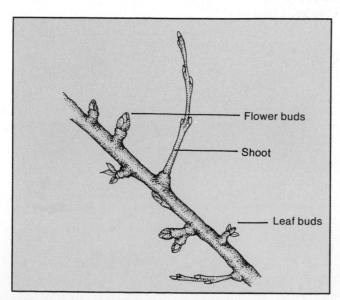

Flower buds are easy to distinguish from leaf buds. Flower buds are rounder and plumper.

ANATOMY OF A TREE

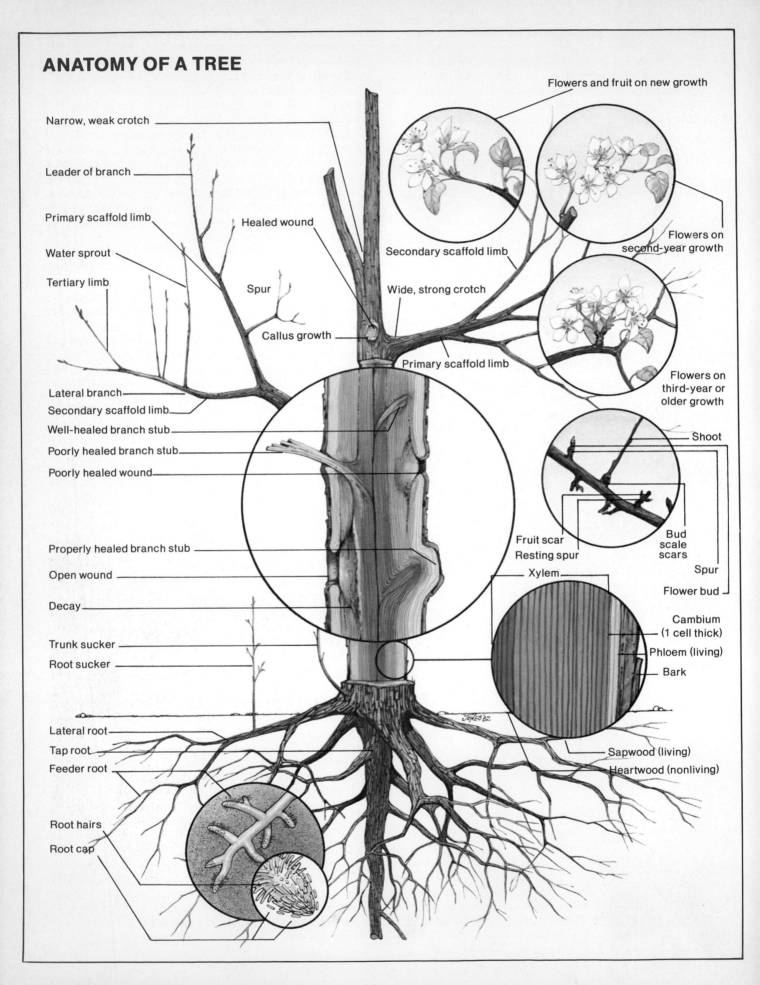

Flowers and fruit on new growth

Narrow, weak crotch

Leader of branch

Primary scaffold limb

Water sprout

Tertiary limb

Healed wound

Spur

Callus growth

Secondary scaffold limb

Flowers on second-year growth

Wide, strong crotch

Primary scaffold limb

Flowers on third-year or older growth

Lateral branch

Secondary scaffold limb

Well-healed branch stub

Poorly healed branch stub

Poorly healed wound

Shoot

Fruit scar

Resting spur

Xylem

Bud scale scars

Spur

Flower bud

Properly healed branch stub

Open wound

Decay

Trunk sucker

Root sucker

Cambium (1 cell thick)

Phloem (living)

Bark

Lateral root

Tap root

Feeder root

Sapwood (living)

Heartwood (nonliving)

Root hairs

Root cap

Cambium—The cambium is the layer of wood between the xylem and the phloem or *inner bark*. Cambium is one cell thick. The cambium is a living part of the tree. The cambium produces new xylem cells on the inside and new phloem cells on the outside. Annual production of new cells by the cambium to form xylem and phloem increases the trunk diameter in plants.

Phloem—The phloem or inner bark is a living part of the tree. It is an important part of the vascular system. The phloem moves food to growing shoot tips and fruit. It also moves food into the starch-storage cells in the bark, xylem and growing roots.

Bark—The bark is the outer protective covering of the tree. Bark prevents the tree from drying out and protects the tree from attacks by insects and disease. If bark is damaged, it may give off large amounts of gum or resin. Resin production is the tree's way of trying to reject or kill intruders.

Bark contains *latent buds* that grow only enough to remain near the outer surface. If a large branch is broken or cut off, latent buds located below the wound will grow and form new branches.

All parts of trees or shrubs are interconnected and dependent on each other. If you remove a section of bark from around a grape vine, called *girdling,* sugars can't move down to the roots. Instead, the sugars move to the fruit, making the fruit larger and sweeter.

By limiting root growth, a heavy fruit crop can require more water. The need for more water increases drought stress. Heavy cropping or summer pruning competes with bark for sugars. Reserves of starch don't accumulate in xylem layers and the tree is devitalized during the next growing season.

Now that you have a basic understanding of how plants grow and develop, take a walk through your garden and observe the perennial plants. Can you see how they are responding to sunlight or wind?

Examine plants closely to see how genetic heritage influences growth and development. Look at growing shoot tips and find terminal buds. See if you can distinguish between flower buds and leaf buds. You should also look for evidence of old or new wounds, insect damage and broken limbs.

Plant Response to Pruning

How different plants respond to pruning depends on apical dominance, type of pruning cuts and growth habits of the plant.

APICAL DOMINANCE RELEASED

Whenever a plant is pruned, you interfere with the process of apical dominance in terminal buds. Pruning terminal buds removes the source of the lateral bud *inhibitor,* a chemical substance that slows or prevents growth. Pruning allows the topmost lateral buds to exert apical dominance over other lateral buds lower on the branch. The upper buds will grow faster than the lower buds, sending shoots upward, sometimes even overtaking and passing terminal buds. This can result in undesirable *water sprouts* on the upper side of branches. Water sprouts are vigorous, vertical shoots that are usually undesirable.

PLANT GROWTH STIMULATED

Pruning in any form stimulates new growth near cuts. Usually several lateral buds form new shoots, or water sprouts, just below pruning cuts. These new shoots result in considerable new growth. Rapid new growth occurs because top growth has been reduced in relation to the size of roots, trunk and main branches. The new growth receives water, minerals and other nutrients stored during the previous season.

Even with new growth, pruned plants always end up smaller. This is called the *dwarfing effect*. Dwarfing occurs because total amount of regrowth after pruning is not enough to replace the amount of plant material removed, plus the growth that would have grown from the original plant material.

Dwarfing is often one of the gardener's main objectives. The dwarfing effect allows gardeners to shape plants. A good example is the popular Japanese *bonsai* plants that are shaped by selective pruning. Bonsai is the art of dwarfing and shaping trees and shrubs.

Pole pruners are useful for reaching the tops of trees. Here pole pruners are used to remove apical tips of branches to control the growth and size of this tree.

When to Prune

A favorite saying about pruning is, "Prune when the shears are sharp." Like most maxims, it oversimplifies and distorts a subject that can be quite complex.

The best time to prune varies with the type of plant, the time of year and the objective of pruning.

First decide what you want to achieve by pruning. Then you can decide when to prune a tree or shrub. The effect of pruning can be different depending on the time of year and the climate.

In general, use the following statements as a guide. For information on specific plants, consult the Encyclopedia section for details on results of pruning and when to prune.

Dormant Season, Late Winter—This occurs during cold winter months in most parts of the country, regardless of the region's climate. Little internal activity is taking place in plants and insects are not active. Pruning during the dormant season usually stimulates extensive regrowth during the active growing season. Prune when temperatures are above 20F (7C).

Late Spring, Early Summer—This period is one of heavy activity for most plants. As days become longer and temperatures rise, food begins to move throughout plants. This growth period puts energy into development of new shoots, buds and leaves. Early summer pruning may stimulate branching with little devitalizing effect on plants.

Summer—Pruning during summer has a devitalizing effect on plants and may cause permanent injury. Pruning wounds cause stress. Energy needed for growth is expended on healing wounds. Wounds are more susceptible to invasion by wood-rot fungi and insects in summer.

Late Summer, Early Fall—Pruning in this season makes plants more sensitive to injury during early freezes. Pruning delays acclimation and reduces starch reserves for next season's growth.

Fall, Early Winter—Pruning in late fall or early winter before plants become dormant increases sensitivity to freezing for at least 2 weeks afterwards. This could result in serious injury and possible death to plants.

WHEN YOU PRUNE AFFECTS PLANT REGROWTH

Plant regrowth after pruning during dormant period.

Plant regrowth following pruning during spring months.

Plant regrowth following pruning in mid- to late-summer.

Plant regrowth after pruning during fall or early winter.

A deciduous tree's response to pruning varies with the season. The most regrowth will occur in spring if pruning is done during the dormant season. Pruning during spring will result in a lot of thin, narrow-angled regrowth the same season. Pruning during mid- to late-summer will result in the most dwarfing and little regrowth. Pruning during fall months will produce results similar to pruning during dormant months.

TYPES OF PRUNING CUTS

All pruning cuts can be classified as either *heading* or *thinning*. Heading and thinning have opposite effects, but both are beneficial to plants.

Heading—This procedure removes part of a shoot or branch, but not at a *branch point*. The branch point is the point of attachment of a branch to the trunk or another limb. Heading increases the number of new shoots formed from lateral buds. Heading stimulates branching and makes plants shorter and denser. Other forms of heading are *pinching, snipping* and *shearing*.

Pinching involves removal of part of current season's growing shoot, usually with the fingertips.

Snipping removes the part of a shoot that grew the previous season.

Shearing refers to many heading cuts made along a single plane, either during the growing season or during dormancy.

Thinning—This procedure removes an entire shoot or limb back to a branch point. Thinning reduces the number of new shoots from lateral buds. Thinning inhibits branching and lets limbs grow longer.

DEGREES OF PRUNING

When asked how to prune a particular plant, expert gardeners often answer "Prune hard or prune light." These are general terms, but they do have consistent meanings. There are intermediate terms, too, and every gardener must interpret these terms in individual applications. The following pruning descriptions and common sense are the best guides.

Light Pruning—Suggests minimal removal of foliage or woody growth. Light pruning usually means less than 1/3 the branch length or amount of growth is removed. Plants that are not tolerant of pruning or are slow-growing should receive light pruning.

Hard Pruning—Usually means removal of two-thirds or more of the foliage or woody growth. Plants that require hard pruning are tolerant of pruning. Growth is usually stimulated by pruning.

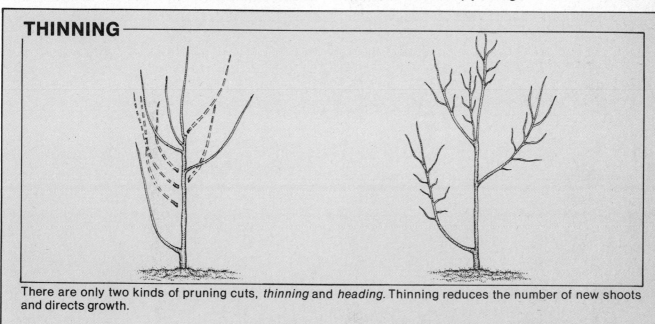

THINNING

There are only two kinds of pruning cuts, *thinning* and *heading.* Thinning reduces the number of new shoots and directs growth.

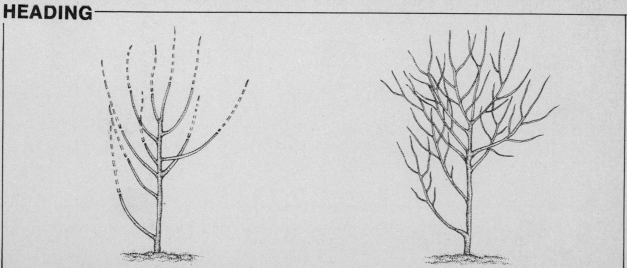

HEADING

Heading increases the number of new shoots formed and stiffens the branches, holding them in position.

How to Remove Large Branches

Good training of young trees and advance planning can help prevent the need for removal of large limbs. However, removal of large, live limbs is sometimes required. The following process is recommended to remove large limbs safely and prevent further damage to trees.

First, use a sharp saw and *undercut* the limb several inches away from the trunk. See illustration at right. When the limb falls away, it won't tear bark from the trunk. If the limb is large and heavy, tie the limb with a strong rope. The rope prevents the limb from crashing down on lower limbs or people and structures.

Make a second cut through the limb from the upper side. This cut should be made several inches past the first undercut. As this second cut is made, the limb will fall without tearing the bark.

Finally, make a third cut through the remaining stub at the shoulder ring. Make this cut close to the tree trunk. Do not make the wound any larger than necessary. See illustration below, right.

If removing a dead limb, make the final cut flush with the bulge of live bark that surrounds the point of origin. Do not cut into live wood to make the cut flush with the trunk.

You can paint pruning wounds with a wound dressing to prevent drying out and deter invasion by insects and disease. However, use of wound dressings has not been proven effective.

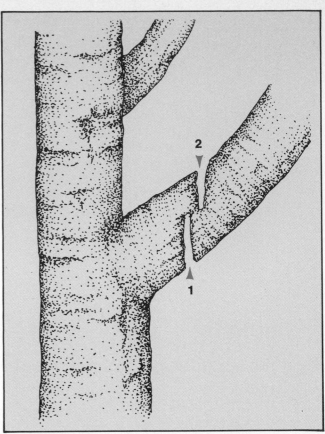

The purpose of making three cuts is to avoid bark tearing. First, undercut the limb until saw begins to bind, then make the second cut down from the top.

Correct removal of large limbs is important to the overall health of trees. Removing limbs incorrectly can damage the protective bark, providing an invasion point for insects and disease.

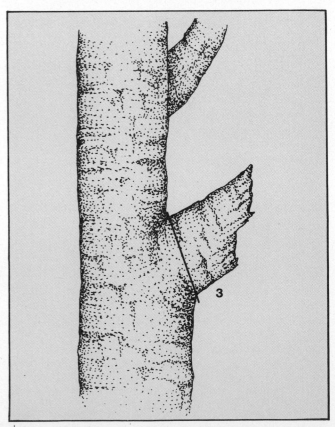

With the second cut, remove the limb completely. If it is a heavy limb, tie it with a rope to help support it. With the third cut, remove the stub close to the trunk.

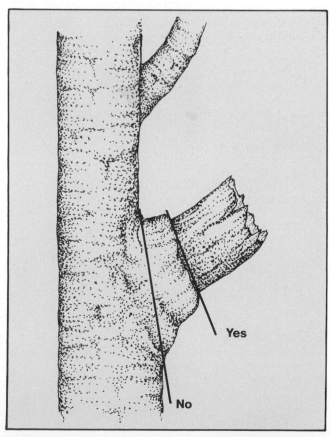

Stubs heal slowly, if at all. When removing an old stub, do not cut into the branch collar.

Cutting into the branch collar increases the size of the wound and the possibility of invasion by decay fungi.

How to Evaluate a Tree

In this section you will find guidelines and a checklist to evaluate the condition of trees and shrubs. Use the checklist to determine the extent of work to be done in your yard. The checklist will help you decide what you can do and what needs to be done by a professional arborist.

You may benefit from the services of a consulting arborist if you still have questions about the condition of plants in your yard. An arborist is a specialist in the planting and maintenance of trees. For a nominal fee the expert comes to your property, identifies plants and evaluates their condition. The expert makes recommendations for tree care and provides specifications for that work. The arborist may or may not be able to do the actual work. This may mean you will need to hire a tree-care service.

If you find trees needing extensive care, ask these questions to determine the need for professional assistance:
- Do I have the knowledge, skill and physical ability to perform necessary work correctly and safely?
- Do I have the tools and equipment necessary to ensure safe and efficient completion of the task?
- Am I able to dispose of debris created by the work?

Carefully examining plants, shrubs and trees can help spot potential problems before they cause irreparable damage to your garden.

Plant Condition Checklist

Evaluate your trees and shrubs using the following checklist before calling a professional arborist. You'll learn how the arborist looks at your trees and shrubs. Communication between you and the arborist will also improve.

NAME OF PLANT

Common _____

Botanical _____

PLANT LOCATION

_____

FOLIAGE

☐ Lush, uniform distribution, vigorous new growth.
☐ Stable, uniform distribution, moderate growth.
☐ Poor, dead tips, sparse distribution, no new growth.

TREE STRUCTURE

☐ No "V" or weak crotches.
Describe size and appearance of weak crotches.

_____

_____

LIMBS

Small—less than 2-inch diameter.
☐ No evidence of dead interior wood.
☐ Moderate, less than 5% buildup of dead interior wood.
☐ Heavy, more than 10% buildup of dead interior wood.

Large—4-inch or larger diameter.
☐ No large dead limbs.
☐ Moderate, less than 10% buildup of dead interior wood.
☐ Heavy, more than 10% buildup of dead interior wood.

Decay or Fungus
☐ No   ☐ Yes

Cavities
☐ None evident.
☐ Less than 10% cavities. Average outside dimensions less than one-half limb diameter.
☐ Many large cavities, 30% or more of limb diameter affected.

Other Factors
Broken limbs
☐ No   ☐ Yes _____

Tree supports or wires
☐ No   ☐ Yes _____

Pruning wounds
☐ No   ☐ Yes _____

Other wounds
☐ No   ☐ Yes _____

Are wounds healing?
☐ No   ☐ Yes _____

ROOTS

Excavations or Obstructions In Root Area
☐ No   ☐ Yes _____

Damage To Roots
☐ No   ☐ Yes _____

Roots Exposed
☐ No   ☐ Yes _____

TRUNK

Decay or Fungus
☐ No   ☐ Yes

Bleeding Stains
☐ No   ☐ Yes

Insect Infestation
☐ No   ☐ Yes

Dead or Sloughing Bark
☐ No   ☐ Yes

Uniform Distribution of Growth Cracks
☐ No   ☐ Yes _____

Cavities
☐ No   ☐ Yes _____

Other Factors

Mechanical damage
☐ No   ☐ Yes

Pruning wounds
☐ No   ☐ Yes _____

USE OF AREA

Past or Future Environmental Changes
Describe: _____

_____

SURROUNDING ENVIRONMENT
☐ Residential Lawn or Garden
☐ Residential Planting Strip
☐ Commercial Planting Strip
☐ Easement
☐ Park

UTILITY LOCATIONS
Overhead
☐ Electrical Power
☐ Telephone Cable
☐ Television Cable
☐ Other

Underground
☐ Electrical Power
☐ Telephone Cable
☐ Television Cable
☐ Water Lines
☐ Sewer Lines
☐ Gas Lines
☐ Other

Past or Future Installation of Underground or Overhead Utilities.
☐ No   ☐ Yes
Describe: _____

_____

INSECTS or ANIMAL PESTS

Location on Plant: _____

_____

Type of Damage:
☐ Boring   ☐ Chewing   ☐ Scratches

Identification of Pest:
☐ Insect _____

☐ Animal _____

☐ Bird _____

Control Measures: _____

_____

What is an Arborist?

A professional arborist is a specialist in planting and maintenance of trees. He performs many different jobs. The most routine task is daily care of the urban forest. This includes all trees, private or publicly owned, that grow in our communities and around our homes.

Care of this urban forest is divided into three categories in the industry: utility, municipal and private.

Utility Tree Care involves careful management of vegetation, usually by a utility company's work crews or by contract with a private line-clearance tree company. These crews maintain trees that grow under or near utility lines.

Municipal Tree Care includes maintenance of street and park trees on city or county property. It may also include state and federal trees. Municipal tree care is carried out by in-house crews or by contract with a private company.

Private Tree Care involves work on trees on a contract basis, usually by a private contractor. Clients are homeowners, commercial developments, condominiums and all agencies and cities that put their tree-care needs out to bid.

Companies that perform tree care are equally diverse. Companies range from one man with a pickup truck to large companies employing hundreds of professional and semiskilled workers. Selecting the right company to care for your trees depends on your needs, the company's abilities, the price you are willing to pay and local availability of qualified companies in your community. Some basic guidelines for selecting a tree service are suggested on page 22.

PRUNING IS FUNDAMENTAL

The most important job performed by the professional arborist is pruning. Other jobs include attaching support cables, bracing trees and limbs and repairing and removing storm-damaged limbs or trees. Arborists transplant trees and apply fertilizers and insecticides.

Specialized tools used include dump trucks and bucket-lift trucks, backhoes, cranes and helicopters. Arborists also use chemical spraying rigs, brush chippers, stump grinders and log splitters.

Most pruning is done by an individual climber, even with the mechanization available. The arborist works from a rope and saddle in the tree using handsaws, chain saws and pole pruners. The quality of work depends on the skill and judgment of the worker guiding these tools. Remember that fact when choosing a tree company to care for your trees.

Proper pruning of larger trees requires expensive equipment and the expertise of experienced arborists. Bucket lift provides easy, safe access to the top parts of trees.

Climbing around the upper parts of large trees is dangerous. Experts use safety belts and ropes while climbing. In case of falls, safety lines prevent serious injury.

How to Choose a Professional Tree Service

Selection of a tree service should be considered carefully. Remember, trees are living entities. Trees and shrubs add beauty and value to your property and deserve the best care.

Read Advertisements—Start your search for a tree service by consulting advertisements in newspapers or the Yellow Pages. This gives you an idea of services available. Size of the advertisement does not indicate size of the company. Often the smallest company runs the largest ad. In any case, the size of the company does not indicate quality of work. Only the experience and policy of the company can ensure proper work.

Pay careful attention to wording of advertisements. Phrases such as "Bucket Truck Available" or "Spray Referral" may mean the company does not have this equipment or service available themselves. Instead, they may subcontract this work to another company.

References to years of experience does not necessarily mean the time the company has been in business. Sometimes three partners, each with five years experience, pool their time and advertise "15 years experience."

Ask Neighbors—If you have neighbors who have had tree work done, ask them about reliability of the firm they used. Find out if they were satisfied with the work done. Did the company keep its agreements? Were workers efficient, courteous and professional? Were workers careful to avoid damage? If minor damage occurred, was it repaired quickly and properly? Tree care is less than precise. Even the best worker can have a gust of wind come up and blow a limb into a window. It's how the company stands behind an accident that is important.

If possible, take a look at work that was done. Was the job cleaned up? Were cuts properly made and in the correct location? Proper placement of cuts is important. This allows trees to compartmentalize and grow callus over wounds with a minimum of decay. Some firms paint cuts, others don't. Painting is not essential. If you think your trees look better with painted cuts, request that painting be done. You should expect to pay extra for this service.

If you are new to an area or don't know anyone who has had recent tree work, call the city park department, street tree division or county extension service. Most cities have used private contractors for tree work. Supervisors know the reputation of local tree services. They probably won't recommend a particular company, but they should be able to give you names of several firms of comparable quality.

Ask For References—Call local tree-care firms and ask for names of recent customers. Call these customers and inquire about their satisfaction with work performed. If a company won't supply you with customer names, forget that company.

Be suspicious if a company offers a free estimate. "Free" estimates don't exist. If you don't pay a fee or service charge for an initial visit to appraise your trees, payment for the call is probably included in the bid.

Firms handle fees for their work differently. Many offer diagnosis and consultation for a small fee. This can be helpful if you have an overgrown property and want to know what to keep and what to remove. Experts come to your property, identify plants and make recommendations for necessary work. There is normally a charge for consultation even if no actual labor is done.

Call several firms and ask for bids. You may find bids vary considerably. The problem is usually poor communication about what work is to be done. For example, one bid of $1,500 might include careful pruning and thinning by an experienced, reputable and insured firm. A bid of $200 on the same job might be a quick butcher-job by an uninsured, disreputable firm.

The highest bid is no assurance of the best job. Often the best-equipped, most-experienced firm is able to perform the job most economically.

Most states have no licensing requirements for tree services. Anyone can purchase an advertisement, buy a chain saw and claim to be an arborist. Be careful whom you select to work on your trees and shrubs. Keep in mind the following points when considering which professional tree service to hire:

- *Source Of Recommendation*—A satisfied client or other impartial recommendation is most reliable. Ads do not indicate reliability.
- *Years In Business*—Keep in mind even the best companies have to start sometime. The worst companies can stay in business for years.
- *Size Of Firm*—If you have one small tree to prune, the small company may be as good as the largest.
- *Affiliation With Trade Associations*—A firm that actively supports trade associations indicates a management policy of keeping informed on the latest technology. However, some of the best arborists are independent loners.
- *Responsibility*—Look for a firm that carries Workmen's Compensation Insurance in accordance with state requirements. Ask if the firm carries Property Damage and Public Liability insurance. Make sure their policies are current. Ask to see a Certificate of Insurance. The reputable contractor welcomes the opportunity to demonstrate responsibility.
- *Established*—Beware of door-to-door tree-care salesmen. Your best investment is a well-known, locally established firm.

Pruning Tools

It's essential to have proper tools to do a good job of pruning plants. The correct tool makes tasks easier and more enjoyable, with less chance of injury to plants.

There are many types of pruning tools available. Tools differ in size, shape and cutting action. Every tool has advantages and disadvantages. Quality can range from poor to excellent, with varied prices.

Regardless of the type, size or price of the tool, buy the best-quality tool you can afford. A good tool costs a little more, but it cuts cleaner, works easier and stays sharp longer. A low-quality tool never works as good as a high-quality tool. A low-priced, low-quality tool can end up being an expensive purchase.

Tools described in this section are common types available in hardware stores, home centers and garden shops.

ONE-HAND PRUNING SHEARS

Two basic types of one-hand pruning shears are available. Both shears are designed for light-pruning cuts. They each have advantages and disadvantages. The choice between the two shears is a matter of personal preference.

Anvil Type—These shears cut by action of a straight blade against an anvil. Anvil-type shears are less likely to be sprung open if used for too-heavy a cut. Some gardeners believe anvil shears have a tendency to crush a stem or branch instead of cutting it.

Hook And Curved-Blade Type—The action of this tool resembles scissors. The hooked blade holds branches and the curved blade cuts branches. These shears have a tendency to spring open if used on large branches.

Anvil-type hand-pruning shears work with action of cutting blade against a solid anvil.

Hook and curved-blade hand-pruning shears cut in the same manner as scissors.

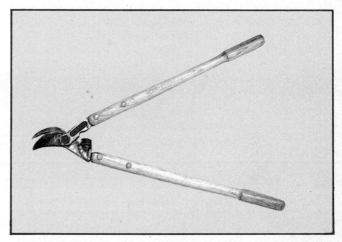

Long-handled lopping shears provide more cutting strength for large limbs. Hook and curved-blade type is shown.

TWO-HANDED LOPPING SHEARS

Long handles and two-handed action of these tools gives greater cutting strength.

Lopping shears are available in anvil type, or hook and curved-blade type. The hook and curved-blade type is more popular. The hook lets you catch hold of the branch.

Loppers can be purchased with 15- to 30-inch-long handles. A pair with short handles is useful for close work. A pair of lopping shears with long handles is better for general use throughout the garden. The limiting factor in selecting size of loppers is weight. Heavy, long-handled loppers are awkward to use at arm's length or above your head.

Expensive loppers have real hickory handles, or possibly fiberglass or metal. Loppers with handles made from hickory, fiberglass or metal are better than loppers with thick, heavy handles of ordinary wood. Desirable features for loppers include a good spring-action or rubber bumper under the jaws. Drop-forged jaws are better than stamped-metal ones.

Compound action, ratchet-type or geared loppers are available. These types of loppers allow more leverage for cutting larger limbs. They are easier to use and cost more than regular hinge-action loppers.

SAWS

Pruning saws come in a variety of styles to fit different situations. Many saws have teeth that cut only on the pull stroke. These blades make it easy to cut overhead branches.

Folding Saw—Smaller folding saws are easy to carry in pockets. Folding saws have fine teeth, usually 8 to 10 per inch. Fine-toothed saws make fine, close cuts on smaller branches. Larger branches can be cut easier with other types of saws.

Rigid-Handle Curved Saw—These saws have blades 12 to 16 inches long and a big handle for a good grip. Curved saws with *raker* teeth have a deep slot after every fifth saw tooth to carry away sawdust. Raker teeth work best for cutting green wood. Curved saws with *lance* teeth are best for cutting deadwood. Lance teeth are all the same size.

Tree Surgery Saw—This saw is similar in appearance to a carpenter's saw. The teeth cut only on the forward stroke. Tree surgery saws are used for trimming larger branches. These saws require a lot of effort to use because of fine teeth.

Bow Saw—Handy, fast-cutting type of saw with a thin, replaceable blade. A bow saw is easy to use and cuts through large branches or limbs quickly. The 21-inch-blade size is the most practical. The main disadvantage of a bow saw is it cannot cut as close as other saws in tight or crowded locations.

Two-Edge Saw—This saw has two cutting edges, one on top and one on bottom. A two-edge saw requires skill and care to use. The two-edge saw can cause more damage than it corrects. The main disadvantage is that when cutting with one edge of the blade, the other edge may also be cutting the tree.

Chain Saw—These modern labor-saving workhorses are quick and easy to use. Chain saws perform a variety of pruning chores around the yard or garden—from light trimming to complete tree removal. Manufacturers have different models and sizes. Many manufacturers offer both electric- and gasoline-powered models.

Chain saw size is determined by length of the *cutting bar*. Chain saws may range in length from small 10-inch models to large, heavy-duty models with a cutting bar over 4 feet long.

Electric-Power Chain Saws are economical to operate, easy to use and quiet. They require little maintenance and can handle many pruning chores around the home. They should be used with a properly grounded, *UL-listed* outdoor extension cord. UL-listed refers to products tested and listed by Underwriter's Laboratories, Inc. See page 157. Avoid tripping over or cutting the electic power cord during operation. The biggest disadvantage to electric chain saws is operating range, which is limited by the length of the extension cord.

Gasoline-Power Chain Saws are larger, more powerful and more expensive. They require more maintenance and adjustments, but offer complete portability and convenience. The 12- to 15-inch-blade is a versatile size for homeowners. This size has enough power to handle all but the largest pruning jobs and is lightweight and easy to maneuver for light pruning operations.

All chain saws, both electric and gasoline, are potentially hazardous. They are sharp, fast-cutting tools and should be operated with extreme caution. Chain saws are safe and reliable if properly adjusted and used correctly, but are difficult and unsafe if used incorrectly. See page 25.

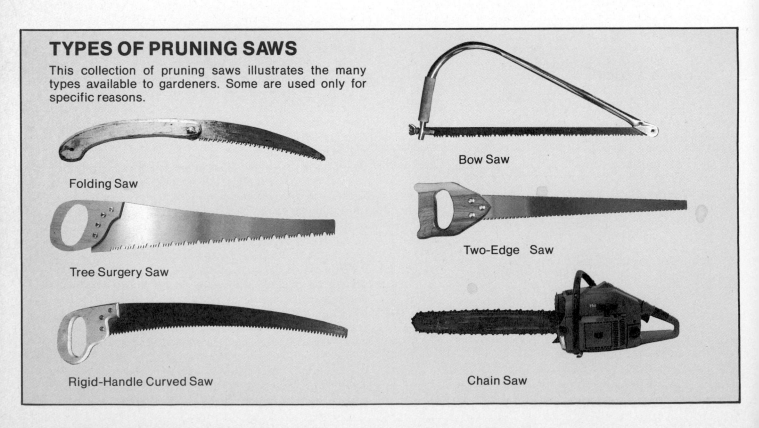

TYPES OF PRUNING SAWS

This collection of pruning saws illustrates the many types available to gardeners. Some are used only for specific reasons.

Folding Saw

Tree Surgery Saw

Rigid-Handle Curved Saw

Bow Saw

Two-Edge Saw

Chain Saw

Safe Chain-Saw Operation

> **WARNING: Chain saws are dangerous! They are powerful, fast-cutting tools that cut through a log or a leg easily. Properly used, chain saws are safe and reliable, saving hours of hard work. Improperly used or maintained, chain saws are dangerous and unpredictable.**

The most important accessory supplied with a chain saw is the Operator's Manual. *READ IT COMPLETELY!* The Operator's Manual contains information on proper care and operation of the chain saw. It also has important safety information.

CARING FOR YOUR CHAIN SAW
Read the Operator's Manual and become familiar with how the saw operates. Learn how to maintain and adjust the chain saw.

Power and Fuel—Electric chain saws require properly grounded electrical outlets for operation. Gasoline chain saws must have the proper ratio of fuel and oil to run efficiently. Fuel and oil should be fresh. Keep fuel in approved, clearly labeled, safety containers for storage.

Add fuel only when the engine is cool. Don't refuel a chain saw in areas that have a fire hazard. Avoid spilling fuel. If fuel is spilled, wipe the saw down immediately. Do not operate a chain saw with a loose fuel cap.

Cleaning—Keep the saw clean and free of oil and dirt on the exterior surfaces. Remove any buildup of sawdust or leaves inside the sprocket cover. Clean any debris from the air intake and pull-starter housing. If the saw will be stored for more than a few months, drain all fuel. Then run the saw until it stops to get all fuel out of the carburetor. Wipe all exposed metal parts with a light coating of oil.

Adjustments—Keeping a chain saw running smoothly and cutting efficiently requires constant adjustments and regular maintenance. Clean and gap the sparkplug at least every 50 hours of operation. Inspect and clean the air filter after each day's use. Make sure oil is changed and the oil and gas filters are replaced on schedule. See your Operator's Manual for recommended servicing intervals.

The muffler should be in good condition and equipped with an approved spark-arrester. Spark-arresters prevent accidental fires. This is especially important if you are working in a wood lot or forest.

A sharp cutting chain is essential for a safe, smooth-cutting saw. A dull or improperly sharpened chain cuts poorly and tends to overheat or stretch. The chain can come off the bar. A dull chain chatters, gets caught in wood and may cause the saw to kickback. Your chain saw is not cutting properly if it makes sawdust instead of chips or is hard to push through wood. If the saw cuts to one side instead of straight through, the chain needs sharpening. Refer to your Operator's Manual for directions on how to sharpen a cutting chain.

The cutting chain may become stretched or out of adjustment if it overheats or gets stuck. Adjust the chain as outlined in the Operator's Manual. Adjust the chain when it is cool, not hot. Tightening a hot chain results in overtightening and possible breakage. The chain bar should be adjusted and lubricated as recommended by the manufacturer.

Any malfunction of the engine or cutting bar and chain should be fixed before further use. Never make adjustments while the saw is running. Shut the saw off and let it cool down.

OPERATOR SAFETY TIPS
Before using the chain saw, become familiar with the Operator's Manual, the saw's features and how to use the saw.

Make sure you have safety equipment such as eye goggles, hearing protectors, gloves and hard hat.

Keep helpers or bystanders away from you and the chain saw. Don't allow children in the vicinity where you are working.

When starting the saw, steady it by placing your knee against the side of the rear handle. Hold the saw firmly on the ground with one hand on the front of the throttle handle. To start the engine, pull up on the starter rope.

Always keep both hands on saw handles when the saw is running. Use the proper grip on the handle bars. Keep your balance and control the location of the cutting chain. Keep clear of the moving chain. Do not touch it! After making a cut, don't move away until the chain stops. Shut off the engine before making any adjustments. Don't carry the saw between cuts with the engine running.

When cutting down trees, select a path of safe retreat before making the final felling cut. Beware of falling limbs and wear a hard hat. Use plastic or wooden wedges to control the direction the tree will fall.

Kickback is the most dangerous situation encountered in operating a chain saw. Kickback occurs when the top-front part of the chain and bar comes in contact with anything during cutting operations. Kickback forces the cutting chain and bar back and up toward the operator. Kickback can cause serious injury or death. Avoid kickback by keeping a good grip on saw handles at all times. Avoid the conditions that make kickback happen. Never let the cutting chain contact the ground or any obstacle, except those you are cutting. Most chain saws come with a kickback-prevention device on the bar. The anti-kickback device is not totally foolproof, so be careful.

Pole Pruner

Combination Pruner and Saw

Pole Saw

Pole pruners and saws provide extra reach for high, out-of-the-way places in towering trees. The hook catches and holds branches; the blade cuts them.

POLE PRUNERS

These pruning tools have a J-shaped hook that catches and holds branches. The branch is cut by a blade operated by a rope or pull-rod. Levers or pulleys can increase leverage of pole pruners. Increased leverage allows large branches to be cut easily.

Pole pruners usually have wooden or fiberglass handles. These handles can be extended by adding long handle sections. Lengths may range from 7 feet to over 20 feet. Longer poles are heavy and difficult to control. Metal handles are to be avoided, especially if there is any possibility of contact with electric power lines.

POLE SAWS

Similar to pole pruners, pole saws are just a extendable handle fitted with a long, curved saw blade. The blade is usually 12 to 15 inches long, with a hook at the base. This hook is used to pull branches down after they have been cut.

COMBINATION POLE PRUNERS

Some pole pruners are made with a pole pruner and a saw in one tool. The two functions of pruning and sawing are combined, but can get in each other's way. The combination tool is heavy and difficult to maneuver.

Extension poles with interchangeable heads—one a pole pruner and the other a saw—are available. Interchangeable heads are a satisfactory compromise, but it might be more convenient to have a pole pruner and a separate pole saw.

HEDGE SHEARS

These shaping tools are used for shrubs, hedges and ground covers. Hand-operated and electric models are available.

Electric Shears—These are easy to use, fast-cutting and accurate tools. Electric shears do a large amount of shearing in a relatively short time. Teflon-coated blades increase efficiency of the cutting action, but add to the cost of the tool. If electric hedge shears do not cut easily and are frequently jammed by thick twigs, use hand shears or loppers.

Be careful not to cut the electric power cord when using electric shears. Always use properly grounded, UL-listed, outdoor extension cords. Do not use electric power tools of any kind in wet areas.

Hand-Operated Hedge Shears—These tools have a serrated blade to keep twigs from being pushed out of the cutting blade. The notch in one blade is used to hold and cut larger twigs. Models with a rubber bumper or shock absorber between blades are easier to use.

High-quality hand-operated or electric shears are more expensive, but are the best investment. They work better and last longer than cheaper tools.

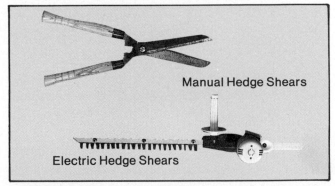

Manual Hedge Shears

Electric Hedge Shears

Hedge shears are used for pruning shrubs, hedges and ground covers.

Pruning Knife

Wood Rasp

Pruning knives and wood rasps are useful for making small cuts and shaping tree wounds.

PRUNING KNIFE

Pruning knives are handy tools. Knives can make small pruning cuts and smooth edges of large pruning wounds. Pruning knives must be extremely sharp to work properly, so handle them with care.

RASP

A coarse-surface wood rasp is useful for smoothing edges of pruning cuts. Get a wood rasp with a good handle. Some rasps have replaceable blades and are self-cleaning.

LADDERS

A good, safe ladder is one of the most important tools for pruning work. A ladder provides a secure platform to work from and lets you extend your reach safely. Ladders come in all sizes, from 4-foot-tall stepladders, to towering extension ladders reaching more than 40 feet high.

The best ladders are made from wood, fiberglass or aluminum. Wooden and fiberglass ladders are heavy and strong. Aluminum ladders are lightweight and strong.

Stepladders—There are two basic styles of stepladders. The most common is the four-leg *household ladder.* The household ladder is not recommended for use in gardens or orchards. Four-leg ladders are unstable and dangerous on uneven surfaces or soft earth.

The best stepladder for gardeners is called an *orchard ladder.* The orchard ladder has three legs and a wider stance. Orchard ladders come in various sizes. The 6- or 8-foot model is most useful. Larger sizes are heavy and difficult to use.

In setting up an orchard ladder, make sure the third leg is an equal distance from the other two. No leg should be resting on soft dirt, a slippery surface or in a gopher hole. If unsure about stability of the ladder, tie the ladder securely to the tree or don't climb on it.

Extension Ladders—These ladders are perfect for reaching higher parts of a tree. Extension ladders have two or more sections nested inside one another. Sections are interlocked by guides. The guides allow one section to slide inside another and extend to the desired height. For general use, extension ladders in 16-foot, 20-foot or 24-foot lengths are most practical. The ladders are tall enough to reach most areas of a tree and still lightweight enough to move easily.

Wooden extension ladders are heavy and expensive. Aluminum extension ladders are lightweight and relatively inexpensive. They are most often purchased. Care should be taken when using a metal ladder outdoors, because aluminum is an excellent conductor. The metal ladder must not contact any electrical wiring or power lines.

Be careful in placing the ladder's feet. One foot in soft dirt can cause a ladder to tip as you climb it. Don't lean too far over to one side when standing on an extension ladder. Leaning can cause the ladder to slip and fall over. To prevent an extension ladder from falling over, tie it to the tree.

SAFETY EQUIPMENT

Protection is the key word here. Any safety equipment that provides protection to you—your hands and fingers, face and eyes, feet or any part of your body—is an essential tool. Safety equipment to protect you during any pruning operation should be the first tools you pick up.

Basic protection items include gloves, boots or sturdy shoes, long-sleeved shirt, pants and perhaps a hat.

One important piece of safety equipment highly recommended is a good pair of safety goggles to protect eyes from pruning cuttings and debris. Safety goggles are essential when using electric hedge shears or a

Orchard ladder is safest model for use in gardens. Three-leg model provides stability on uneven or soft ground. For safety, never stand on the top two steps of any ladder.

chain saw. Ear plugs are also essential when using any chain saw, gas or electric powered.

Some type of safety belt is recommended if climbing a tree without a ladder. Professional safety belts are expensive, but so is a hospital stay from a broken leg or concussion. A strong rope can be used to secure you to a tree. The rope may be uncomfortable, but it can save you from a fall and serious injury. Tie the rope around your waist securely, then tie it around the tree trunk.

If you are uncomfortable about climbing a tree or working on a tall ladder, consider calling an arborist or tree service to handle the job. See the section on *How To Evaluate A Tree* on page 19 for more information.

Electricity Kills

Pruning a tree can put you in touch with sudden death! Each year thousands of homeowners are electrocuted when pruning tools, ladders, or bodies come in contact with energized power lines. A 230-volt houselead can kill, and so can an ordinary 115-volt extension cord.

Carefully check to see if a line of any passes through a tree before attempting to prune. Look carefully. Sometimes lines and cables are difficult to locate. Consider all lines to be energized and carrying lethal voltage. Call the local utility company for help. Commercial line-clearance companies are required by law to maintain 10 feet of clearance between tree limbs and all electrical wires.

Tree Wounds and Diseases

This large, spacious tree has received good care and proper pruning to reach this size. It is healthy and attractive, providing plenty of shade for its owners.

The following information has been provided by W. Douglas Hamilton. He is horticultural advisor for the University of California's Cooperative Extension Service, serving Alameda, Contra Costa and Santa Clara counties.

Trees are an important part of our natural surroundings. If undamaged, trees can live for years. Unfortunately, trees are damaged by a wide variety of natural and unnatural causes. This damage creates wounds, which are a normal part of a tree's life. If tree wounds are treated promptly and correctly, only scars will remain. Wounds can destroy entire trees if left untreated. This section explains what tree wounds are and discusses treatments to help heal wounds.

Additional information is provided on diseases, decay and treatment to prevent further damage to trees. This information is based on research results plus practical suggestions from arborists. This section should help you make decisions for treatment of tree wounds.

CAUSES OF WOUNDS

Scars are left by fallen leaves and limbs. Stubs are left by fallen dead branches. Orchard and city trees are subjected to damage from automobile accidents and lawn mower blades. Trees are beaten by baseball bats. Holes are made by nails and fence staples. Branches can break during storms. Limbs can split and burn from lightning. Fire, insects and animals create small and large wounds such as scrapes, punctures and breaks. In many cases, trees are neglected by society. All these wounds provide entrance points for insects, disease, wood-rotting fungi and decay.

A tree wound is any injury that damages living tissue. Living tissue includes external bark, phloem, cambium and sapwood in the xylem. Non-living heartwood in the xylem may also be damaged.

Branch stubs are especially susceptible to infection by decay-causing organisms. These organisms create discoloration and decay in living trees.

RESPONSE TO DAMAGE

Trees have active defenses against wounds. When a wound occurs, specific chemical and physical changes take place in tissues around the wound.

A waterproof covering of *suberin* is quickly produced over the tree's live cells. Suberin protects tissues from sunburn and prevents drying out. In many cases, resin or sap may flow from wounds. Resin helps defend non-living heartwood from invasion by fungus and bacteria.

As wounds heal, cells begin to divide from the cambium layer. Cells create protective tissue called *callus*. Successive layers of callus form over wounds from the outside to the inside or center of wounds. Callus prevents entrance of decay organisms into inner tissue of trees.

Callus growth is encouraged by protecting wounds from heat, light and drying for four to eight weeks after injuries. This is where suberin plays an important role—protecting injuries from heat, light and drying.

After callus has formed over wounds, an additional covering is created by normal production of new phloem, xylem and *cork*. Cork is sometimes called *inner bark*. If wounds are covered rapidly, deadwood in wounds is protected before decay-causing organisms become established. At present, there is no proved way to increase rate of wound closure, except to increase vigor in trees.

Protective wound dressings are often added to the tree's natural protective responses. Wound dressings are discussed in greater detail later in this section. See page 31.

NON-DECAY ORGANISMS FIRST

Fresh wounds provide an attractive habitat for many microorganisms. Bacteria and non-decay fungi are first to appear on wounds. Few of these specific microorganisms can grow into wood. Crown-gall bacteria and cankers caused by *Ceratocyctis* and *Cytopspora* fungi are good examples of non-decay fungi.

Organisms that do grow into wood must pass through protective chemical barriers produced by trees. These chemical barriers are called *phenolic compounds.* Some organisms can pass these chemical barriers. Most organisms never get inside trees.

Deep wounds in a tree's heartwood produce no protective response from non-living tissue. Deep wounds are highly susceptible to invasion by decay fungi.

DECAY ORGANISMS SECOND

Decay fungi, *Hymenomycetes,* are the next microorganisms to invade tree wounds. Decay fungi appear after wood around wound has died. This makes sense, because decay is the breakdown or decomposition of dead organic matter. When tree wounds are not covered by callus, decay usually occurs.

Decay can occur within one year in some trees. Decay can take from two to ten years to appear in other trees. Protection of open wounds should continue until wounds have healed.

Healthy, vigorous trees slow decay. Years of research and practical experience suggest the more vitality a tree has, the stronger the protective response is to decay. In weak trees with little vigor, decay is rapid. Decay is rapid in older, mature trees with slow growth. Decay is also rapid on wounded trees that have been defoliated during the growing season.

LIMITS TO DECAY

Decay does not normally involve the entire cross-section of a tree's limb or trunk. There are natural limits to the spread of decay in a tree. The greatest diameter of decay in any tree is the diameter of the tree at the time of the injury. New tissues form each year, always outside the injured area. Decay does not spread into new, living tissues formed after injuries. In effect, trees are compartmentalized multiple plants, capable of walling-in injured areas.

BARRIERS TO DECAY

Tree decay is slowed and halted by four distinct barriers. The first barrier is the plugging of live cells immediately above and below the wound. This barrier is easiest for decay organisms to breakthrough. Live cells must be plugged before decay occurs to prevent damage to the tree. Plugging is a dynamic process that depends on many factors. Long, discolored compartments are formed when the plugging process is slow. If plugging is fast, compartments are shorter.

The second barrier to decay is the live, inner growth ring. This is the first layer of living cells under the bark of trees. The growth ring is continuous from the top to the bottom of a tree. The inner growth ring is the second weakest barrier. If wounds are deep, this layer of cells is damaged. Decay fungi are not stopped from entering.

Side walls of trees form the third barrier. Sidewalls are *ray tissues,* or sheets of cells that form across tree rings. Rays form from the center of trees out to the sides. Discoloration and decay does not appear to follow ray tissues into the center of trees beyond injured rings, but the edges of ray tissues usually appear ragged.

The cambium layer is the fourth and strongest barrier. The cambium layer is found just inside the bark. Strength of this barrier depends on many factors, including size, type, position and severity of wounds.

The time of year when wounds occur and a tree's genetic sensitivity to damage have some influence on effectiveness of these barriers.

Decay is slowly spreading throughout the trunk of this large tree. Entry was provided through a wound created by improper removal of a large limb.

Callus growth helps prevent the entrance of decay organisms. Callus also protects wounds from sunlight and drying out.

These four barriers compartmentalize damaged tissue, keeping damage confined. These barriers are particularly effective in young, vigorous trees. Confinement is less in older trees or trees with large amounts of heartwood.

WOUND CLOSURE IS IMPORTANT

A tree's most important defense against decay is rapid closing of wounds. A tree is never safe from invading decay fungi until wounds are completely covered with living tissues. Decay continues to eat away at tree trunks long after wounds have sealed. Many factors influence how quickly tree wounds close. These influences include:

● *Current Growth Rate*—This refers to how fast trees grow in height, diameter and root spread. A good indicator is rate of callus formation over wounds.

● *Wound Size*—If pruning cuts are made flush with the trunk, wounds are large and slow to heal. If short stubs are left, wounds are small and close rapidly.

Pruning cuts should be made outside of shoulder tissue, slightly away from the larger limb. These cuts are made just outside the first protective barrier. See page 19.

● *Number of Wounds*—The more wounds, the longer wounds take to close over. The fewer the wounds, the quicker the closure.

● *Location of Wounds*—If all other factors are equal, wounds low on a trunk will close quicker than wounds higher on the trunk.

● *Genetic Influence*—Some trees decay more rapidly than others. Willows, cherry and other short-lived trees decay quicker than conifers or oaks.

● *Tree Age and Vitality*—Young, vigorous trees close wounds quickly. Older, slow-growing trees close wounds slowly.

● *Season Wounds Occur*—Wound closure is usually quickest when wounds are made just before or at the beginning of spring growth. This means pruning should usually be done in late winter or early spring. See page 16 for more information on when to prune.

The second-fastest healing period occurs in early summer, after new leaves have expanded fully. Late fall and early winter are the worst periods for wounds, primarily due to large amounts of fungal spores in the atmosphere. Tree wounds also close slower if wounds occur when buds and leaves are expanding. This is because food reserves are lowest at that time. Plant energy is directed into growth instead of healing.

WOUND TREATMENT

Wound Shape—Proper treatment of wounds promotes callus growth and ensures rapid healing of wounds. Some arborists shape bark wounds on branch and trunk surfaces in an elliptic pattern. Research shows the shape of the perimeter of bark wounds does not influence callus formation. In other words, it makes no difference if wound shape is elliptic, round, or square. Some arborists do advise against making sharp angles on wound edges. Don't widen wounds more than necessary. Trim loose bark parallel to the wood grain. Use a rasp or coarse sandpaper to smooth rough edges.

Removal of large limbs creates fresh tree wounds. Rapid closing of wounds with callus growth or an artificial covering is an important defense against decay.

All bark around wounds should be tight. Remove all loose bark or press the bark into place.

Chemical Treatments—Trees diseased or infested with insects may require treatment with chemical insecticides, fungicides or nutrients. Chemical treatments cause varied reactions in different trees. Injection of some insecticides can be highly *toxic,* or harmful to young wood tissues. Nutrient injections of manganese, magnesium, iron and zinc cause a minor amount of damage to some trees. Application of Benzimidazole fungicides encourages decay in some trees.

Limited research indicates applying large amounts of the fungus *Trichoderma harzianum* may delay invasion of wood-decaying *Hymenomycetes* for at least two years in red maples. After two years, decay fungi gains dominance and wood decays. Under natural conditions, *Trichoderma harzianum* directly invades decaying wood at the edge of injured tissues, but it is not effective at slowing decay. The artificial application of *Trichoderma,* followed by covering treated wounds with black plastic sheeting, may have promise as a wound treatment. It needs to be studied by scientists to determine just how effective it can be.

Arborists recommend chemical treatments to prevent spread of the following diseases be applied to pruning wounds. The diseases are:

Crown Gall is a bacterial disease of young, established trees of many species. Anti-bacterial preparations, such as Galltrol and Gallex, are effective in preventing infection.

Eutypa is commonly called *dieback* in apricot trees. Dieback is characterized by tips of twigs and branches dying backward toward the center of trees. Dieback is a wound-invader. Dead branches should be cut and removed. Prune infected branches at least 8 to 12 inches below visible damage. Apply benomyl fungicide to cuts.

Wound Dressings—A classic definition of a wound dressing says: "Ideally, it should disinfect, prevent entrance of wood-rotting fungi, stimulate callus and be toxic or harmful to parasitic organisms." Unfortunately, no one treatment meets all those qualifications.

Tree pathologists have found some compounds, such as copper and creosote, to be harmful to living tissues. Water-soluble asphalt emulsions are believed to stimulate callus growth in some cases. But asphalt-based dressings tend to crack and provide less protection against drying.

Newer paints are made with a polyvinyl-acetate base. These paints maintain an elastic, durable, crack-free protective coat.

Some tree pathologists suggest that tree-wound dressings are strictly cosmetic and have no positive influence in healing wounds. Others pathologists disagree, recommending use of wound dressings for all wounds and pruning cuts. Conclusive scientific evidence is lacking.

Drains—In most situations, it is not advisable to install drains through live and uninjured tree tissue. Installing drains may create new wounds. Drains may not have any influence on the healing process.

Cavities—In almost every case, it is better to leave cavities open. One exception to this is installation of a smooth surface across a large cavity. This provides a surface for callus to grow on and the shortest distance to cover wounds. Arborists have used concrete, asphalt and even *polyurethane foam* with success. Polyurethane foam is a synthetic material.

Careful training and correct pruning practices have helped produce these beautiful ornamental trees. These trees illustrate good form and height control. They will maintain their health and beauty for years.

chapter two

Ornamental Trees and Shrubs

Training Ornamentals

There are several reasons for training young ornamental trees. You may want to grow an attractive specimen or spreading shade tree. Perhaps your garden needs a background or privacy hedge. Whatever your objective, the plant should have a specific training program.

Hedges require little training, but they must be sheared frequently to develop shape and height. Potentially large shade trees usually require staking and pruning at planting.

Some specimen trees can be allowed to assume natural forms with little training. Other trees must be trained carefully to avoid limb damage as they grow

Japanese maple, foreground, and flowering dogwood have been pruned to complement each other. Japanese maple is pruned high over walkway to keep path clear. Flowering dogwood is pruned to promote flowering.

Left: This large, attractive tree typifies the beauty obtained by carefully training and pruning ornamental trees and shrubs.

older. It is usually best to encourage development of natural-looking trees instead of geometric forms.

The basic idea in training ornamental trees is to develop strong branches in proper places.

Training helps trees grow at a controlled pace. Training allows development of pleasing, natural-looking shapes. Proper positioning of scaffold branches and lateral limbs should be done early in a tree's life. Positioning of scaffolds helps the tree maintain an attractive shape as the tree grows older. Training requires careful use of pruning practices, supports and applications of nutrients and water.

Early training contributes to the long life of trees. Development of strong, healthy branches reduces the need to make large pruning wounds when removing broken or weak limbs. Large pruning wounds in mature trees invite entrance of wood rots.

Take It From The Top—Most ornamental trees arrive from nurseries balled and wrapped in burlap, or in a container. There could be considerable root loss from the balling procedure or transplanting.

Compensate for any root loss by pruning the treetop. If the top is not pruned, trees may grow slowly during the first few years.

Many gardeners want newly planted trees to look like mature trees. For this reason, gardeners often leave too many branches when pruning. None of these branches will be dominant. Branches are often too close together and form narrow angles with trunks.

These tree forms may be attractive for a few years, but serious problems will develop as trees grow older and larger. The trees will eventually grow large, heavy limbs. These limbs have a weak attachment to the trunk. Too much weight may cause limbs to break. Limb breakage causes more damage to the trees, to people and to property.

Don't be too concerned about the shape of young trees during the training phase. In early years, about 1/3 of the foliage should be located in the lower 1/2 of trees. Observing this pruning practice develops strong trees with straight, tapered trunks.

Developing The Central Leader—Train most ornamental trees to develop a strong *central leader* during the first few years. Select one strong, upward-growing branch to become the leader during the first or second growing season. Remove all branches that form narrow crotch angles with the trunk. Use wooden spreaders to spread other side limbs with wider crotch angles. Spreading develops a permanent scaffold structure.

Developing Scaffold Branches—Determine how high you want to develop permanent scaffold branches. Head the newly planted tree 1 or 2 feet above that height. This establishes the *head height*. The point of origin for a branch remains at approximately the same height throughout the tree's life. Scaffold branches normally begin growing 1 or 2 feet below the heading point. The lowest scaffold limbs on a deciduous or

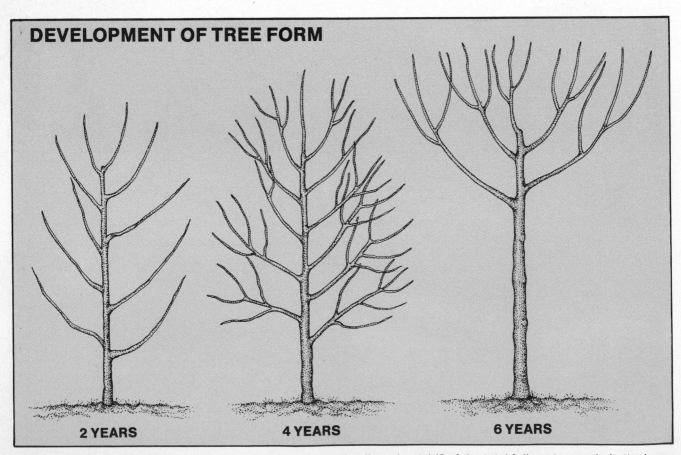

DEVELOPMENT OF TREE FORM

2 YEARS   **4 YEARS**   **6 YEARS**

After planting and throughout a tree's early years of growth, allow about 1/3 of the total foliage to remain in the lower 1/2 of the tree. The tree may appear unattractive during these early training years. As the tree grows, remove foliage and branches gradually over the years. The mature tree will be strong and attractive.

DEVELOPING A CENTRAL-LEADER TREE

Left: Developing a central-leader shade tree from nursery stock requires heading during the first year after planting. Center: During second year, allow new central leader to grow. Prune back lower branches to develop strong secondary branches and establish head height. Right: During third year of growth, continue development of central leader. Carefully prune secondary branches and water sprouts.

EFFECT OF HEADING HEIGHT ON YOUNG TREES

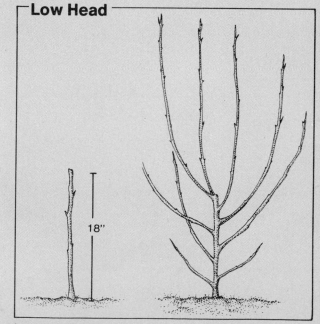

Low Head

18"

Low heading at planting stimulates many new shoots. Shoots may be too low to use.

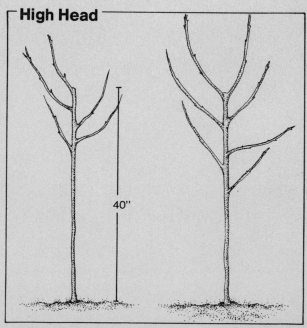

High Head

40"

High-headed trees are likely to lean in the wind and have sun-scalded trunks. High heading produces a few shoots high on the trunks.

The scaffold limbs of some central-leader trees tend to be close together. Spreaders applied when limbs are young can prevent weak crotch angles from developing.

broad-leaved evergreen tree should be several feet above ground.

If low limbs are desired, head the tree 2 or 3 feet above ground. If higher permanent scaffold branches are wanted, head the tree higher. If you want clearance beneath limbs for automobiles or pedestrians, head the tree at 3 to 5 feet. Heading at this point develops one strong, upright leader. Permanent side limbs also form at the desired height later.

The degree that trees are naturally upright or spreading influences where the height head should be located. Naturally upright trees with narrow or columnar shapes should have a low head height. Wide-spreading trees require a higher head, and weeping-type trees require the highest head.

All side limbs should form wide angles with the main leader to develop strong, permanent scaffold branches. If side limbs don't form wide angles, remove the limbs. These limbs can also be treated as temporary side limbs and removed later. Temporary side branches should be kept short until the permanent scaffold system is fully developed. These temporary branches help feed the trunk and roots.

Even with a strong leader and scaffold branches, most trees develop another set of branches high above lower scaffold branches. If a strong framework of branches has been developed below, new upper limbs won't become too large.

HEAD HEIGHT AND TREE GROWTH HABIT

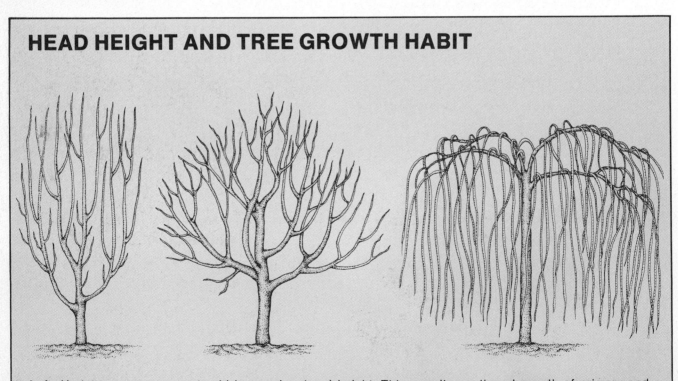

Left: Upright, narrow trees should have a low head height. This permits continued growth of primary and secondary branches, without the tree growing out of reach for pruning purposes. Center: Spreading trees should have a higher head height. This allows growth and development of strong upper branches, and sufficient clearance for people and automobiles. Right: Weeping trees require the highest head height. Drooping, low-hanging branches will grow and hang toward the ground without touching it.

Growth habit of trees influences how many permanent scaffold branches may be safely left in trees. Growth habit also determines the amount of attention required for training trees.

Trees with strong central leaders or narrow, upright trees should be pruned carefully, leaving a large number of young limbs on the trunk. These trees require less training than wide-spreading trees.

Wide-spreading trees should be pruned to develop four or five limbs for permanent scaffold branches. Each spreading branch must be strong enough to carry a heavy load of foliage.

If main scaffold branches are crowded close together in young trees, secondary branches develop too far from the trunk. This could result in excessive spreading and broken limbs because of foliage weight.

Reducing the number of primary scaffold limbs will allow strong secondary branching close to the trunk. This helps distribute foliage evenly and prevents broken branches.

Ideally, major scaffold branches should be evenly spaced around the trunk. Scaffold branches should also be a foot or more apart vertically. This spacing allows main branches to grow in diameter without coming into contact with each other.

Prune trees with a weeping growth habit to a single leader. Allow the leader to grow until it reaches a height of 10 to 12 feet. There will be plenty of room for cascading branches above that height. It may be necessary to stake the single leader until the desired height is reached.

Several years of proper training and pruning eliminates the need for additional pruning of a young ornamental tree until it is almost fully grown. Avoid pruning young trees after training, except for occasional corrective cuts. Remove crossed-over limbs, dead branches and undesirable water sprouts to prevent future damage.

Sometimes, young trees begin to grow rapidly a few years after planting. This rapid growth results in long, flexible limbs and an abundance of heavy foliage. Prevent broken limbs and avoid scaffold damage by supporting these branches with straps or ropes. Scaffold limbs can be tied to the leader or to stronger supporting limbs. This prevents them from breaking. In extreme cases, prune the ends of branches.

SPECIAL CASES

Pollarding—This system of pruning large ornamental trees keeps trees small and manageable. *Pollarding* creates dwarf trees and ruins the natural shape of trees.

In pollarding, trees are headed at a height of 8 to 12 feet above ground. All scaffold limbs grow above that point. Scaffold branches are headed when they reach a length of 2 to 5 feet.

Shoots growing from these scaffold branches are pruned back to scaffold branches *every year*. Cuts are always made into wood less than 1 inch in diameter. Cutting small branches ensures there are no pruning wounds large enough for entrance of wood-rotting fungi.

Pollarded trees require annual maintenance. Trees that respond well to pollarding include sycamores, elms, horse chestnuts, poplars, willows and limes.

Making many saw cuts throughout the top of trees without considering branch points is called *stubbing*. Stubbing is not an approved pruning method. Arborists refer to stubbing as *butchery*.

Attractive weeping form and low height of this weeping cherry have been carefully controlled by proper pruning. Pruning emphasizes and helps trees develop natural growth habit.

Severe and systematic cutting back to the same point is called *pollarding*. Sycamores, as shown here, are among the most tolerant of trees to this process. Pollarding is a convenient way to control tree size and produce a picturesque winter silhouette.

POLLARDING

True pollarding begins with severe heading of all scaffold limbs when the tree is young and stubs are small enough to heal. Each year thereafter, all shoots are removed. Pollarding dwarfs the tree.

Espalier—This is a specialized training method for young ornamental and fruit trees. Espalier is used to grow trees or shrubs in specific patterns, usually close to a fence or wall.

At planting time, a *trellis* or support system is installed. The trellis provides a place for young tree limbs to be attached and trained.

Espalier training is usually done in late spring and early summer. Young, flexible shoots are tied to the trellis. Surplus shoots are *pinched back* as they arise. Pinching is done with thumb and forefinger. Some dormant pruning is required. For more information on espaliers, see page 61.

PRUNING MATURE ORNAMENTAL TREES

Mature ornamental trees usually do not need pruning every year. Main exceptions are pollarded trees and espaliers. Deciduous trees usually need pruning more often than evergreens.

Trees should be examined once a year to check for damage or serious problems. In many cases the average gardener forgets about pruning mature trees. Several years may pass before serious thought is given to the need for pruning. By that time, trees may have developed severe problems. For ornamental trees, prevention of problems is more desirable than curing problems. Let's look at some potential problems and see how these problems can be prevented.

Well-pruned carob trees provide an attractive pattern between the street and sidewalk.

Wisteria is extremely easy to shape and form by pruning. Just pinch and snip vines in a consistent manner.

TREE PROBLEMS

Excessive Height—Controlling height of many ornamental trees is not often desirable or easy. Some of these trees include firs, poplars and other large species. It is desirable to control height of smaller ornamentals, especially flowering plums or crabapples. If these small trees grow higher than a house's roofline, they can be damaged by strong winds or too-heavy foliage.

Tree height can be reduced by a method known as *drop-crotching*. The gardener tries to maintain the general direction and growth pattern of each major scaffold limb. This is done by *dropping* the highest crotch formed by a scaffold limb and the trunk to a lower crotch on the trunk. Make a cut through the trunk between a high scaffold limb and the next lower, upright, inside scaffold limb. Make the cut just *above* the lower crotch. It's important the lower upright limb be an *inside* growing limb. The crotch angle of the lower scaffold limb now becomes the highest.

The upright, inside limb inhibits growth of undesirable *water sprouts* near the cut. If limbs are cut without considering *branch points*, a large mass of water sprouts can surround the area of the cut. Water sprouts alter the natural shape of trees. If cuts are made above outward-spreading branches, those branches will soon be filled with water sprouts. All branches below the cut will be less vigorous because of shading from new foliage.

Excessive Spreading—This condition in ornamental trees is as undesirable as excessive height. Large spreading limbs high in trees are likely to break and fall. Falling limbs are dangerous to people and property and can damage trees. When pruning to reduce overall size of trees, remove limbs from the highest, outermost parts.

Low Limbs—Low-hanging limbs are removed from trees to allow people or cars to pass underneath, or to make gardening or lawn-mowing easier. Remove low limbs before they become large. Early removal avoids large wounds and scars on trees. Small wounds reduce the chance of invasion by insects or wood rots.

Removing part of low limbs is not recommended. Instead, remove all of a limb back to the trunk. Dense shade from the upper part of trees causes partially removed limbs to weaken or die. Weak limbs are susceptible to disease.

Removing low limbs can damage the health of trees. This pruning operation is considered convenience pruning rather than maintenance pruning.

Dead, Weak, Extra Limbs—All deadwood in trees should be removed to the nearest branch point containing live wood. Presence of any deadwood in a live tree indicates something is wrong. Look for the cause of deadwood and take appropriate action.

Remove individual weak branches. If an entire tree appears weak, give the tree a general thinning out. The inside, lower limbs of some trees are easily shaded out. Thin the top of the tree to allow more light into the tree's interior. **Caution: Don't overdo the thinning-out process. Removal of too much wood in tree tops can lead to sunburned limbs.**

If two branches are crossing and rubbing, remove

Water sprouts grow near stubs and cuts on trees. They also appear on top of drooping limbs. Remove water sprouts unless needed as replacement limbs.

the upper one. If you want the tree to become taller, remove the lower limb.

To enhance a tree's overall shape, thin extra limbs back to side branches.

Crowded Trees—Most gardeners want to fill landscapes with young trees and foliage. When trees mature, the end result is a garden containing more trees and shrubs than the space can accommodate.

Crowding spoils the shape of trees and shrubs. It causes plants to grow excessively tall. Overcrowded trees are subject to limb breakage and blow-down. Overcrowding usually occurs before the gardener realizes it is happening. By the time it is recognized, low limbs on permanent trees have been damaged.

It's important to recognize an overcrowding problem early and realize that removal of some trees will be necessary. Complete removal of crowded trees is difficult and may not be desirable or safe.

Removal of some trees can create large voids in the landscape. Surrounding trees or property could be damaged by removal of these trees. Consider those trees as temporary and prune them severely. Allow surrounding trees to grow into the space left by removing the temporary trees. After two or three years of heavy pruning, temporary trees will be dwarfed. Dwarfing makes trees relatively easy to remove. Permanent trees will fill in areas left by temporary trees.

REDUCING HEIGHT OF LARGE TREES

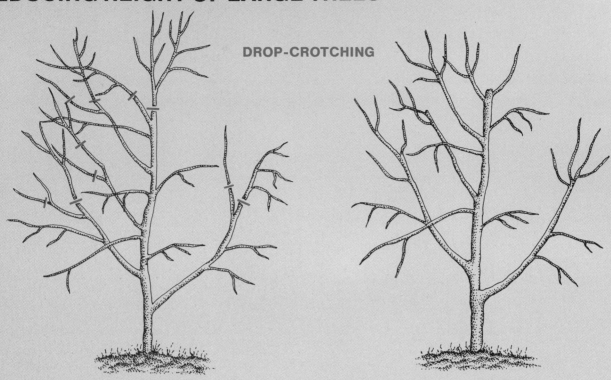

DROP-CROTCHING

Drop-crotching produces a smaller tree that is in better balance and reduces the chances of damage to the tree and property.

Drop-crotching and removing the outermost branch ends reduces the overall height and size of tree. It is the preferred method of pruning large trees.

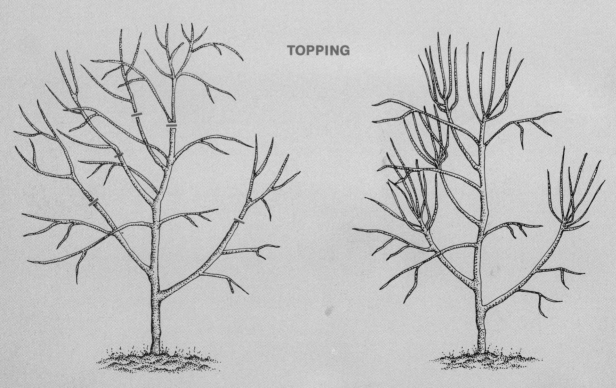

TOPPING

Topping or pollarding a tree leaves unattractive stubs. It is not recommended except for overgrown trees.

Water sprouts will grow from the stubs left by pollarding. They should be removed.

Pruning Conifer Trees

Coniferous, or cone-bearing, trees require little training and less pruning than flowering evergreens or deciduous trees.

Many conifers develop a single, dominant central leader. This growth gives conifers a tall, narrow, pyramidal shape.

Pruning that changes this natural shape will probably ruin the looks of conifers. Conifers used as single specimen trees or screens and backdrops require no pruning for training.

Planting Precautions—Most conifers arrive from nurseries balled in burlap or in metal containers. Conifers may have lost roots in the balling or transplanting process. Compensate for this root loss by carefully removing part of the top. Don't destroy the tree's natural shape during this pruning operation.

There is no practical way to reduce height of a central-leader conifer without destroying the natural shape. If the leader of a conifer is damaged or destroyed, select a branch below the damaged leader. Tie this branch to an upright stake. This branch will exhibit apical dominance and become the new leader.

Such is not the case with conifers that have several natural leaders or look natural without a central leader. Digger pines, piñons and junipers fit into this category.

Pruning conifers to non-symmetrical forms creates interesting landscape specimens. Selective pruning helps control size.

Coniferous trees naturally assume a tall, narrow, pyramidal shape. Conifers are commonly used as individual specimen plantings or as Christmas trees.

Weeping pine is an unusual form planted for unique effect. Training consists of staking the trunk until the tree develops to the desired height.

BASIC PRUNING PRINCIPLES

The most important pruning rule for conifers is to always cut back to visible live buds. Never leave stubs. Pruning conifers requires advance planning. When a limb is removed, another limb will not grow to replace the pruned limb. If a large limb is obstructing traffic or is too close to a building, remove the limb completely. Don't leave a stub.

Careful pruning of lower branches may be necessary in locations where shade-loving plants are wanted under conifers. Where the wind is strong, leaning and breakage of trees can be minimized by thinning limbs. Thinning allows wind to pass through trees easily.

Fast-growing conifer trees with dense foliage make excellent hedges. Yews are a good example. Maintaining the natural form of these plants is not important. Prune these plants to interesting shapes.

Lower limbs of closely planted conifers will die from too much shade. To prevent death of lower limbs, thin stands of conifers by removing trees planted too close together. Thinning must be done while there are still lower limbs to be saved. When lower limbs are lost because of shading, pruning will not restore branches and foliage.

Only a few conifers produce growth from dormant buds on old wood. Examples are yews, hemlock, retinospora and arborvitae. Even though these plants will sprout new growth from old wood, pruning makes them unattractive and should be avoided.

This large monkey-puzzle tree, *Araucaria araucana*, presents an eye-catching pattern against the sky. Minimal pruning combined with natural growth habit has produced an attractive, well-balanced tree.

When To Prune Conifers—Most conifers such as pines, spruces, cedars, cypress and false cypress normally have only one period of rapid growth—in the spring.

Prune these trees annually in spring or early summer. Pruning restricts size and make trees compact. Head back and thin new growth to maintain natural shapes. Pinch new growth between your fingertips.

New growth in pines, firs and spruces is called *candles*. Candles should be pruned or pinched back to maintain the symmetrical form of trees. Christmas-tree growers normally cut candles approximately in half. See page 49 for information on pruning Christmas trees. Don't head into previous year's growth of wood.

Conifers that grow too large for their space can be held to a convenient size for several years by selective pruning. These trees eventually become too large to be contained by pruning and need to be replaced.

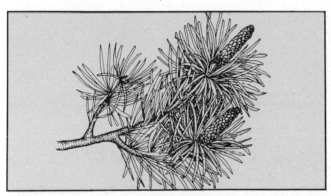

Pine tree size is easily controlled by pinching back new candles in spring, before needles have expanded.

This tall, narrow Douglas-fir tree has received little or no pruning except to remove dead branches. Pruning these trees often destroys the natural form.

Left: These are candles or new growth on a pine tree. To promote height, remove all but the longest, central leader. Shorten all candles by 1/2 to 2/3 to promote dense, bushy growth.

Ornamental Trees and Shrubs **43**

These attractive evergreen shrubs have been shaped by selective pruning and shearing to produce an imposing hedge. Related plantings provide contrasting form, texture and color.

Large landscapes with lots of hedges require extensive pruning and shearing. In many cases, expert assistance is the best solution.

PRUNING BROAD-LEAVED EVERGREEN AND DECIDUOUS SHRUBS

In this section, we will provide some general advice on when to prune shrubs. We'll discuss how to achieve specific objectives and how to solve some problems.

Broad-leaved evergreen shrubs normally need less pruning than deciduous shrubs. Fast-growing shrubs need more frequent and severe pruning than slow-growing shrubs.

Most deciduous shrubs are fast-growers. Some evergreens grow so slowly they seldom need pruning. Rate of growth determines the amount of pruning required. Rate of growth depends on soil conditions, sunlight, water and care given by the gardener.

It's not logical or practical to fertilize and water to encourage fast growth in a plant, then prune away new growth. Moderation in amounts of fertilizer and water, along with minimal pruning, will achieve good results with less effort and expense.

Deciding how to prune a shrub depends on three things. One, the kind of shrub. Two, how the shrub fits into the landscape. Three, what must be done to keep the shrub attractive and healthy.

In some cases, severe pruning might improve the

health and beauty of a shrub. If severe pruning eliminates a shrub's purpose, pruning should not be used. If severe pruning is necessary to contain a shrub, the shrub's looks could be ruined. It would be better to remove the large shrub and replace it with a smaller plant. Prune shrubs only after objectives are planned.

Learn What You Have—There are hundreds of different kinds of trees and shrubs available for planting throughout the United States. You may have several species and varieties in your garden already.

If you don't know the names of plants in your garden, there's an easy way to learn the names. Clip off a few shoots, with flowers if possible, and go to a nursery. Examine plants offered for sale and find ones that match your samples. If you can't find all your plants, ask the nurseryman to help identify them. If he can't help, the next stop is your local county extension agent or public library.

When you've identified the plants, label each specimen. At home, label each tree and shrub in your garden. Make a yard map with space for notes. Throughout the year, fill in important information such as time of bloom or fall color.

Knowing the different shrubs and trees in your garden will increase your enjoyment of gardening. Observing growth and flowering habits of each plant will help determine when and how to prune. Knowing your plants will help you use this book to make your trees and shrubs healthy and attractive.

At Planting Time—Container-grown shrubs *do not need pruning* at planting time. But it is important to continue watering container-grown shrubs for a month or longer after transplanting. Roots take at least a month to grow and spread through surrounding soil.

Bare-rooted shrubs do need pruning at planting time. Remove 1/3 to 1/2 the top shoots to compensate for lost roots. Failing to prune tops will result in shrubs that stop growing soon after leafing out. Bare-rooted shrubs won't grow again until roots are well-established in moist soil.

Pyracantha are evergreen shrubs that respond well to pruning. They can be trained in almost any shape.

Japanese spindle tree, *Euonymus japonica,* can be pruned high to accent branching or serve as a small tree. Shear this plant to any shape or size.

Pruning Mature Shrubs—The best time to prune mature shrubs with a definite period of bloom is immediately after the bloom period has passed. Begin by removing all deadwood. As you prune, try to determine why wood died. If limbs died from shading, remove foliage that shaded the area. If limbs died from disease, remove diseased parts and apply chemical treatments.

Forsythia, a shrub that blooms in early spring, should be pruned as soon as flower petals fade. It blooms only on wood formed the previous season. Pruning forsythia before bloom eliminates too many flowers and ruins the natural beauty.

Pyracantha blooms on spurs of wood two or more years old. Most pyracantha are slow-growing types. They should be pruned in winter, *before* buds break out. Pruning pyracantha later stimulates less growth and bloom.

Slow-growing shrubs require less severe pruning than fast-growing shrubs. Slow-growing shrubs may go a longer time between prunings.

Fast-growing species tend to be loose and scraggly, requiring frequent, severe pruning. Such shrubs can be cut to short stubs and regrown.

Red-osier dogwood is valued for bright-red shoots in winter. It should be pruned severely, even down to the ground, just before bud-break. Pruning severely before bud-break allows more time during the winter months to enjoy the brilliantly colored shoots.

Shrubs admired for fall colors need less pruning. These shrubs can be allowed to become more twiggy than other shrubs.

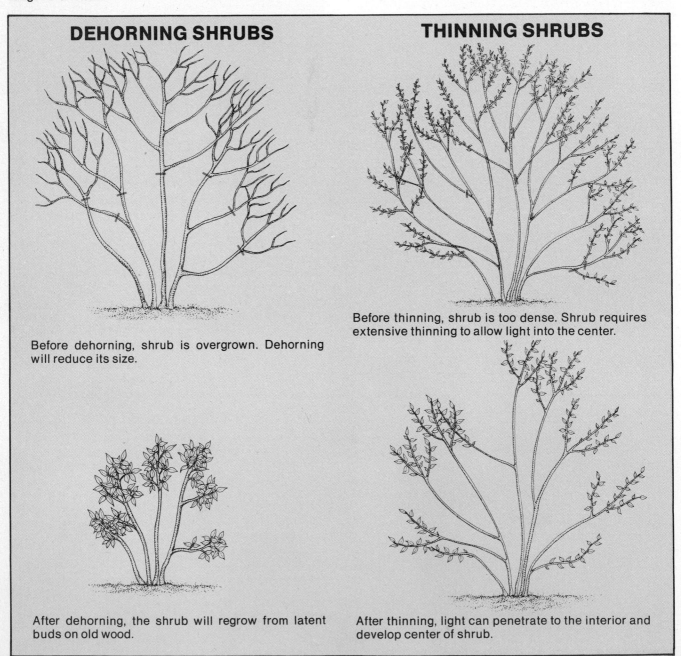

Pruning overgrown shrubs requires careful selection of branches to be removed. Make inside cuts, removing longer branches.

CORRECTING SHRUB PROBLEMS

Shrubs have several problems that can be corrected with proper pruning procedures. Here are some common shrub problems.

Shrub Is Too Large—Reduce size by thinning to short side branches. Thin several inches to a foot inside the *canopy* of the shrub. The canopy is the dense area of foliage that creates the shrub's overall shape. Reduce overall diameter of the shrub's upper part more than the lower part.

Remove all unwanted branches. Remove the oldest and weakest branches without leaving large holes in the shrub. Visualize what the final effect will be before making a cut.

With species that sprout readily from old wood, *dehorn* the shrub to within 1 or 2 feet of the ground. Dehorning means to remove all large branches in the top of a shrub. Follow-up dehorning in subsequent sea-

DEHORNING SHRUBS

Before dehorning, shrub is overgrown. Dehorning will reduce its size.

After dehorning, the shrub will regrow from latent buds on old wood.

THINNING SHRUBS

Before thinning, shrub is too dense. Shrub requires extensive thinning to allow light into the center.

After thinning, light can penetrate to the interior and develop center of shrub.

sons with thinning and pinching. This gives a compact, pleasing shape to the shrub.

Shrub Is Too Dense—A shrub with a thicket of weak, spindly shoots and small leaves is not the most attractive plant. Thin the shrub's top. Head remaining shoots to the plumpest buds.

Thin less severely as you prune down through the bush. Leave upright shoots in the top so light can pass deep into the center. Give the shrub water, mulch and fertilizer after pruning to stimulate new growth.

Shrub Is Too Loose—Shorten outermost branches severely, pruning to a short side branch. Head all wayward branches back to the natural outline. Remove branches that spread along the ground. Where shoots have bent over, cut to upright laterals.

Shrub Is Twiggy—A shrub may be twiggy, without being dense. Shrubs are twiggy because of weak, slow growth. Make sure the shrub has sufficient water, light and nutrients. Light pruning may help stimulate growth. Thin small, weak branches and leave the strongest branches.

PRUNING CONIFEROUS SHRUBS AND HEDGES

Conifers used as shrubs require little pruning, unless they are beginning to grow beyond the allocated space. Coniferous hedges do require regular shearing, The method of pruning coniferous shrubs depends on the shrub's branching pattern.

Shrubs that branch once a year, and only at the start of season's growth, produce a *whorl* or circular growth of branches at the growing tip. Pines, firs and spruces are good examples.

Heading into current-season's growth in early spring is the acceptable method of pruning coniferous shrubs. The distance between whorls of branches formed the next season can be shortened by pinching. Nothing can be done to shorten the distance between existing whorls. Heading at an existing *internode*, the space on a stem between two leaf nodes, results in a stub with no *viable* or living buds. Shorten or pinch back candles on whorls after candles have grown out, but while needles are still small.

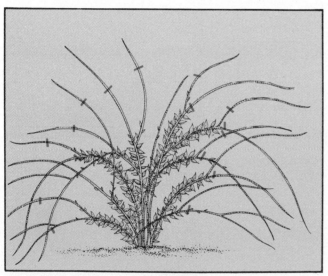

Too-loose shrub is sprawling. Shrub requires severe heading to control growth.

Heavy pruning of a conifer that doesn't sprout from old wood will result in a shrub with no foliage on top. Shape is ruined.

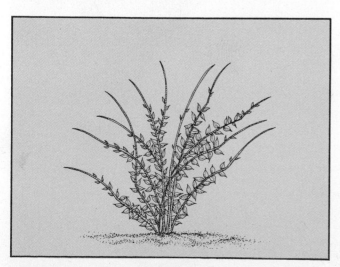

After heading, shrub will be more compact and upright.

Most conifers that branch once a year lack latent buds on old wood. That's why these shrubs won't regrow when they are cut back severely. It is important that these shrubs be pruned to control size before the shrub grows too large for its space. Shorten branches that are too long, but leave others unpruned to shape the tree.

Shrubs that branch as growth proceeds will produce new shoots at the point of pruning. Examples of this type of shrub are junipers and arborvitae. Shearing and thinning are used to prune these shrubs.

With species that sprout from old wood, severe thinning or shearing slows growth. It leaves these plants unattractive for one or more growing seasons.

Shearing is the most common way to prune evergreens during the growing season. It is quick and easy. Shearing can be done twice during the season if extra dwarfing is wanted. When shearing any shrub, taper sides outward from the top down to the base. Tapering ensures good light distribution to lower foliage. The illustration on page 49 shows how to taper.

Shearing shapes shrubs in regular, more formal shapes instead of loose, more natural forms.

Thin evergreen shrubs soon after a period of growth. Thin to side shoots near the plant's center to give a natural appearance, especially for shrubs that branch irregularly.

Start thinning in the top of the shrub and work downward. Prune less severely as you proceed. Find a short branch on the upper side, lift the branch and remove a larger branch below. Prune alternate branches on all sides of the trunk as you move down through the tree.

By doing this, pruning cuts are hidden by remaining foliage. Shorten longest growth first to make it easy to see the effect on overall shape. Finish by cutting shorter branches as needed. Remember to keep the top smaller in diameter than lower parts. Tapering prevents overshading of low foliage.

In some cases, it may be possible to reduce the overall size of a conifer by removing some longer limbs. Don't stub these limbs. Stubs won't sprout new growth, and insects and disease are attracted to fresh wounds.

Another way to make a conifer compact and bushy is to remove the terminal buds. Remove these buds after they have formed in summer. New growth next spring will come from buds several inches back on shoots.

Low-growing conifers, such as prostrate junipers, are often used as ground covers. When branches reach a walkway, don't shear them off straight. Instead, thin back and shorten shoots from underneath. Thinning back keeps a more attractive, natural look to the shrub.

Prune roots before new growth starts in spring. Root pruning keeps fast-growing conifers under control. Prune roots with a sharp shovel. Cutting about 2/3 of the way out between the trunk and ends of the longest branches. For easy access to roots, tie up lower limbs and water the root area thoroughly.

Well-designed plantings of different evergreens create a pleasing informal landscape design. Varied shapes, sizes and textures provide interest and continuity to the sloping site.

SHEARING CHRISTMAS TREES

Christmas-tree customers consistently prefer dense, uniformly shaped conical trees. Conical trees are produced by shearing. Most Christmas trees are grown on commercial tree farms or plantations and are sheared to the ideal, conical shape.

Natural-growing conifers, spruces and pines are used for Christmas trees. Unless these trees grow slowly, unsheared trees will have too much distance between whorls of branches. Distances between whorls vary noticeably, and tree are usually not symmetrical in shape. Unsheared trees usually won't fit inside a room with an 8-foot ceiling without severe pruning.

The objectives of shearing Christmas trees are to obtain:

- a symmetrical tree.
- uniform spacing between branches.
- uniformly dense foliage.

Uniform distance between whorls is established by heading the central leader. The central leader is maintained by thinning or tying up a new leader as needed. See the illustration on page 51.

Christmas trees are normally pruned several times during the years trees are under development.

Christmas trees are grown on commercial tree farms.

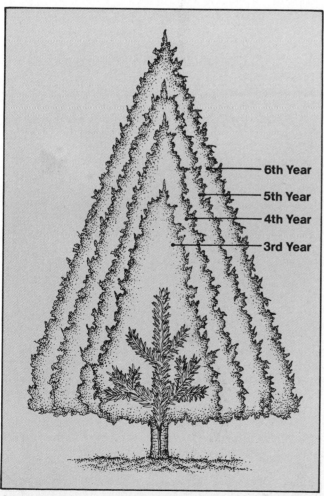

Christmas trees are sheared to approximately a 50% taper. Four shearings are required, starting in the third season after planting. By the sixth year, a 7- to 8-foot tree will be produced.

6th Year
5th Year
4th Year
3rd Year

Typical Christmas-tree shape is achieved by shearing.

SHEARING CHRISTMAS TREES

A 7-year-old Douglas-fir Christmas tree before shearing. Width should be 40% to 60% of height.

Same tree after shearing. Shear after bud-set in mid-summer or before bud-burst in April.

Timing of Shearing—Shearing usually begins in the third growing season, but depends on how fast trees are growing and developing. Slower-growing trees might not be thinned until the fourth growing season.

Shear pines in late spring or early summer or when new needles are half as long as old needles. Pines won't form buds near cuts unless pruned during a period of active shoot elongation. Pine shoots sheared out-of-season may die back to the next inner branch point.

Spruce and fir trees may be sheared after new growth begins, and even after terminal buds have set. These trees form new buds all along new growth. When spruce and fir trees are sheared, shoot growth stops and buds develop. Usually, new growth does not appear until the following season. Occasionally, summer rains will stimulate regrowth in a tree sheared early in the season.

Douglas fir can be sheared from mid-July to the following spring. The first shearing should not take place until the tree is at least 3-1/2 feet tall. During harvest season, stop shearing trees by mid-October. This gives trees time to recover from pruning. Trees won't be full of fresh cuts when they go to market.

Shearing Pines—Pine trees normally require more annual shearing than fir and spruce. Pines tend to grow loose and shapeless. Begin shearing when young pine trees are 1 foot tall. Pines should be sheared annually for four years.

Start by shortening the central leader to about 12 inches. Each year after the first shearing, head the lead shoot the same length as the previous year. The lead shoot determines distance between whorls of branches. Controlling this distance helps control density or thickness of trees. Trees will be denser if the lead shoot has been cut short. These are usually more attractive trees.

If trees are in short supply and tall trees are needed quickly, cut the lead shoot to be a little longer than 12 inches. The whorls of branches will develop farther apart. The trees will take fewer growing seasons to reach harvesting height.

Normally, only the first and second whorls of branches below the leader need to be sheared. Head side shoots to half the length of the lead shoot. Cuts can be made at any point on new growth, because there are no buds to cut off. Cut lower whorls *only* if they are too long or need to be shortened to develop a well-balanced tree.

The overall shape of a sheared pine should be rounded or teardrop-shaped. When pruning long-needle pines, use hand clippers instead of shears. Hand clippers give better control and you won't prune ends of the previous season's needles. When pruning pines, never cut a shoot in the previous season's growth.

Shearing Firs and Spruces—Firs and spruces tend to grow tighter than pines. They need fewer annual prunings. Start by cutting lead shoots to about 12 inches in length. Cut at a point approximately 1-1/2 inches above a lone *internodal bud*. These are the buds located between two leaf or branch nodes. Internodal buds form new leaders the following year.

The 1-1/2-inch stub protects the top bud from dieback or damage by birds. The stub also provides a convenient tying post to support the new leader.

Christmas-tree growers normally preshear the leader and top whorl of branches with hand clippers before shearing the sides of the tree. Preshearing helps establish a dominant central leader. It also makes it easy to cut lower branches to desired lengths.

Shear the sides to obtain an approximate 50% taper. This means tree height should be twice as tall as tree width at the base. Remove any buds on the top side of a sheared branch. Buds in this position produce unwanted inward-growing shoots. Don't cut inside current season's growth.

Problems can occur after shearing firs and spruces. Multiple leaders commonly appear after the third or fourth shearing. Cut multiple leaders back to the lowest, strongest, most-vertical leader to re-establish a single central leader. Don't be concerned if this leader produces a crooked dog-leg. The leader will become straighter with further growth. Any minor crookedness can be hidden by foliage.

If the central lead shoot is damaged, prune it down to the closest internodal bud. Bend a flexible lower shoot upward and tie it to the pruned stub. One shoot usually turns upward without encouragement, becoming the new central leader.

To prevent development of multiple leaders, head all shoots just below the new leader. Cut off any *suckers* or unwanted shoots back to their first branch point.

Basal Pruning—Basal pruning develops a short section of smooth trunk below the first main whorl of branches. Basal pruning removes lower limbs up to the first whorl of branches at the tree's base. Removing these lower limbs creates a short area of trunk free of branches. This open trunk area makes harvesting and handling of Christmas trees easier.

The bottom whorl of branches should have four or five strong branches and be about 10 to 12 inches above ground. Basal pruning is done after two seasons of growth and before base limbs are too large. Cut lower branches completely off. Don't leave stubs. By the time trees are harvested two or three years later, wounds should be healed.

TOOLS

Shearing tools include hedge shears, hand clippers, power trimmers and shearing knives. Any one of these tools is adequate if you have a few trees to shear.

Shearing knives, 12 to 16 inches long, are sharp and easy to use. They are used on large Christmas-tree farms or plantations. Because knives are sharp and dangerous, workers should wear leg guards and keep away from other workers.

Preshearing the leader and top whorl of branches by hand permits better control of conifer shape.

Remove any branches that compete with the central leader as soon as they appear on Christmas trees.

If the leader of a conifer is lost because of breakage or other causes, a new leader may be developed by tying up a lower side shoot to the stub of the old leader.

Bonsai culture requires careful and creative blending of the art of pruning and the science of plant growth. Bonsai dwarfs plants, emphasizing the natural forms and directing growth.

Bonsai Pruning

Bonsai is an art form that originated in China sometime during the 14th century. Bonsai is now considered a Japanese art form. A bonsai is a carefully cultivated tree or shrub that has been miniaturized by pruning and growing techniques. Sometimes a bonsai appears in nature. Usually plants are kept smaller than nature intended using artificial methods.

Bonsai culture includes root-pruning, leaf-cutting, selective watering and fertilization, and wiring. Because this book deals with pruning, discussion is limited to top-pruning, leaf-picking, leaf-cutting and root-pruning.

The two main purposes of bonsai culture are to create a work of art using living materials and to give a view of nature on a small, intimate scale. The goal of the bonsai artist is to create nature in miniature. Bonsai artists work to grow eye-fooling distortions of scale with a large trunk diameter, small limbs and small leaves. A root system fits into a shallow pot, strengthening the dwarfing effect by making the tiny tree seem taller.

Nursery Stock purchased for bonsai culture should already have some character or be a less-than-perfect specimen. Carefully consider how you can prune and direct the plant to enhance and develop a special character. Study the plant. Never cut a branch unless you consider the total effect on the plant's character.

Fruiting and Flowering Trees should have all new growth reduced to two or three sets of leaves per branch. Remove excess leaves immediately after flowering. Exceptions are apple and pear trees that are pruned after leaves have fallen.

Deciduous Trees such as maples and oaks are pruned yearly and throughout the season as necessary. Begin in early spring and leave two or three leaves or sets of leaves per branch.

Needle Evergreens are pruned throughout the growing season by pinching with fingertips. Prune most of the new growth. Pines are pruned in spring by carefully cutting 1/2 to 2/3 of the young candles with scissors.

Broad-Leaved Evergreens are pruned by pinching away 1/2 of the succulent new growth in spring. Do this immediately after flowering. Remove flower buds by pruning in fall or early spring.

Conifers are pruned to give the appearance of an aged tree. Consider topping young trees so they do not have the conical form associated with young conifers.

If possible, remove opposite branches without ruining the overall form. Alternating or whorled branch patterns are natural to conifers and opposite branches eventually die.

Dead branches on bonsai conifers do not need to be removed unless diseased. Bark on dead branches can be carefully removed by rubbing branches between thumb and forefinger. Bare branches whiten with age, adding character and an aged look.

Top-Pruning—Top-pruning contains the plant's size and shapes it artistically. Top-pruning also keeps a plant healthy by removing weak, diseased or crossing branches.

There are two kinds of bonsai top-pruning operations: *New-growth pruning* done throughout the growing season on new young shoots, and *branch* or *old-wood pruning* done during the dormant season. When top-pruning, use standard forms or natural forms of the tree. Don't try to make one tree look the same as or take the form of another tree. Remember the general shape of the entire tree. Use sharp, sterile tools and cut just beyond leaf nodes and 1/4 inch beyond branch points. Pruning tools can be sterilized in alcohol. Top-pruning starts at the top. Work down and around the tree. Protect wounds with pruning sealer.

Leaf-Picking—This involves selectively removing leaves from certain branches and limbs to influence branch size. Leaf-picking observes the horticultural rule that the greater the number of leaves per branch, the larger the branch grows. In this way, certain portions of trees can be encouraged or discouraged. Only 1/5 of the leaves should be removed from a branch.

Leaf-picking should be done only on healthy trees.

Leaf-Cutting—This process removes all leaves from a bonsai, once and perhaps two or three times during the growing season. Leaf-cutting is used when leaves get too big and out of scale. When the leaves are taken off, the leaf-stalks or *petioles* are left behind. Small buds in the petiole's axil produce new leaves.

Root-Pruning—Bonsai root-pruning provides only the roots the plant needs to survive and stay healthy. Root-pruning is done at repotting time. It is done every year or every other year for fruiting trees, flowering trees, other deciduous trees and broad-leaved evergreens. Every three or four years is often enough for needle evergreens.

Young, vigorous bonsai are root-pruned frequently. More mature specimens are not pruned as often. If the plant is root-bound, knock it out of the pot, prune the roots and repot it. Repotting freshens the soil and aids in miniaturization.

To prune roots, carefully remove 1/2 to 1/3 of the soil with dull sticks, called *chopsticks*. Remove any dead roots. Trim the bottom roots flat with the bottom of the soil. Untangle and prune side-bound roots. Leave 1-1/2 to 2 inches of the roots exposed. Side-bound roots are entwined with one another in a tangled mass. Roots become side-bound after being in a container too small to allow adequate growth. Use sterile, sharp tools and make downward-slanting cuts. Repot the bonsai plant and repack the container carefully. Push soil around roots firmly with chopsticks.

Water the repotted plant until water drips out the bottom hole. Using a gentle spray, spray the leaves and protect the plant from direct sun and wind for a few days. Water bonsai whenever needed. Never allow bonsai to dry out after root-pruning and repotting.

Japanese gardeners often train pine trees into distorted, asymmetrical forms. The results resemble old, wind-torn trees found in alpine or seashore areas. Starting with a newly planted tree, limbs are bent to obtain the desired forms. Wires and ties hold limbs in position. Pruning exposes the interestingly shaped limbs.

chapter three

Training and Pruning Fruit Trees

Fruit-bearing trees and vines combine beauty and practicality. These plants serve as attractive and colorful focal points in gardens and provide delicious fruit.

Fruit trees and vines require proper care and plenty of attention. This includes frequent watering, fertilizer applications and careful pruning.

Pruning keeps trees and vines attractive, under control, healthy and productive throughout their lives.

This chapter is divided in two sections. The first part explains basic principles of training and pruning for fruit-bearing plants. The second part provides specific pruning information for common fruit and nut trees.

Planting and training semidwarf apples at this acute angle increases productivity and makes harvesting easier.

Left: These beautiful, delicious Washington navel oranges were produced through proper training and pruning of healthy fruit trees.

TRAINING YOUNG TREES

Training young fruit trees is important. Training develops branch frameworks and helps trees fit in the proper spaces in gardens. Training also helps trees arrange leaves for maximum exposure to sunlight. Training involves many things, including pruning, bending, spreading and tying branches. Training normally takes three to five years of work from planting.

Strong Branches are developed through training. Strong branches hold heavy fruit crops without breaking or needing support. Some training methods, such as *trellis-palmette* and *espalier,* use some kind of support for trees.

Training shapes trees to fit the space allowed. The size of a garden and the role of trees in the landscape determine how to train trees.

Trees can be trained to be large and spreading, spherical and small, or narrow and upright. Trees can flatten against a wall or fence, or grow high to allow gardening under them. Fruit trees can be trained into hedges or as large specimens. Many fruit trees are grown in patio containers. Different training methods are required in each case. These methods are explained throughout this chapter.

Commercial orchards train fruit trees for ease of pruning, spraying and harvesting. Methods are quick and efficient, with little concern for the tree's appearance. As a home orchardist, you should train trees to be beautiful and practical.

It is not always necessary to train peach trees in a vase shape, or grow apple trees in an orchard. Peach trees can be trained to an espalier form. Apples can be grown in large patio containers. Knowing the fundamentals of tree growth and a tree's fruiting habits can help you train trees successfully. See page 9 for more on basic principles of plant growth and development.

Productivity of a tree is affected by pruning. A fruit tree that has never been pruned begins to produce at an earlier age. The tree also produces more fruit in its early years. But production of fruit decreases dramatically after several years and the quality of fruit is not as good. In addition, heavy fruit loads in early years of growth may cause limbs to develop poorly. This overabundance of fruit could result in weak or damaged branches susceptible to breakage.

A tree that has been carefully pruned produces more and better fruit over a longer period with no injury to the tree. Training involves light pruning to delay fruit production as little as possible.

Nursery trees are trained differently depending on whether limbs are well-branched or poorly branched. A well-branched young tree has limbs spaced evenly around the trunk. Limbs are 8 to 12 inches apart vertically. Well-branched trees have scaffold limbs selected at planting time. The rest of the limbs are removed. Side limbs are headed back at least 1/2 their length.

Poorly branched nursery trees have unevenly spaced branches. All side limbs should be removed at

This apple tree is an excellent example of an open-centered, well-pruned mature fruit tree. Note the balance of the scaffold and terminal branches.

Dwarf and semidwarf fruit trees often produce more fruit than they can support. Use some kind of support system so crop weight does not ruin the trees.

A hedge or fence of apples is an efficient, space-saving training method. Pruning, spraying and harvesting require no ladder. Training is simple, but requires constant attention.

planting time. If young trees will be watered frequently during the first summer, leave more branches on top at planting time.

Staking is necessary to develop normal upright trees on windy sites or with certain species such as walnut. Tie trees loosely so they do not become too dependent on stakes for support.

TRAINING METHODS

Bending, spreading, tying-out and pruning are methods used to train fruit trees to be stronger, healthier, more productive and attractive. The four methods may be used in combination.

These methods reduce influence of apical dominance by terminal buds. These methods partially or completely allow buds and shoots to grow from below terminal buds. If a limb is bent, shoots might form flower buds during the current season or the next. Spreading helps to increase fruit set if blossoms have formed.

Bending—Limb bending has certain effects on trees, depending on degree of bend. Bending changes the number, length and position of side branches formed on limbs.

Bending limbs to about 30° from vertical slightly decreases length of terminal shoots. Bending also increases the number and length of side branches.

Bending limbs 45° to 60° from vertical suppresses terminal shoot growth Bending to 45° to 60° increases shoot growth on the upper side of branches away from

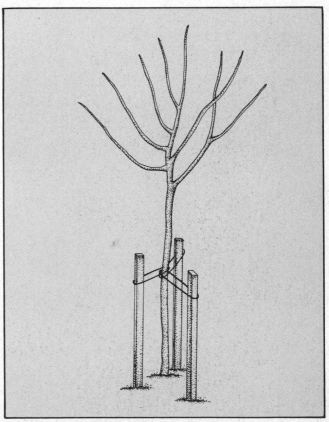

Loose staking of young trees permits some movement in wind. Movement helps develop strong trunks.

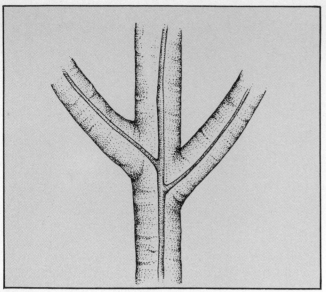

Original wide crotch angles of young tree, shown inset, will develop into wide, strong crotches as tree grows in thickness.

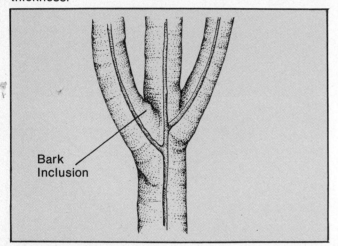

Bark Inclusion

When the original branch angles are narrow, shown inset, bark inclusions form as the tree grows. This results in weak crotches.

One of the easiest ways to train young trees to develop wider crotches is to use spring-type clothespins. Install clothespins when shoots are 6 to 8 inches long and still flexible.

terminal buds. This degree of bending does not allow extremely vigorous growth of side shoots.

Bending limbs down to 90° horizontal or more, stimulates growth of vigorous shoots or water sprouts close to the trunk. Remove these water sprouts by pruning.

Spreading—Spreading young shoots in the first or second season of growth creates wide crotch angles. Wide crotch angles are structurally stronger than narrow angles. As limbs grow and thicken, wide-angled crotches develop strong supporting wood. Narrow-angled crotches develop bark *inclusions*. Inclusions are weak or damaged areas covered by callus growth.

Wide-angled crotches reduce the chance of limb breakage, especially when limbs carry a heavy load of fruit. In cold Northern climates, strong crotches support snow and ice better. Narrow-angled crotches with bark inclusions break apart when ice forming in them expands.

Tying-Out—This method is used in conjunction with bending and spreading. Tying-out involves tying branches into desired positions. Branches can be tied down with ropes or wire cable to help develop wider crotch angles. Branches can be tied to the central leader to help support them.

Pruning—Pruning is used as little as possible for training purposes. Pruning reduces tree size and delays onset of production. For best results, use pruning moderately in conjunction with spreading.

Spread trees first, then determine which limbs to keep and which limbs to remove. In spring, pinch back poorly placed shoots when they have made only a few inches of growth. Pinching poorly placed shoots directs the energy of trees into usable scaffold branches. Don't remove unwanted shoots entirely, just pinch back to discourage growth.

Use simple wooden spreaders to bend young branches outward during training of young fruit trees. Cut a V-shape in each end of a short piece of 1x4 lumber, or drive nails in the ends of boards. Clip off the nail heads to form sharp points. The sharp points will hold spreader boards in position.

Because midsummer pruning has a dwarfing effect, it is not used for training trees. Dormant-season pruning plays the major role in training.

TRAINING SYSTEMS

Different training systems have been developed to fit various plants and situations. Some systems are simple and easy; others are more difficult.

Vase or Multiple Leader—This system is widely used by commercial orchardists. The mature tree assumes a vase shape if properly trained.

Head the tree between 18 and 30 inches above ground at planting. During the first dormant season, select three or four lateral shoots to develop as primary scaffold limbs. Scaffold limbs should originate about 1 or 2 feet above ground level and be evenly spaced around the trunk. The height of limbs remains at the same point above the ground throughout the tree's life. Make sure there is enough space between young shoots to grow without pressing on one another.

The vertical distance between primary scaffold limbs should vary 6 to 8 inches for the tree to be structurally strong. Too little vertical distance between primary scaffold limbs is a common weakness of vase training.

Primary scaffold limbs should be unequal in length and thickness. Equal forks and branches are structurally weak. Prune hard on the most vigorous limb to balance it with the others.

Three or four primary scaffolds are enough. More scaffolds results in a tree with an excessive spread and weak, unproductive branches. Scaffold limbs do not bear fruit. Only *fine wood* is productive. Fine wood is small-diameter, young wood that develops on secondary and tertiary scaffold limbs.

During the second dormant season select three or four secondary scaffold limbs 12 to 18 inches above the primary scaffold limbs.

If there are too many scaffold limbs, fine wood develops at branch tips, instead of near the trunk. Each scaffold limb will be smaller and weaker. Heavy loads of fruit will grow near the end and limbs will spread excessively outward. An ideal vase-trained tree spreads little under the weight of a heavy fruit crop.

One problem with vase or multiple-leader training is easy to see in naturally upright trees. Leaders tend to close in on one another in the center. To correct this condition, place limb spreaders between primary scaffold limbs when limbs are flexible enough to bend. Bend scaffold limbs about 20° to 30° from vertical to open the tree's center.

Modified Leader—This training system is better for upright and closed-center trees. A leader is developed from a central axis and is kept in place until the basic framework is established. This temporary central leader helps develop well-spaced, wide-angle scaffold limbs.

If necessary, scaffold limbs are spread with boards

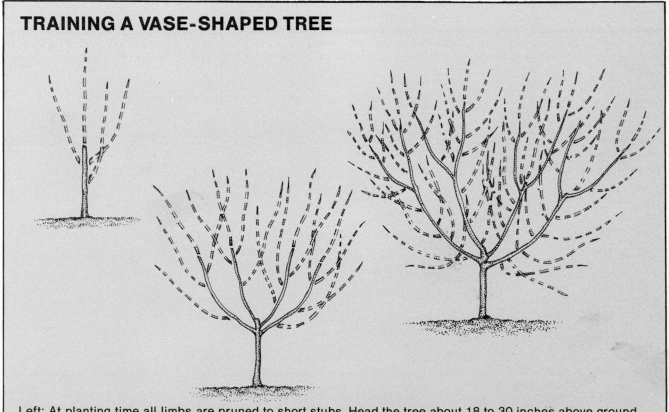

TRAINING A VASE-SHAPED TREE

Left: At planting time all limbs are pruned to short stubs. Head the tree about 18 to 30 inches above ground. Center: Select three or four permanent scaffold limbs in the first dormant season. Remove all other limbs. Scaffold limbs remain at the same height throughout the life of the tree. Right: During the second dormant season select three or four secondary scaffold limbs 12 to 18 inches above the primary scaffolds. Training this way forms the basic vase shape.

In the modified-leader system, the central leader is removed after main scaffold limbs have formed.

Central-leader trees, such as this 'Red Delicious' apple, tend to grow into upright, columnar trees. You can counteract that tendency by placing small boards or spreaders between branches, forcing the branches to grow apart.

placed against the central axis. Later, the central leader is pruned back to a lateral. This seldom-used method takes longer and requires more pruning than the vase system. The end result produces a tree similar to the vase system.

Central Leader—Central-leader training will develop a framework for a tall, narrow tree. A conical shape is produced for efficient utilization of light. Central-leader training avoids most problems caused by tree spreading.

Central-leader training is easier with certain species of trees than with others. This method is especially useful with dwarf and semidwarf trees because harvesting is easier with smaller trees. Central-leader training is not recommended for large trees. It is difficult to reach the center of a tree when the center is 10 feet or more above ground.

To develop a central-leader tree, remove or spread competing shoots to establish the dominant position of the central leader. This is best done in the summer following planting.

Each year during the dormant season, head the central leader 2 or 3 feet above the lower whorl of branches. The ideal distance between whorls of branches is related to the distance branches must spread. The larger the tree, the greater the spread and distance required between the branches.

Before pruning, use wooden spreaders to hold limbs 45° to 60° from vertical. Some central-leader fruit trees do not need limb spreading because side limbs naturally form wide angles.

Spreaders can be moved to higher limbs the following year. Remove spreaders in midsummer. Three main whorls of branches on a 12-foot-high central-leader tree is common. About four to six side branches develop per whorl. Some temporary limbs can be left for early fruiting. Remove these temporary limbs later. Remove about 1/3 of the terminal shoot on side limbs

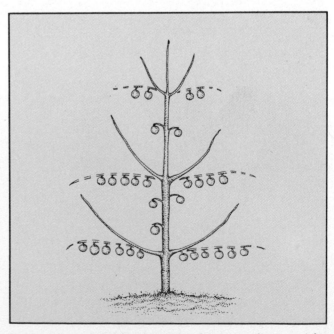

Limbs of a central-leader-trained tree won't spread far off center with weight of crop.

TRAINING CENTRAL-LEADER TREES

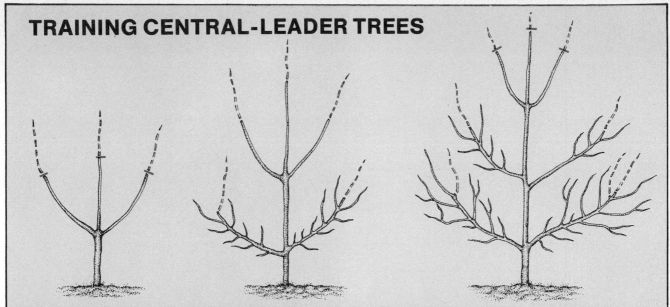

Left: To grow a well-trained central-leader tree, select the first layer of scaffolds during first dormant season. Install spreaders and head scaffolds to stimulate branching. Center: During third or fourth dormant season, install longer spreaders on the lower branches. Develop and prune the second tier of limbs the same as the first tier. Right: During fourth or fifth dormant season, prune higher branches the same as lower tiers.

each year. Head to outward-pointing buds on varieties that do not branch well.

Remove water sprouts growing on upper sides of spread limbs. The presence of water sprouts indicates limbs are spread too far apart.

Remove all fruit from the upper 1/3 of the central leader. If fruit is not removed, the leader bends to the side and growth stops.

Trellis Training—There are many ways to train a tree to a trellis. The trellis may be constructed against a wall or fence, or between posts. Usually a trellis has three or four wires strung horizontally and spaced 2 or 3 feet apart vertically. The tree is trained onto the trellis while shoots are limber.

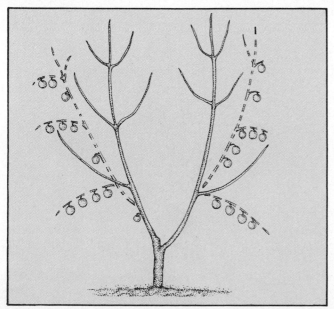

Limbs of a multiple-leader-trained tree spread wide under the weight of a heavy crop.

Numerous methods are used to fasten limbs to the trellis, including wire staples, cloth strips, masking tape and twine. Avoid using ties made of materials that could injure growing limbs. Ordinary masking tape is good for flexible shoots because it does not need to be removed to prevent damage to limbs. Large, U-shaped wire staples are useful for permanently fastening limbs large enough to hold staples. The limb grafts itself to the wire where staples are attached.

Horizontal Espalier training requires heavy pruning to control shoots on top of horizontal limbs. Create a horizontal espalier by heading the central leader just below the lowest wire. This will develop two horizontal shoots and one vertical shoot. Spread the two lower shoots horizontally along the wire. As the horizontal shoots grow, continue attaching them to the wire. As the vertical central leader grows to the next horizontal wire, head below that wire, and repeat the process.

Baldessari Palmettes are developed by heading the tree 4 to 6 inches below the first wire. Use the uppermost shoot for the central leader and the next two lower shoots to form side limbs at an angle of about 45°. As the tree grows, head the leader just below the next wire. Repeat the procedure at each wire level until the top wire is reached. Pinch back or remove all other shoots. Don't head side limbs of the palmette. See the illustration on page 62.

A simple variation of the palmette involves developing only two limbs in a V-shape. This is done with some trees such as peaches. Training in a V-shape can be done without a trellis.

If shoots are cut or pinched back in summer, flower buds may form at the next bud below the cut. This happens only when shoots are in a certain stage of development. The best time for pruning varies among species and varieties. If you can determine the right time to pinch back shoots arising from horizontal espaliers, flower bud formation is stimulated.

Drapeau Marchand is another system of training plants to a trellis. The tree is planted at a 45° angle, rather than straight. The tree is not headed, but all side shoots are removed. The trunk and side limbs are developed at about 45° from vertical. The tree may be planted straight, but all side limbs are attached to trellis wires at 45° from vertical.

Limbs are bent and spread with spreaders. Limbs are trained across the axis of the next tree in the row. Train secondary scaffolds at 90° to primary scaffolds.

The drapeau-Marchand system controls growth well, but the plant is dependent on the trellis. Staples are used to hold limbs permanently to the wires.

Cordon systems are started the same as horizontal espaliers, but the side limbs, after a short distance of horizontal growth, are turned 90° upward. Numerous variations on these basic systems have been tried. All have advantages and disadvantages.

Another way to fit fruit trees into limited space is to develop the head high so flowers or vegetables can be grown underneath. Start with a central-leader system, but don't develop lower limbs. Instead, gradually remove lower limbs as the head of the tree is developed higher on the central axis.

DEVELOPMENT OF BALDESSARI PALMETTES

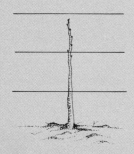

1. Allow young fruit tree to grow 12 to 18 inches tall during first season.

2. Head central leader of young tree 4 to 6 inches below first support wire.

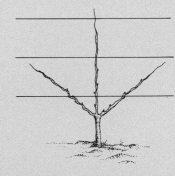

3. As first scaffold limbs develop, attach limbs to lowest wire with ties.

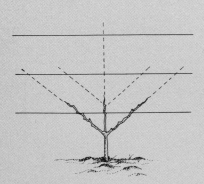

4. As tree grows, head central leader just below second wire. Pinch back first scaffold limbs and develop second set of scaffold limbs.

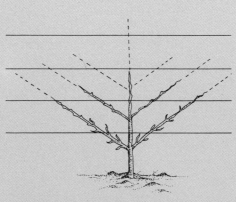

5. Continue heading and pinching process at each wire level until the top wire is reached.

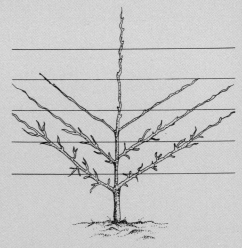

6. Pinch back all leaders to encourage growth of fruiting wood for fruit production.

SUPPORTING FRUIT TREES

Weak scaffold limbs with too-wide or too-narrow crotch angles can sometimes be corrected by radical tree surgery. In an extremely old and weakened tree, there is nothing to do but hope for the best. No amount of pruning will correct advanced age or deterioration of a tree. Weak scaffold systems can be held together by wiring a strap around the outside of the limbs.

The tree can be used to support heavy or weak scaffold limbs by twisting water sprouts together from nearby scaffold limbs. The water sprouts become grafted to one another, forming a living bridge of support. If too many scaffold limbs are found in a young tree, remove one limb per year.

Wind—Wind is a complicating factor in tree training. To support a tree in windy locations, angle a stake into the ground downwind from the tree. Tie the trunk and any major limbs on the windward side to the stake with loose ties. If the site is extremely windy, a trellis system may be the best solution. Wind can make it almost impossible to grow some varieties of fruit.

TREE SUPPORT SYSTEMS

Here are several different effective support systems used for fruit trees. Using these methods can prevent breakage from heavy crops in young fruit trees and help support older trees.

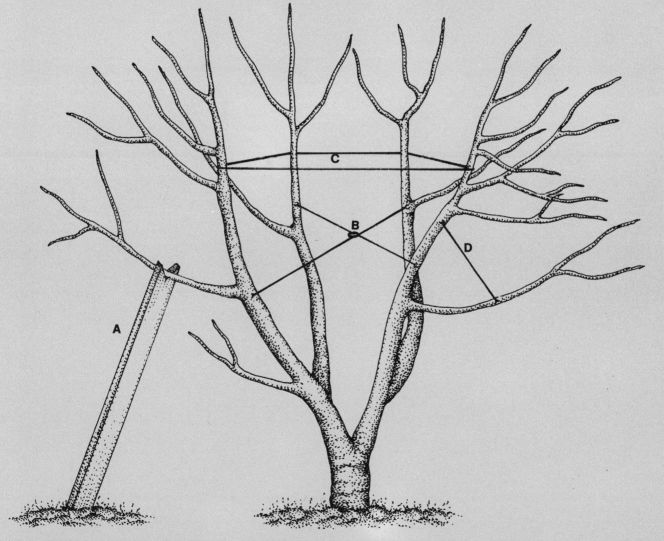

A. Limb props made from old 1x4 or 2x4 lumber with notched ends.
B. Center wiring uses screw eyes in limbs and a washer between wires.
C. Straps or wire placed around the outside of main scaffolds.
D. Limbs tied up with wire and screw eyes in limbs.

Bearing Trees

Pruning for training should be completed in three to five years. Although it is important to remember training goals, pruning has other objectives.

The prime purpose of pruning a bearing tree is to renew fruiting wood. Another purpose is to reduce the need to support fruit-laden branches. Prune a young bearing tree as little as possible so crop production is not reduced. Lightly pruned peach trees produce twice as much fruit as heavily pruned trees. Unpruned peach trees will soon stop producing. Peach trees bear only on wood that grew the previous season. This is not true for trees that bear on long-lived spurs.

Pruning is necessary to keep trees accessible for spraying, thinning and harvesting. Tree height must be limited and openings made for ladders. Foliage must be thinned so chemical sprays penetrate and coat foliage and branches. This is especially important to control scale insects and spider mites. Pruning also helps maintain good-quality fruit.

Determining Age—You can determine the age of any portion of a branch up to 4 or 5 years old by counting rings of bud-scale scars back from the terminal shoot. Counting rings is more difficult with trees that branch frequently. The distance between rings of bud-scale scars tells the years the tree grew well and years of poor growth.

Bearing Habit—This refers to position and age of wood that carries fruit. Fruit is borne on current-season's wood, last-season's wood, long-lived spurs or on a combination of shoots and spurs.

Plum blossoms are among the first to bloom in spring. Knowing the flowering time of fruit trees helps you learn the location of fruiting wood. Fruiting wood helps you determine the location of pruning cuts.

DETERMINING AGE OF FRUIT TREES

Determine the age of fruit trees by counting the rings of bud scale scars. By examining stems of this fruit tree you can see that it bore fruit every other year. This means most of the flower spurs rested, with little or no fruit borne on them during the first year. The spurs produced a lot of fruit the following year. The rest of the flower spurs produced a small amount of fruit, and these spurs will not bear fruit the following year.

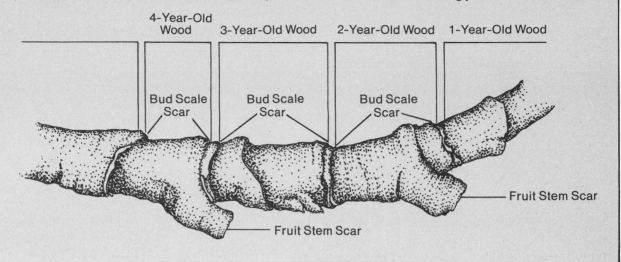

Fruit-bearing wood is positioned terminally, laterally or both. See the table below for fruiting habits of various fruit trees. Bearing habit influences the number and kind of pruning cuts.

Species that fruit only on current-season's or previous-season's growth require more pruning than trees that fruit on spurs. More pruning is required to renew fruiting wood on trees that bear on short-lived spurs. See pruning of individual species for details.

Pruning to Increase Fruit—Deciduous fruit trees differentiate flower buds from leaf buds the year before the spring when these buds open, bloom and set fruit.

In midwinter, flower buds are easily distinguished from leaf buds. Flower buds are larger and rounder than leaf buds. Normally, more flower buds are produced than are needed for a good crop.

Pruning helps improve fruit size by reducing the number of fruit-setting flower buds. Some fruit trees produce few or no flower buds during the year when trees bear a crop. These are alternate-bearing trees that bear fruit every other year. Pruning heavier in winters with abundant flower buds promotes more regular bloom and bearing. Fruit-thinning early in the growing season encourages trees to bear consistently.

FRUITING HABITS OF COMMON FRUIT AND NUTS

This chart shows the position on the branch where fruit will be borne and the type and age of wood that bears fruit.

Current-Season's Shoots	Previous-Season's Shoots	Previous-Season's Spurs and Shoots	Long-lived Spurs
Fig—second crop	Avocado	Apple—minor	Almond
Grape	Blackberry	Cherry, sour	Apple
Lemon	Black Currant	Gooseberry	Apricot—short-lived spur
Orange	Black Raspberry	Pear—minor	Blueberry
Persimmon	Fig—first crop	Pomegranate	Cherry, sour
Quince	Filbert	Red Currant	Cherry, sweet
Raspberry—ever-bearing	Nectarine	White Currant	Pear
Walnut	Olive		Pecan
	Peach		Plum, European
	Pistachio		Plum, Japanese
	Quince		Pomegranate

Supporting Heavy Crops—The growth rate of trees usually slows considerably after trees begin to produce heavy crops. Even if trees are well-trained and properly pruned, the first few crops often bend or break limbs. Prevent limb breakage by stringing a light rope or flexible wire around scaffold limbs about 2/3 of the way up the tree. Hold ropes in place by tying them to limbs. Strings or ropes can be tied to the central leader of trees. Or, tie a pole in the tree's center and run strings or rope out to the limbs to hold and support them. Other support methods are described on page 63. After scaffold limbs have reached sufficient thickness, support is not necessary.

Heavy fruiting pulls upper limbs down into horizontal angles. As limbs become horizontal, buds on the upper side are released from apical dominance. Long water sprouts form. Top-growth shades and weakens lower parts of the tree. To avoid this, cut upper limbs back to upright shoots where limbs arch over.

Young bearing trees tend to produce more shoots than fruit during fruit-bearing years. But as trees grow older, this gradually changes and trees begin to produce more fruit than wood. Pruning encourages trees to produce more wood and less fruit. Avoid excessive pruning of young trees that are slow to set fruit. Prune vigorous young trees by thinning, with little or no heading. If early heavy fruiting has stunted tree growth, stimulate growth by making many heading cuts.

This mature peach tree has been well-trained and pruned. It will require little support to carry a heavy crop.

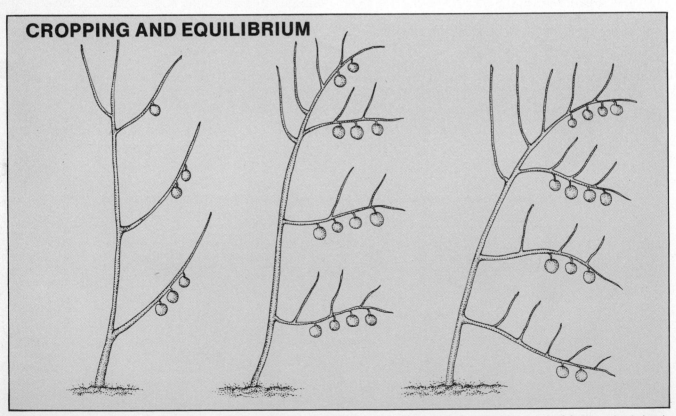

CROPPING AND EQUILIBRIUM

This illustration shows how heavy cropping affects equilibrium. As limbs bend under the load of fruit, apical dominance is lost. Water sprouts appear. Use of the leader-renewal system and tree supports will counteract this effect. See opposite page for more information on establishing renewal leaders.

SUMMER PRUNING

Summer pruning of vigorous young trees reduces tree vigor, but does not interfere with flower-bud formation. Pruning during or soon after bloom stimulates as much regrowth as dormant pruning. Later summer pruning creates a dwarfing effect up to the time when shoot growth stops.

Early summer to midsummer heading or pinching of shoots promotes branching. Regrowth after pinching is often too thin, weak and parallel to be useful fruiting wood. Pinching is essential to control growth with some espaliers.

Heading current-season shoots on apples and leaving a 1/4-inch stub at the base ensures regrowth from less-well-developed buds near the shoot base. Regrowth from these buds is weak, and vigor is controlled. Excess vigor in the tops of young trees can be controlled by summer pruning.

Pruning from midsummer to late summer delays acclimation of trees to fall cold. Pruning at this time increases vulnerability to an early freeze. Don't prune trees in fall, especially if winter cold threatens. Summer pruning slightly increases the amount of chilling required to ensure normal leafing-out in spring. This factor is important in areas with warm winters. Although summer pruning of young bearing trees has some useful applications, most pruning of young trees is best accomplished during the dormant season.

DORMANT PRUNING

When trees are dormant, it is easier to see the amount of new growth and distinguish scaffold-limb structure.

Start by pruning a ladder bay. This is an area in the tree's center that allows access for ladders, with room for you to work. Set the ladder and climb to the highest point you wish to work.

Establish the permanent renewal point for each leader at a place that can be easily reached with your loppers. See below for information establishing renewal points. Select a single vertical shoot and head it. Remove all other shoots above or around the vertical shoot. The headed shoot that forms at the renewal point is now the highest point on the leader. The growing tips of these leaders will hormonally suppress growth of shoots below.

Descend through the tree, thinning shoots and leaving shoots needed for renewal of fruiting wood. Prune hardest in upper, outermost parts of the tree. Thin to an outward-headed terminal shoot where more spreading is needed. Thin to a more upright shoot where spreading isn't needed. Most productive wood tends to migrate upward and outward away from the trunk. This is due to a tendency for the greatest growth in well-lighted parts of the tree and for fruit weight to spread the tree.

This trend is counteracted by maintenance of a series of renewal leaders. As the secondary scaffold

ESTABLISHING RENEWAL POINT

To establish a renewal point, thin the central leader to a single upright shoot with a few scaffold limbs and then head it. Repeat this procedure the following season, always moving up or down the terminal leader a few inches. The renewal point can be re-established each year with three or four cuts.

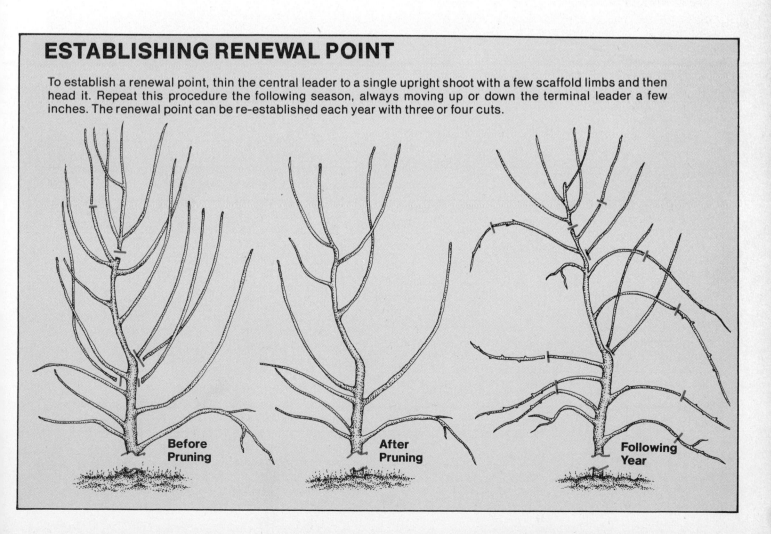

Before Pruning

After Pruning

Following Year

Low, wide-spreading branches are the key to successful training of peach and nectarine trees. Developing two or three primary scaffolds in a Y-configuration saves space and makes harvesting easier.

Optimum light distribution is the key to high productivity in mature fruit trees. The pyramidal-shaped tree at left gives better light distribution down the sides and toward the inner part of the tree. Only the center and bottom parts of the tree receive little light. Tree at right has good light distribution only throughout the top. Light does not reach the center and lower parts.

bends down, remove the old leader that has become nearly horizontal.

Keep higher limbs upright so light can pass into the center of the tree. Lower limbs may be horizontal or angled downward. Don't allow one limb to develop directly over another. The lower limb will be shaded and weakened. Prune so there is space for light to pass between secondary-scaffold limbs and main scaffolds. Most pruning of bearing-age trees is done by thinning, not heading. See descriptions of individual plants for details and exceptions.

Two general problems often arise with young trees. Either the top of the tree overgrows and dwarfs the lower portions, or lower limbs grow up around the top and stunt tree development. This last problem is especially true with certain central-leader-trained varieties. Both problems are solved by more severe pruning of excessively vigorous parts. Such corrective pruning is more effective if done in midsummer.

PRUNING MATURE TREES

Once trees have settled into a regular pattern of production and attained adult size, trees are said to be mature. If given space, trees can continue to become larger long after regular production begins. This concept of maturity cannot be defined with precision. The principal objective of pruning mature trees is to contain trees in a specified space. Regular pruning lets you reach the tops of trees from the top of a ladder. If the

HOW PRUNING IMPROVES LIGHT DISTRIBUTION

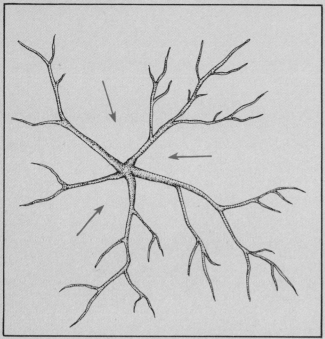

Bird's-eye view down on a tree pruned without equal forks shows how light easily penetrates into the tree's center. Light penetration improves growth and fruit production.

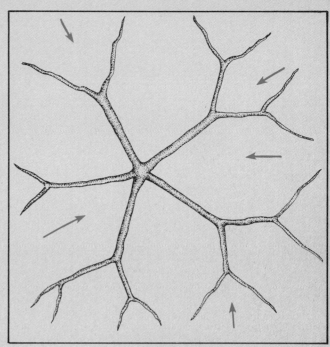

Same view of another tree pruned with too many equal forks. Light penetration is blocked. Result is poor fruit production and eventual death of interior growth.

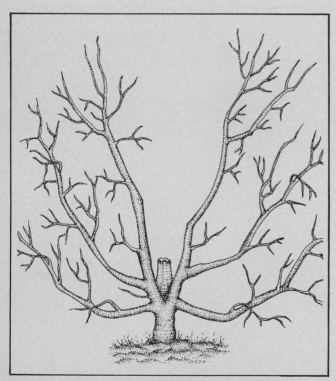

Pruning improves light distribution throughout this tree. Upright limbs do not shade the lower limbs.

Horizontal limbs in the top of unpruned tree block light before it can reach lower limbs. Growth is sparse.

PRUNING FOR FRUIT PRODUCTION

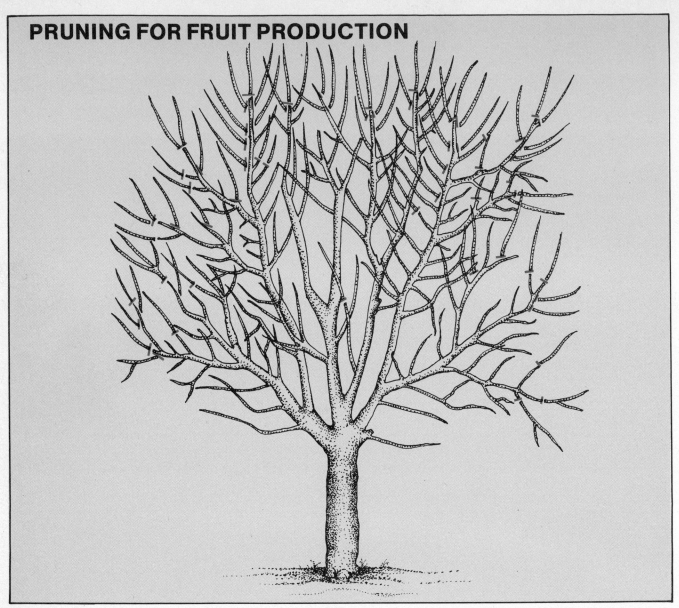

Prune hardest in upper, outermost limbs to allow light into interior of tree. This keeps fruit producing on heavier wood. Larger branches can support fruit without bending.

tops grow out of reach, you either get a taller ladder or lose control over the trees.

Correct pruning promotes production from the top of the tree all the way down to the crotch, not just in the highest, most difficult-to-reach parts of the tree. A tree pruned to bear all over will be covered top to bottom with bloom in spring. A well-pruned tree doesn't need limb props that a poorly pruned tree requires to prevent limb breakage.

Correct pruning increases fruit size, sugar content and improves color and skin texture. Pruning for good light penetration and accessibility for thinning and picking improves disease and insect control because the sprays penetrate better. Correct pruning does require a lot of time. A large apple or pear tree may require 1 to 3 hours of detailed work. The time is well spent if you value the tree's beauty and the quantity and quality of fruit.

Vigor And Fruiting Zones—In large, mature trees it is usually possible to discern three main zones in regard to the balance of fruiting to vigor:

Zone 1: Greatest vigor in the top.

Zone 2: Good balance between vigor and fruiting.

Zone 3: Generally low in vigor. Blooms well, but sets few fruit.

As trees grow older, Zones 1 and 3 enlarge at the expense of the more ideal Zone 2. Principal reasons are shading of lower limbs by upper limbs and weight of fruit pulling limbs off-center.

Pruning hard in upper, outermost part of trees helps counteract this trend. As trees age, upper limbs grow thicker and tend to produce longer shoots. Occasional saw cuts are needed to keep heavy wood out of treetops. Heavy, horizontal wood should not be allowed to develop in treetops.

As trees grow older and limbs stiffen, the need for

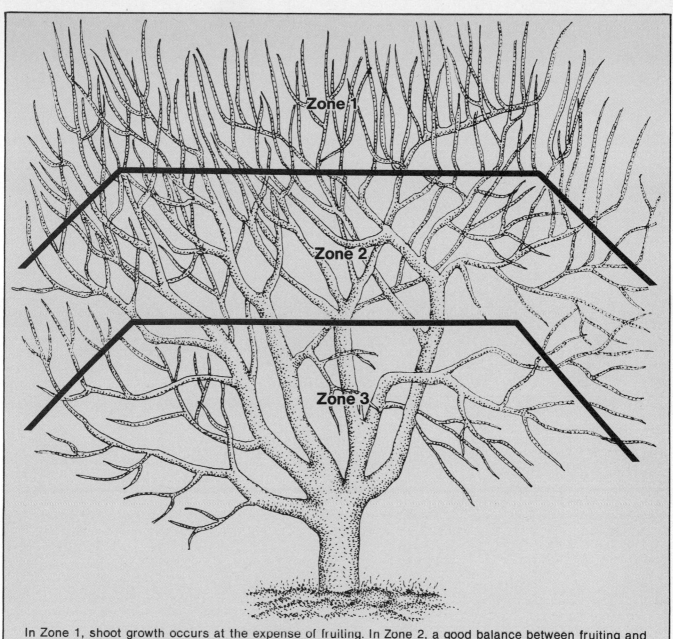

In Zone 1, shoot growth occurs at the expense of fruiting. In Zone 2, a good balance between fruiting and growth exists. Zone 2 produces high-quality fruit. Zone 3 is shaded and weak, lacking vigor and producing poor-quality fruit.

replacement leaders diminishes. It is important to maintain the upright angles of higher limbs.

The overall shape of the fruit trees should be conical or trapezoidal. The widest part should be at the base and the tree should taper inward toward the top. Unless upper limbs are pruned to be shorter than lower ones, this shape relationship is quickly reversed.

Remove long water sprouts and suckers during summer. Well-pruned trees have few suckers because apical dominance has been maintained. Water sprouts can be entwined limb to limb to form a living brace. Tying water sprouts together strengthens the internal limb structure of trees. If water sprouts are bent over and tucked under a spur or other limb, they usually form a flowering spur. This increases productivity of that part of the tree.

Here are some steps to take in pruning large, mature trees:

1. Prune shoots and limbs that extend into ladder bays.
2. Working from the top of a ladder, head vertical shoots of leaders on each major scaffold.
3. Remove outward and downward-angling fruiting wood on limb ends. Cut to replacement leaders—or at least cut in that direction.
4. Remove old fruiting wood, especially on the underside of limbs.
5. Selectively remove shoots, leaving well-spaced branches to renew fruiting wood.
6. Create space between limbs for passage of sunlight.

Common Fruit Bearers

This section provides specific information on pruning requirements of common fruit-bearing trees and vines and several nut-bearing trees. Trees and vines are arranged in alphabetical order by common name. The botanical name follows.

ALMONDS
Prunus dulcis

Almonds bear laterally on spurs that usually live about five years. Train an almond tree with three or four leaders and an open center.

Prune the tree to renew about 1/5 of fruiting wood each year. Cut into wood 1/2 to 1-1/2 inches thick throughout the tree. Remove older, more horizontal wood, especially in upper parts of the canopy. Prune the tree low enough so you are always able to remove some of the highest wood. Prune both upper and lower limbs to ensure adequate renewal of bearing wood.

When reducing the height of a tall tree, look for upright side limbs lower on the leaders. To continue growth in that direction, make pruning cuts just above side limbs. This reduces water sprouts and speeds stub healing.

Before pruning, this almond tree has become too dense for good light penetration and fruit set.

When pruning mature pears, clear ladder bays and re-establish renewal points. Thin shoots but leave enough to renew fruiting wood. Head long shoots and remove old spur systems. Remove water sprouts. See page 94.

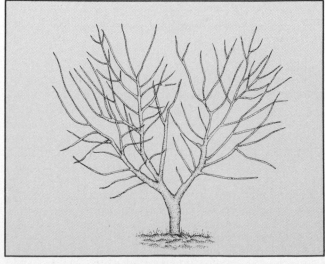

After pruning, the almond tree is well-thinned. The tree will produce nuts throughout the canopy.

APPLES

Malus species

Apple varieties have been classified into four types:

Type I—spur-types, characterized by 'Starkrimson Red Delicious' and 'Jonagold' apple.

Type I trees tend to be upright with narrow crotches and sparse branching. Fruiting occurs on many long-lived short spurs. The fruiting zone is close to the trunk.

Type II—non-spur-types, characterized by most *standard* non-spur strains of 'Delicious'.

Type II apple trees are a variation of type I, with branching more frequent. There is a tendency for the fruiting zone to move away from the trunk.

Type III—spreading-types, characterized by *standard* 'Golden Delicious' and 'Mutsu' varieties.

Type III apple varieties tend to be wide-spreading with wide crotches and frequent branching. Type III apples bear on spurs and shoots at 1 to 3 years of age. The fruiting zone moves rapidly away from the trunk to the outside of the tree.

Type IV—tip-bearers, characterized by 'Red Rome', 'Granny Smith' and 'Tydeman's Early Worcester'.

Type IV varieties have upright main scaffolds, with narrow crotches and frequent branching. Fruit is borne on the end of last season's shoots. The lower half of shoots may be without leaves or fruit. Fruiting wood moves to ends of branches, causing the tree to spread.

Type I, spur-type, 'Jonagold' apple.

Type II, non-spur-type, 'Red Delicious' apple.

Type III, spreading-type, 'Mutsu' apple.

Type IV, tip-bearer, 'Red Rome' apple.

Training and Pruning Fruit Trees   **73**

EARLY TRAINING, ALL APPLE VARIETIES

At planting time, all varieties should be headed at 18 to 24 inches to develop main scaffold limbs. Training can begin in the first summer.

Dwarfs are trained to a central leader. Use a stake or wire to support espaliers.

Semidwarfs are also trained to a central leader. Use a temporary support only if the tree is exposed to strong wind. Spread side limbs if necessary.

Non-dwarf training involves developing three or four leaders at 20° to 30° from vertical. Head leaders annually and remove competing shoots. Spread secondary scaffolds if necessary.

Training and Pruning, Individual Types—Each type of apple tree requires different methods of training and pruning to develop a strong structure and good fruiting habits.

Type I Varieties naturally grow few branches. These varieties tend to be sparse and leggy. Head primary scaffolds to stimulate branching or retain a large number of primary scaffold limbs from the central leader without heading. Dormant-season heading must be followed by thinning branch ends to single shoots after new growth begins.

Once trained, type I varieties require little pruning. Spurs remain productive 10 or more years. However, this is true only if trees have adequate light and don't have a disease that kills most of the old spurs. This dis-ease is known as *dead-spur disease*. If dead spurs occur, renew trees by sawing off entire limbs. Regrow limbs from a nearby water sprout.

Type II Varieties should be trained with few limbs. Use spreaders on scaffold limbs to develop wide crotch angles.

Mature type II trees require moderate to heavy pruning to renew fruit buds. To renew fruiting wood, thin to relatively upright replacement shoots. Nearly horizontal branches may be headed to 2-year-old wood to prevent breakage under heavy fruit loads.

Type III Varieties should be trained with no more than three primary scaffold limbs. After the first fruit crop, head secondary scaffold limbs to stiffen.

Mature type III trees require extensive thinning each year. Thin to upright shoots that appear on 2- or 3-year-old wood. Thinning renews fruiting wood. Lighten branch ends every year by thinning to single, upright shoots.

Type IV Varieties should be trained to no more than three leaders. Head leaders annually, about 2 feet from the previous heading. Heading causes branching and stiffens leaders. Midsummer heading also helps in training.

Mature type IV trees require heavy thinning to replace fruiting wood. Make thinning cuts to upright shoots in 2- or 3-year-old wood around the outside of the tree canopy.

This mature apple tree has been carefully trained and pruned to control size and produce a balanced crop of fruit. The tree is low and easy to harvest.

FRUITING HABITS OF APPLE TYPES

Arrows indicate the direction in which fruiting wood tends to migrate away from the tree trunk.

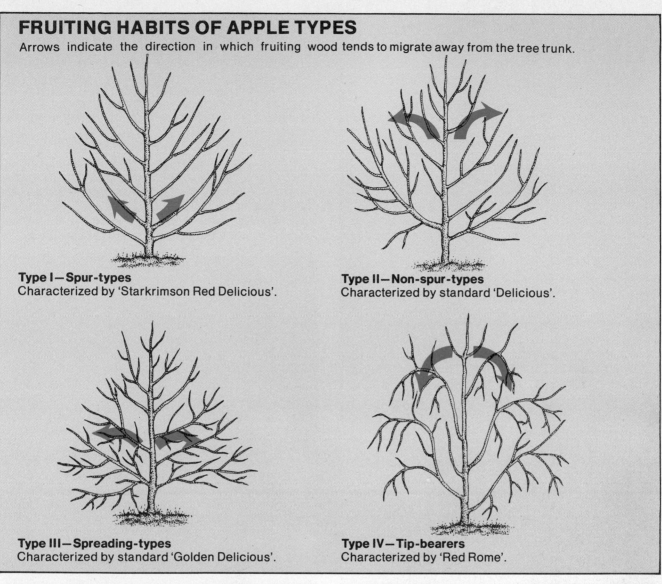

Type I—Spur-types
Characterized by 'Starkrimson Red Delicious'.

Type II—Non-spur-types
Characterized by standard 'Delicious'.

Type III—Spreading-types
Characterized by standard 'Golden Delicious'.

Type IV—Tip-bearers
Characterized by 'Red Rome'.

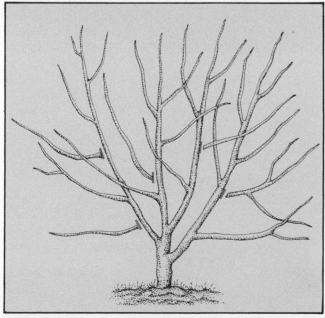

Fruiting wood can be renewed in type I apple varieties by an occasional large cut. New branch forms at cut.

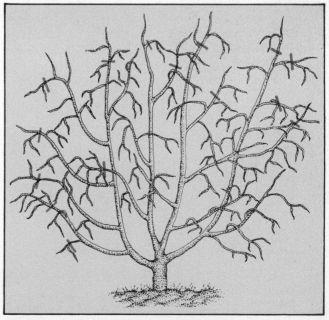

Type IV apple varieties, or tip-bearers, require many small cuts throughout the tree to renew fruiting wood.

Healthy apricot fruit.

APRICOTS
Prunus armeniaca

Train to vase shape with three leaders. Apricot trees tend to spread excessively, so thin to upright wood.

Apricots bear laterally on spurs that usually live for no more than three years. Annually thin bearing trees to upright shoots. Thinning renews fruiting wood and improves light distribution. Don't head remaining branches unless branches are excessively long. Head long branches lightly to contain them.

Mature apricot tree.

AVOCADOS
Persea americana

Train to a multiple leader with three or four main scaffold limbs. Some species have a sprawling growth habit. Control this sprawling habit by selecting upright shoots for framework branches. Remove long horizontal limbs that interfere with development of a sturdy framework. Most varieties produce a strong framework with little training.

Prune mature avocado trees to restrict height and spread and for convenience in harvesting. Pruning maintains productivity of lower limbs by admitting light. Lighten ends of excessively spreading branches to prevent breakage caused by a heavy crop load. In tall, slender varieties, remove or shorten long branches in the top of the tree to prevent breakage.

Mature avocado fruit, ready for harvest.

Mature avocado tree has rounded form.

Blueberries require little pruning. Fruit is sweet, juicy and delicious.

BLUEBERRIES
Vaccinium species

High-bush blueberries are slow-growing, long-lived woody shrubs that require little pruning. Head rooted cuttings at planting with no additional training. Prune bearing plants close to the ground in winter or early spring. If shoots are too crowded, remove some older shoots entirely. To increase fruit size, head shoots that have an abundance of flower buds.

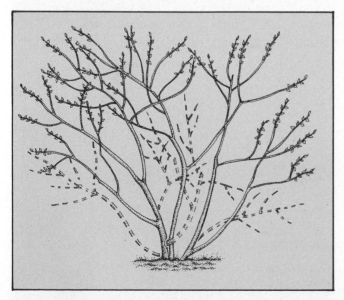

Prune blueberries by removing oldest, weakest shoots in winter or early spring. Remove weak side shoots in top of plant. Increase fruit size by heading back shoots that have an abundance of flower buds.

CANE FRUITS
Rubus species

The genus *Rubus* includes blackberries, boysenberries, loganberries, red raspberries and others. With few exceptions, these plants share common growth and fruiting habits. Canes grow one season and produce blossoms and fruit the next season. A few everbearing raspberries produce fruit in late summer on canes produced the current season. Wild, untrained and unpruned blackberries are difficult to pick because of thorny canes.

Train and prune these fruits with these objectives:

Support fruiting canes for ease of harvest. When fruiting canes are supported, new canes spread out below fruiting portions.

Separate fruiting from non-fruiting canes for ease of harvest. This makes removal of fruit easy and protects non-fruiting *primocanes* from pickers and cultivation. Primocanes are canes that appear during the first season of growth and before flowers appear.

Prevent spreading of fruiting canes throughout the garden. New canes are headed to force fruiting close to the plant's base. The farther berries are borne from the base, the smaller the fruit are at maturity. Keep canes in the trellis row and protect canes from being trampled by pickers, mangled by cultivation or sunburned.

Blackberries are produced on slender, thorny canes. The canes require support.

Blackberries—Immediately after harvest, remove fruited canes and train the strongest new canes loosely on a two-wire trellis. Remove weak canes, keeping 8 to 10 strong canes. A fanlike arrangement of canes is best because it allows for the best fruit and leaf development. Group several canes together in bundles for easy handling.

In addition to new canes that rise from the crown, erect blackberries send up root suckers. Pull out all root suckers. Head canes at about 6 to 8 feet in hot climates; 8 to 10 feet in cool climates.

In winter, after leaves fall, remove all laterals within 2 feet of the ground. Head any long laterals from 12 to 15 inches. Head shorter laterals less to increase fruit size.

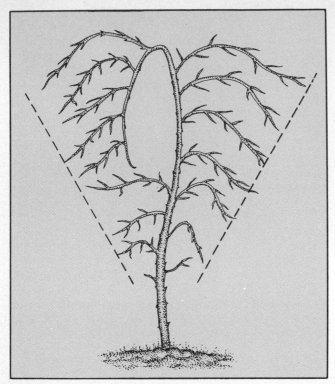

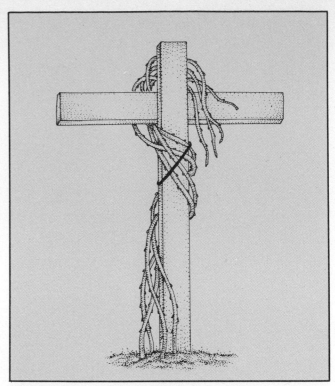

To prune blackberries, remove all laterals within 2 feet of the ground in winter, after leaf fall. Head long laterals to 12 to 15 inches long. Head shorter laterals less to increase fruit size.

Where space is limited for growth of blackberries, canes can be tied to a post with a crossbar. Don't tie canes too tightly, or they can be damaged as they grow.

Red Raspberries—After planting, prune the top to a 1- or 2-inch stub. If no pruning is done at planting time, the plant may set a few fruit. But the plant may fail to produce new growth in following years. Although a crop may be harvested the second year, it takes three years before full bearing is reached.

Raspberries may be trained to a *hill,* a *linear-row* or a *hedgerow* system.

The hill requires the least space because all suckers are pruned off with a shovel. Removing suckers prevents the plant from spreading beyond the hill. Six to 10 bearing canes are kept each year to form the plant. Hills are spaced about 5 feet apart. New canes are produced from large leader buds at the base of the old canes.

In the linear-row system, only leader buds are used

Raspberries should be grown on supports of posts and wire.

to produce canes. Plants are set 2 or 3 feet apart.

In the hedgerow system, plants are set 3 feet apart. Both leader buds and suckers in the row are allowed to develop.

All three systems require support from stakes, or posts and wire. Supports are important where canes grow to heights greater than 4 or 5 feet. If canes grow less than 4 feet, canes will stand without support after light heading. Supports help keep berries clean, make picking easy and help separate fruiting canes from primocanes. Remove fruiting canes immediately after harvest.

Red raspberries are often supported by two parallel, horizontal wires about 18 inches apart. The wires are held by crossbars. Headed canes are pulled up between wires as fruiting canes are removed.

Canes of ever-bearing varieties fruit on the tips the first year. More fruit is produced on the basal portions in following years. Annual pruning consists of removal of second-year canes after canes have fruited. First-

Beautiful fruit of red raspberries are delicious. Pruning helps canes produce bigger, better fruit.

TRAINING AND PRUNING RED RASPBERRIES

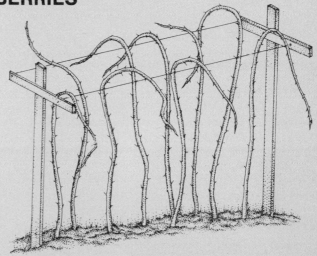

Single red raspberry plants can be trained by tying canes to a stake.

Red raspberries can be supported by two parallel, horizontal wires. Wires are spaced 18 inches apart and held by crossbars. Pull headed canes between wires.

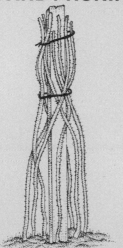

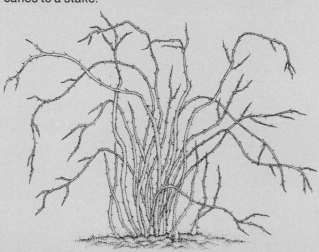

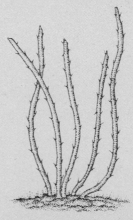

Red raspberries can be left free-standing. If plants are allowed to grow too long, fruit rubs against ground.

To prevent loss of fruit from free-standing raspberry bushes, head all canes over 4-1/2 feet long.

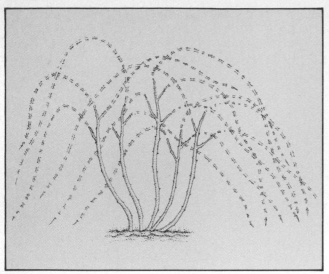

Before pruning, black raspberries have long canes. Fruit rests on ground and can be ruined.

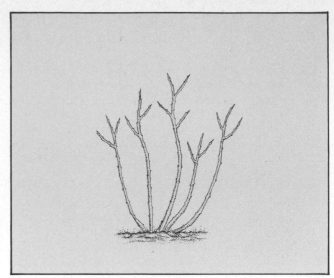

After pruning, raspberry canes are free-standing. Plants will produce more and better fruit.

year canes should also be headed several inches behind the area of fruiting.

Black Raspberries—Black raspberries do not produce suckers. These plants are pruned differently from red raspberries. Canes are left free-standing because they are stiffer and less vigorous than red-raspberry canes.

Fruiting canes are headed to spurs annually. Laterals on small canes should be headed to two buds. Larger canes may carry 8 to 12 buds per lateral.

CHERRY, SOUR
Prunus cerasus

Training Immature Trees—Sour-cherry trees have weak wood and tend to form crotches that break easily under a load of fruit. Head nursery trees at 18 to 24 inches and select three or four shoots with wide crotch angles. Train to a multiple leader. Because sour cherries branch freely, heading is not required after the first dormant heading of scaffold limbs.

Pruning Bearing Trees—Contain height and spread by thinning as needed. Sour cherries also tolerate hedging if not allowed to become too dense.

CHERRY, SWEET
Prunus avium

Training Immature Trees—Sweet-cherry trees ordinarily branch only at the start of a season's growth. Sometimes, sweet cherries won't branch at all. If not pruned, these trees quickly become tall with few branches close to the ground.

Head trees about 18 to 24 inches above ground at planting. Head all shoots to 24 to 36 inches after the first and second year's growth. Remove terminal buds of shorter shoots to promote branching. In the third and fourth years, head only the vigorous shoots. When fruiting begins, gradually remove a few scaffolds until seven or eight remain. Head all shoots annually in dormant season. Heading develops low, spreading trees that are easy to pick.

Pruning Mature Trees—Sweet cherries fruit on spurs

Mature cherry tree.

that live up to 10 years. Thin tops as necessary to let in more light and keep upper limbs in reach. Prune old, devitalized trees harder, using both heading and thinning cuts to increase vigor.

Fruit from a healthy sweet-cherry tree is round and juicy, bright-red in color.

TRAINING A CHERRY TREE

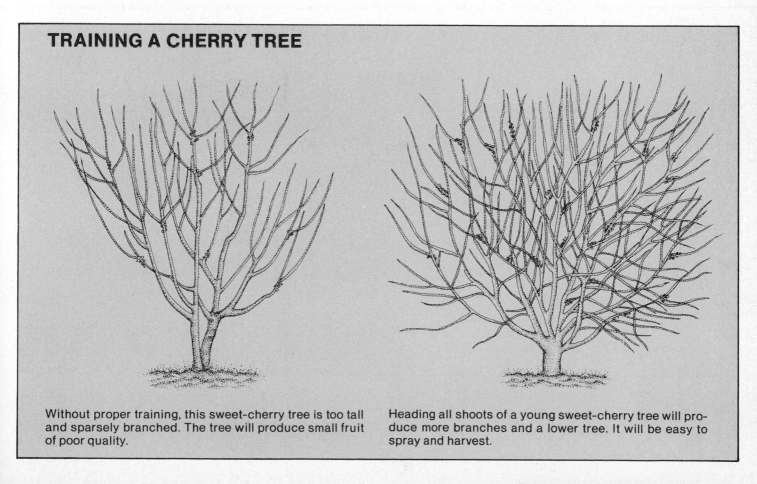

Without proper training, this sweet-cherry tree is too tall and sparsely branched. The tree will produce small fruit of poor quality.

Heading all shoots of a young sweet-cherry tree will produce more branches and a lower tree. It will be easy to spray and harvest.

Burred hulls and toothed leaves of chestnut.

CHESTNUT
Castenea mollisima
The edible chestnut needs little encouragement to grow with a single straight trunk. Develop wide-spreading permanent scaffolds about 6 feet above ground. Mature trees seldom need pruning.

CITRUS
Citrus species
Oranges, grapefruit and lemons are closely related members of the citrus family. These plants have similar growth and fruiting habits.

Citrus are evergreens and do not have reserves of starch for growth. Citrus grow, bloom and fruit at any time when weather is favorable. This makes pruning for renewal of fruit unnecessary. Citrus are pruned to let light and chemical sprays into the center of the tree, for containment and for appearance.

Prune tops regularly to keep trees from becoming too tall. Avoid pruning lower, outer limbs. These limbs produce most of the fruit. Train by thinning to maintain a compact shape. Thinning ensures that early fruiting takes place on wood strong enough to support weight of fruit. Thin to strong laterals or to main branches at any time in frost-free areas or after danger of frost in cold climates.

Oranges—Training is necessary to prevent breakage under weight of heavy crops and to keep lower limbs high. Train trees to a central leader. Gradually remove lower side limbs and raise the head. Train until trees are high so lower limbs can spread out and downward without touching the ground.

Once established, oranges need little pruning except to remove dead, twiggy growth.

Grapefruit—Prune the same way as oranges.

Lemons—Because lemon trees grow more open and rangy than other citrus, more pruning is needed to

Mature evergreen lemon trees produce tangy, colorful fruit.

keep lemon trees under control. Lemons respond to pruning with vigorous new growth.

Head young trees at about 3 feet and select three or four main leaders. Head leaders severely to balance the top if many roots have been removed through transplanting. More leaders may be selected as trees grow. Thin and head as required to develop compact trees.

Lemon trees produce strong-growing water sprouts on the trunk. Water sprouts run up through the center of trees and cause crowded conditions. Properly spread, water sprouts can be used to fill gaps in the canopy. Pull water sprouts over before they are too stiff or tie them in place. Remove all unwanted water sprouts several times annually. Prune rangy branches to solid wood closer to the trunk. This lightens branch ends and prevents breakage.

Orange tree with fruit, ready for harvest.

Rejuvenating Citrus Trees—As citrus trees get older and larger, they produce fewer and smaller fruit. This happens because inside and lower limbs become weaker from shading. Topping and hedging are used to correct this problem. Pruning can be done all at once, with a consequent loss of yield. Or pruning can be done gradually, removing parts of the tops and sides each year. Removing deadwood allows more light into the interior and stimulates new growth. In areas with a frost hazard, don't prune until after the frost-free date.

Old, weak trees can be renewed by *skeletonization*. Skeletonization removes all foliage and all wood less than 1 inch in diameter. It stimulates the production of much new wood. A coating of whitewash must be applied to the entire tree immediately after skeletonization to prevent sunburn of the limbs.

If wood in lower limbs becomes weak and sickly, remove branches by undercutting. Leave new upper foliage.

Red currants.

CURRANTS
Ribes species

At planting, cut tops back to two or three canes. Head these canes to stimulate shoot development. On bearing bushes, remove any borer-infested wood and destroy it immediately. Remove weak shoots and head other shoots a few inches.

On a mature bush, thin to keep two to four third-year canes, three to five second-year canes and four to six first-year canes.

With black currants, remove all canes over 1 year old and thin the rest. Head 6 to 10 of the strongest canes, removing approximately 1/4 of the growth.

FIG
Ficus carica

Training Young Trees—Figs can be grown as bushes with multiple trunks or as trees. In cold regions, fig bushes regenerate faster after a freeze than single-trunk trees.

Mature 'Mission' figs.

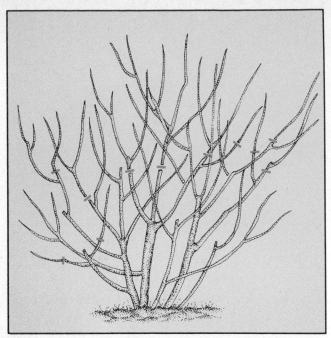

Pruning bush-form figs is easy. Thin to control height. Head to stimulate new fruiting branches.

To train as bushes, plant in a depression and head 12 inches above the ground. After several branches have formed, fill in the depression and mound soil so the bases of the shoots are below ground. Head shoots annually at 2- or 3-foot intervals to stimulate branching. This ensures fruiting close to the ground.

Train fig trees to the multiple leader system with three or four main scaffold limbs and two or three secondary scaffolds on each main scaffold. Remove suckers and basal sprouts annually.

Pruning Mature Trees—The first crop of some fig varieties is borne on previous-season's wood. Because most of this old wood would be removed by heading, prune mature trees by thinning. Remove any suckers.

Some fig varieties produce primarily on current-season's shoots. Head all of the previous-season's shoots to one or two buds during the dormant season. Remaining buds produce long shoots that bear 10 to 15 figs.

GOOSEBERRY
Ribes species

Cut back to several strong shoots at planting time. Train to a spreading bush. Thin shoots to allow space for picking berries without being stuck by thorns. On bearing bushes, remove branches over 3 years old.

Bright-green clusters of 'Seneca' grapes.

Deep-purple clusters of 'Zinfandel' grapes.

Grapes grown on arbors provide shade and fruit for enjoyment by all.

New grape leaves in spring.

GRAPE
Vitis species

Three species of grapes are grown in the United States: *Vitis vinifera*, the European grape; *Vitis labrusca*, a native of northeastern America; and *Vitis rotundifolia*, known as *muscadines* and grown in the southern parts of the United States. Some hybrid varieties are also grown. The principal *Vitis labrusca*, or *slipskin*, variety is Concord. This grape is used in making grape juice, grape jelly and for fresh table fruit.

Many table grapes such as Thompson's Seedless and Tokay, as well as most wine grapes, are varieties of the European or *Vitis vinifera* group.

One important difference in fruiting habit influences training and pruning of these species. Although buds on the base of the previous-season's wood of European varieties are fruitful, basal buds of American varieties often are not fruitful. This means that while *vinifera* can be pruned back annually to two to four basal buds on each cane, *labrusca* and *rotundifolia* varieties must keep much longer stretches of cane.

Grapevines are trained and pruned for two reasons. One is to train vines for the gardener's needs. The second is to increase fruit production. Grapevines can serve other purposes too. On a multilevel trellis, grapevines can shade and cool the sunny side of a house in summer. In winter, when leaves are off, grapevines admit light and warmth. Grapes can be used to screen areas from view, increasing privacy. Grapevines on an arbor can shade a patio or a bed of begonias. Be careful where you plant grapevines. Vines may need to be sprayed for disease and insect control and sprays can drift onto surrounding areas.

Swollen grape bud in early spring.

Training and Pruning Fruit Trees   **85**

Grapevines after about 1 month of growth.

TRAINING GRAPEVINES

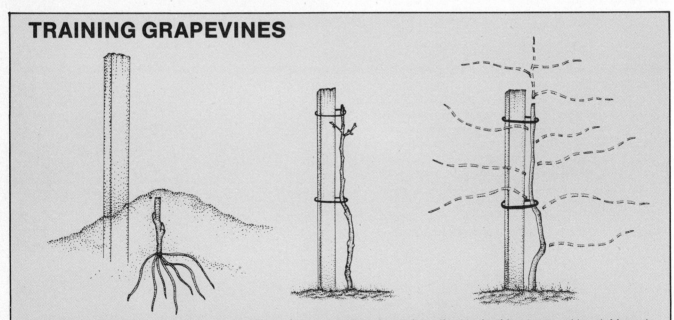

Left: When planting a rooted, pruned cutting of grape rootstock, set it so the top bud is at ground level. Mound soil over the plant. Developing buds will push through to the surface. Center: This shoot is trained to a stake. Tie shoot loosely to the stake and allow laterals to develop. Remove suckers from roots or crown. Right: At the first dormant pruning of the grapevine, remove all but one strong cane. This single cane is pruned back to two or three buds.

Training New Plantings—Grapevines are usually obtained as rooted cuttings and trained to a stake. Head cuttings to three buds and prune roots to about 6 inches. Plant top buds level with the soil surface. Mound loose soil over the top of plants to protect from sunburn, especially in hot climates. At this time, insert a stake next to plants. As canes grow, the stake supports them. The growing shoots push out of the ground.

At the first dormant pruning, remove all but one cane from vines. Cut single canes back to two or three buds. After a few inches of growth have been made in the second summer, the best-placed and strongest shoots are saved and others are removed. Shoots are tied loosely to the stake that was set at planting time. Remove suckers from roots and old stems. Allow tied canes to branch freely. Vines to be head-trained, cordon-trained or cane-pruned are trained to stakes.

HEAD-TRAINING GRAPEVINES

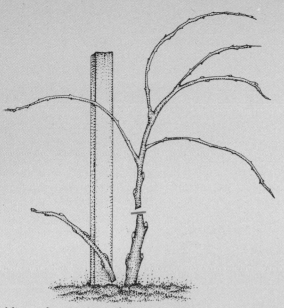

After a few inches of growth in the second summer, the best-positioned and strongest shoot is saved. Other shoots are removed.

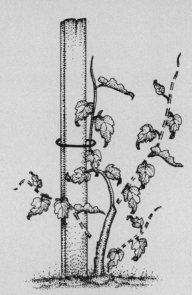

Canes of head-trained vines are cut off at the node or dormant bud. Cut through nodes to destroy buds above where the head is to be formed.

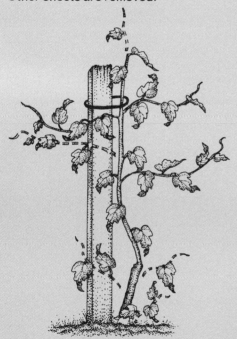

Mature, head-trained vines of European grapes are usually spur-pruned. Prune vines severely to control sprawling growth.

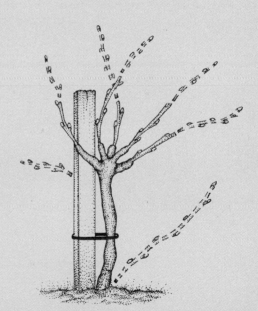

All lateral canes below the middle of the trunk are removed entirely. Weak laterals in the upper half of the vine are also removed.

Head Pruning is used for training European grapes when plants are confined to a small space.

Canes of head-trained vines are cut off at the node *above* where the head forms. Cut through the node to destroy the bud. Tie canes tightly to the top of supporting stakes and loosely about halfway to the ground.

Remove all lateral canes below the middle of the trunk. Weak laterals in the upper half should be removed. Two to four of the stronger laterals may be headed to two or three basal buds. The greater the diameter of vines, the more buds that can be left.

Mature head-trained vines of European grapes are spur-pruned. Spur pruning restricts the space vines occupy. Depending on vine vigor, remove all but three to six of the strongest canes that developed in the third summer. Head remaining canes to leave two, three or four basal buds, based on vine vigor. These are the fruiting spurs. More spurs, from 10 to 20 per head, are left each year as vines age.

Cordon Design is a modification of head training.

CORDON-TRAINING GRAPEVINES

Cordons have two permanent laterals that stretch in opposite directions along a support. This support may be a wire trellis, a wall or the top of a fence.

Choose two strong laterals, one on the main shoot and another strong lateral, at a point 8 to 10 inches below the support. These are the cordon arms. All other laterals and the main shoot are pinched back. Fasten cordon arms to the support at least a foot back from growing tips.

During the third dormant season, retain fruiting spurs on cordon arms. Space spurs about 8 to 12 inches apart, along the arm. Head the spurs to two or three buds depending on the cane vigor.

After heading spurs, refasten and straighten the cordon arm. Canes that grow from spurs often break off because of weight. To avoid breaking and twisting the cordon, tie side arms to wires above and to the sides of the cordon. Pinch back vigorous canes.

Cane Pruning is similar to head pruning. Instead of heading canes to leave only a few basal buds, a few long canes are left. The remaining canes are headed to 6 to 18 buds, depending on vigor. Select canes in a fan-shape instead of evenly around the trunk. This system is used for European and American varieties. Many European varieties are more productive if pruned by the cane system.

In the third dormant season, two canes are selected and tied to a support. Head two other canes at basal buds. Growth from basal buds supplies next year's fruiting canes. As vines become older, more canes may be kept.

The Kniffen System, commonly used for American varieties, is basically the same as cane pruning. A second, higher pair of canes is selected and tied to a higher support. Tie the central leader to a cane to keep it straight. Head canes just above top vines.

After the next season's growth, remove all but two canes at each level. Head canes to four to eight buds and fasten canes to the support.

In later years, remove all canes that have fruited. Select vigorous new canes for next year's fruiting. Tie canes to the support and head the canes to 6 to 10 buds, depending on vigor. From the base of old fruiting canes or arms near the trunk, select two or three strong canes. Head these canes to two or three buds each. Growth from these buds supplies next year's fruiting canes.

Top: A cordon is a permanent, horizontal branch on a wall or trellis. In the second summer, cordon-trained vines are allowed to go unheaded. Two strong laterals are chosen. Pinch back all other laterals and the main shoot.

Center: Two laterals are trained in opposite directions along the trellis. Space ties a foot away from the growing points.

Left: During the third dormant season, fruiting spurs are spaced 8 to 12 inches apart along laterals. Spurs are cut to two or three buds, depending on cane vigor.

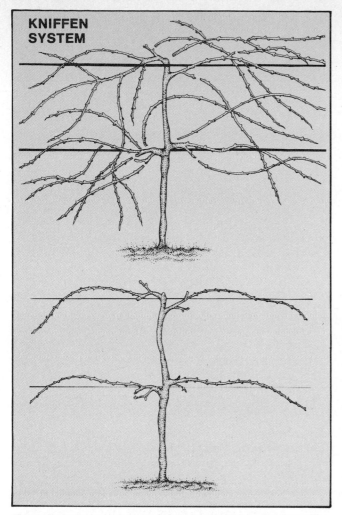

KNIFFEN SYSTEM

Top: American grapes are trained by the Kniffen system. This system is similar to cane pruning, but with an additional upper wire. Tie the central cane to a stake and head cane just above top wire. After next season's growth, prune away all but two canes at each wire level. Cut canes to two to four buds and tie to trellis.

Bottom: In later years of Kniffen pruning, remove old fruiting canes and select vigorous canes for next year's fruiting. Tie canes to trellis and cut back to 6 to 10 buds. Select two or three strong canes from base of old fruiting cane or arms near the trunk. Cut canes back to two or three buds each. Growth from these buds will supply next year's fruiting canes.

Training To An Arbor is similar to the Kniffen system. The leader is not headed until it has grown across the entire trellis. Once the basic framework of vines is established, side arms can be cane-pruned or spur-pruned.

HAZELNUTS
Corylus species
Training Young Plants—It is easier to train hazelnuts as bushes than as trees. At harvest time it's more difficult to rake nuts from under bushes than to harvest trees. To train hazelnuts as bushes, plant trees and let them grow without removing suckers. To grow trees, remove all 6- to 12-inch-long suckers close to the trunk. Remove suckers in spring. Remove suckers annually throughout the tree's life. Train trees to a multiple leader with four or five main scaffold limbs.

Pruning Mature Trees—Prune mature hazelnut trees severely once every four or five years. Remove all twiggy, horizontal wood of poor vigor. Make thinning and heading cuts into wood 1 to 2 inches in thickness throughout the top. Thinning and heading stimulates vigorous new growth that produces heavily the second season after pruning.

KIWI
Actinidia chinensis
Training Young Plants—The kiwi is a vigorous vine that requires careful training on supports. Vines must be pruned properly to renew fruiting wood. Vines should be grown where they are not exposed to high wind. Construct a trellis 6 feet above ground or train vines to a wall or fence. Permanent arms are trained

Mature hazelnut tree requires heavy pruning to maintain form and control growth.

Pick kiwi fruit as color turns from green to brown.

Training and Pruning Fruit Trees **89**

along the trellis. Fruiting occurs on side branches. Kiwi may also be trained on flat-topped *pergolas*. Pergolas are arbors with an open roof of crossed rafters or wires.

Stake kiwi at planting time and train a single leader up the support system. During the growing season, remove all side growth not needed for the main stem. When the leader reaches the permanent supports, train two leaders in each direction. Remove all other shoots. A single leader in each direction is satisfactory, but more fruit is produced when two are used together. As leaders grow, twist them around the wire with a full turn every 18 to 24 inches. Leaders can also be tied into position. A system of temporary fruiting arms develops at 12- to 15-inch intervals along these leaders.

Head fruiting laterals to seven or eight buds early in the season. Shorten excessive growth back to the same point. Laterals are grown for three seasons and fruited for two before they are removed. When kiwi are grown

Olive fruit is borne laterally on last season's shoots.

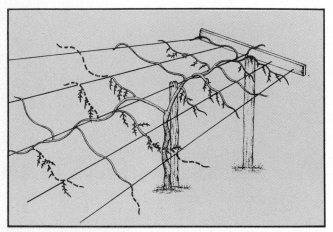

Kiwi fruit are trained on fruiting laterals. Laterals produce fruit for three years, then should be removed.

on pergolas, head spurs harder and more often to keep them as short as possible.

Prune kiwi in midwinter to avoid bleeding. Remove all 3-year-old fruiting arms each year. Head younger fruiting arms, but leave two buds past where the fruit was borne. Head new canes to clear the ground.

To train kiwi on a pergola, plant vines down the middle and train single stems to the top of the pergola. Let vines branch and train one or two branches to become main leaders. Allow these leaders to grow lengthwise up and down the center of the pergola. Develop a series of permanent, horizontal, fruiting-secondary laterals at right angles to the main leaders. Fruiting-secondary laterals should be 24 to 30 inches apart. Temporary fruiting spurs are developed along permanent secondary laterals.

To ensure adequate pollination, graft in a male *scion* in place of every ninth fruiting arm. Scions are buds of stems of the kiwi plant. Scions develops into *staminate arms* or male pollen-bearing organs.

Pruning Bearing Vines—Summer and winter pruning is needed to control the exceptional vigor of kiwi vines. Fruiting occurs on the first two buds of current-season's growth. Although new canes may appear at

almost any point on vines, only canes from previous-season's growth bear fruit.

Strong, upright shoots on some kiwi varieties are slow to bear. Remove these shoots soon after growth starts. Strong uprights on other varieties can be tied down and fruited. Shorten long, pendant fruiting arms about 18 inches above ground.

OLIVES
Olea europaea
Training Young Plants—At planting, remove poorly placed suckers and shoots. Select three scaffold limbs and remove or pinch back all other limbs. If young olive trees receive heavy pruning for training purposes, they will not bear fruit. Avoid pruning until after trees have begun to bear.

Once trees start to produce, gradually select about nine well-placed secondary scaffold limbs. Thin out surplus limbs. Too-severe thinning during a year forces trees into a non-fruiting, vigorous-growing condition.

Bearing Olive Trees—Olives are borne laterally on shoots produced the previous season. Prune to

Mature olive tree is ornamental and productive.

Peaches require severe pruning during training to develop a strong, healthy tree. Here are results of hard work.

remove wood that has fruited. Pruning stimulates production of new fruiting wood. Prune in years of potentially heavy crops after fruit has set in spring or early summer. Thinning to renew fruiting wood and improve light penetration is helpful. Don't prune too heavily because trees may become vegetative and produce few olives.

PEACHES AND NECTARINES
Prunus persica

Training Young Trees—Peach and nectarine trees require more severe pruning for training than any other kind of fruit tree. Trained to a central leader, these trees may overgrow in the top and lose lower limbs due to shading. Y-shaped two-leader trees are practical and may fit limited spaces better than trees with more limbs. Three-leader trees are strong and easy to care for. Trees with four or five leaders definitely have too many leaders. Genetic dwarfs require thinning to four or five scaffolds with little other training.

Head young peach and nectarine trees 6 inches above ground at planting if you want a short tree. Head up to 2 feet above ground for gardening space underneath. Central-leader trees can be developed without heading, but all side limbs must be removed.

After heading at planting, shorten side shoots to 2 or 3 inches where you want a scaffold branch. Remove all others. Space scaffold limbs evenly around the trunk and several inches apart vertically. Scaffold spacing is

This peach tree has been well-pruned. It will require little support for a heavy fruit crop.

TRAINING YOUNG PEACH TREES

During the first two dormant seasons, peach trees require heavy pruning. Pruning helps trees develop a few, strong scaffold limbs for supporting heavy crops.

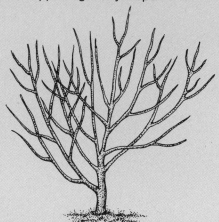

First dormant season, before pruning.

First dormant season, after pruning.

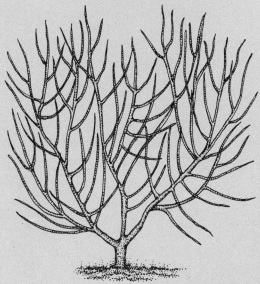

Second dormant season, before pruning.

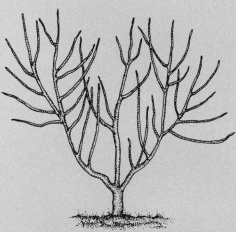

Second dormant season, after pruning.

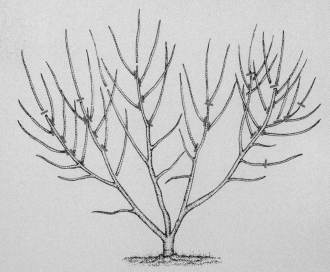

Third dormant season. Thin and head to develop strong secondary and tertiary scaffold limbs.

Fourth dormant season. During this and following seasons, thin and head to develop strong fruiting wood.

important because peach trees tend to have weak crotches. These crotches break if limbs originate at the same height on the trunk.

Pinch unwanted shoots in summer to direct most new growth into scaffolds. During the first dormant season, head scaffold limbs at 24 to 30 inches away from the trunk. Heading stiffens scaffolds and ensures development of strong secondary limbs.

Remove all vigorous shoots that compete with secondary scaffolds. Thin shoots again in the second dormant season and develop secondary-scaffold limbs. In the third dormant season, thin fruiting wood to prepare for next summer's fruiting. Favor the outward-growing wood so sunlight can reach into the tree's center.

Pruning Bearing Trees—Because peach and nectarine trees bear only on previous-season's wood, trees must be pruned extensively every year. Heading upper, outer shoots in midsummer to late summer helps bring sunlight to lower limbs and prevents dieback from shading. During the dormant season, remove fruiting shoots. Cut back to shoots of medium vigor. Prune to counteract strong tendency of fruiting wood to move upward and outward, away from the trunk.

Remove or thin strong-growing shoots in the tree top. Thin these shoots back to more upright shoots. Upper, outermost branches tend to spread too far apart. Thin weakest shoots, leaving shoots of pencil-thickness far enough apart for good light distribution and fruit production.

This genetic-dwarf peach tree produces delicious fruit.

PRUNING MATURE PEACH TREES

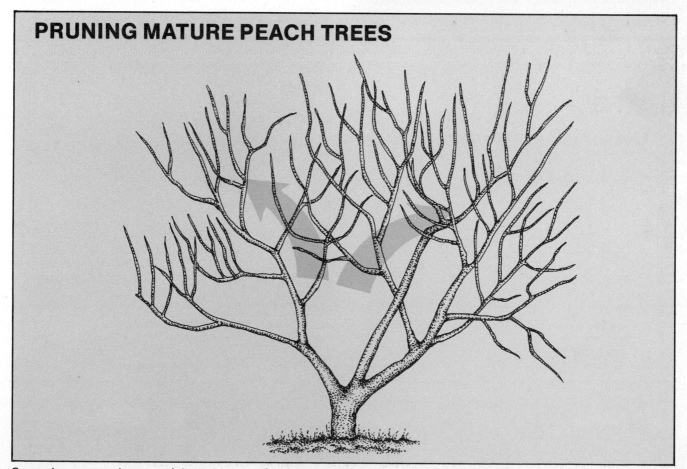

Severely prune mature peach trees to renew fruiting wood each year. Pruning also counteracts the tendency for fruiting wood to migrate away from the trunk. Arrows indicate direction of migrating fruiting wood.

Remove more wood from early maturing varieties than from later-maturing varieties. Clingstone peaches may be allowed more fruiting shoots than freestone peaches. Leave more fruiting wood in rainy regions of the country where fruit-set is likely to be light. Head longest shoots back to 2 feet or less, especially when excess shoot growth is a frequent problem.

PEARS
Pyrus species

Training Young Plants—Pears can be trained to a central-leader, multiple-leader, espalier or palmette. Central-leader trees are likely to be damaged severely by a disease called *fireblight*.

Bartlett pears have soft, flexible wood that bends down easily with the weight of leaves. This makes central-leader training difficult because limb-spreading must be followed promptly by tying-up of limbs. Other varieties of European pear are more easily grown as central-leader trees.

Head pear trees 24 to 30 inches above ground at planting. Select three well-spaced scaffold limbs. Shoots below these limbs can be left to fill in the bottom of trees. Remove any shoots between scaffold limbs. The central leader may be kept for one or two years to help spread permanent scaffolds. The central leader should be suppressed and eventually removed.

Head scaffolds each year at 2-1/2 to 3 feet above previous year's heading. Do not head side shoots. If leaders are growing rapidly, summer pinching can stimulate branching. Tie or strap scaffold limbs together to prevent breakage while limbs are young and flexible.

Pruning Bearing Trees—Pears bear on long-lived spurs. However, pear trees generally require heavy pruning to stimulate fruit-set.. This is particularly true if there has been no provision for cross-pollination. Fruit-set is usually extensive on young spurs on 2- or 3-year-old wood. Don't head shoots unless shoots are over 2 feet long. Remove or head shoots to about 18 inches in length.

Head shoots to flower buds on 2- or 3-year-old wood. Remove wood that fruited heavily in the previous season. Leave a well-positioned, 1-year-old shoot to replace the wood removed. Remove water sprouts and suckers to replace fruiting wood.

PECANS
Carya illinoinensis

Head at planting time to about 4 or 5 feet. Remove about 1/3 of the top, depending on size of the nursery tree. Limb breakage can be a problem because of narrow crotches and brittle wood.

Mature 'Comice' pear tree has well-balanced crop.

'Comice' pear.

LEADER DEVELOPMENT IN YOUNG, BEARING PEAR TREES

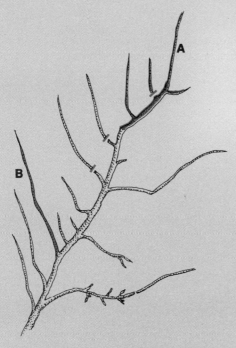

Scaffold limbs are pulled outward by fruit. Thin shoots and locate leader A and renewal leader B.

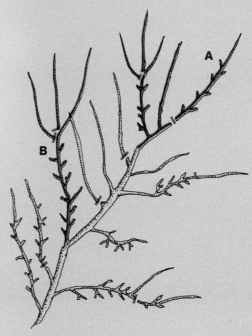

Following season, remove water sprouts and fruiting wood. Thin to single, upright shoots. Remove leader A.

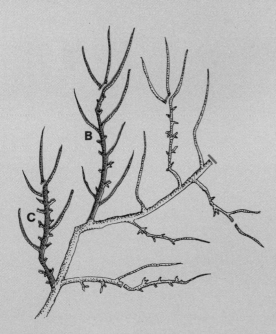

Following season note dominance of renewal leader B. Branch C will become the new renewal leader.

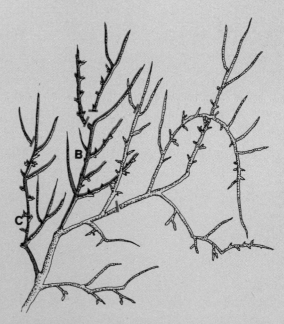

Remove outward fruiting wood to establish dominance of leader B. Renewal leader C will soon replace leader B.

Colorful 'Hachiya' persimmon fruit.

Train pecans to a central leader, avoiding narrow-angle crotches. Head scaffold limbs to stiffen and strengthen. Prune lightly the first five or six years. Remove limbs that are crowded, have poor angles, are too low or compete with the leader. Mature trees need little or no pruning except to remove low limbs.

PERSIMMONS
Diospyros species
Head the nursery tree at 2-1/2 to 3 feet at planting. Select five or six shoots spaced over a foot or more up the trunk to form scaffold limbs. Suppress other growth below scaffolds. Head scaffolds 1/3 to 1/2 after

the first growing season. Avoid further pruning until the tree begins to bear fruit. Remove occasional crossing or poorly placed limbs.

Bearing trees require little pruning. Thin to more upright shoots to lighten branch ends. Thin out tops of old, weak trees to let in sunlight and stimulate growth.

PISTACHIO
Pistacia vera
Train to a modified central leader with well-spaced lateral branches. Stake the tree the first two or three years. Develop three to five main leaders with the first leader about 4 feet above the ground and the others

'Brooks' European plum.

'Satsuma' Japanese plum.

spaced at about 1-foot intervals. Pinch off undesired growth the first few years. Avoid large wounds. Wounds heal slowly. Trees bear on wood formed the previous year. Pistachio trees are slow growing. Little pruning is required to contain them. Male trees are required to pollinize female trees. Male trees are vigorous and may need more pruning than female trees.

PLUMS and PRUNES
Prunus domestica, P. salicina
Training Young Trees—Plum and prune trees are trained to a multiple leader with three or four main scaffold limbs. Head trees at 18 to 24 inches at planting and select shoots to be leaders. If shoots are upright with narrow crotches, use spring-type clothespins to spread limbs during the first growing seasons.

Most European plums—some are called *prunes*—require only one light heading of scaffold limbs about 2 to 2-1/2 feet from the crotch to stimulate branching. These plums bear heavier and earlier if they are pruned lightly instead of heavily.

Japanese plums require more severe heading of scaffold limbs to stiffen limbs and promote branching. Thin to keep outside spreading limbs. Avoid severe *bench-cutting* because this pruning method weakens scaffolds. Bench-cutting is a method of spreading trees by heading leaders to outward-growing shoots. Keep secondary branches that are well-positioned. Head primary scaffolds just above secondary branches. Head at 24 to 36 inches from the crotch to stimulate branching.

During the third dormant season, thin *tertiary* or third-year scaffolds to one or two per secondary. Because Japanese plums tend to be narrow and upright, it helps to thin interior shoots to spread the tree.

Pruning Bearing Trees—Prune European plums to lighten branch ends as needed to prevent breakage. Fruiting wood renewal comes from long water sprouts. These water sprouts arise on the upper side of arched fruiting limbs. Cut back to the arch on these limbs to reduce tree height and renew fruiting wood.

Pruning mature Japanese plums consists of thinning out 1-year-old shoots. Leave some 1-year-old shoots to renew fruiting wood. Remove a few branches carrying old, weak spurs.

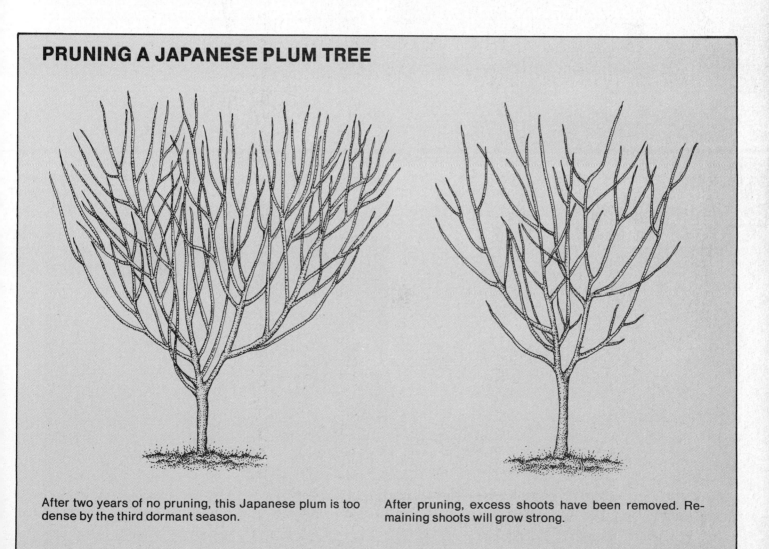

PRUNING A JAPANESE PLUM TREE

After two years of no pruning, this Japanese plum is too dense by the third dormant season.

After pruning, excess shoots have been removed. Remaining shoots will grow strong.

'Wonderful' pomegranate fruit.

POMEGRANATES
Punica granatum

Pomegranates may be pruned to bushes, or to single-trunk or multiple-trunk trees. Bushes are easier to maintain because pomegranates produce many basal suckers. A single trunk is likely to be killed in a freeze, but some of the multiple trunks could survive. If one or two trunks are lost, new ones can be developed from suckers.

Bearing trees require annual thinning to keep them open for harvesting and to renew fruiting wood. Light, annual thinning leaves slow-growing mature wood with flower spurs and maintains production. Remove basal suckers annually.

QUINCE
Cydonia oblonga

Quince can be trained as shrubs or small trees. Multiple-leader trees with four main scaffold limbs are easiest to manage. Head young trees at 18 to 24 inches. Space branches about 6 inches apart.

Quince fruit is borne terminally on shoots that grow the same year. Thin branches to improve penetration of sunlight and chemical sprays. Do not head shoots.

WALNUTS
Juglans species

Training Young Trees—Walnut trees are large and wide-spreading. It is best to develop main scaffold branches about 5 or 6 feet above ground. Because nursery trees headed at 5 or 6 feet would grow little, if ever, it is necessary to head trees lower and develop a new trunk.

Head trees at planting to four or five buds. Install a 2x2 stake extending 6 feet above ground. Tie the

Immature English walnuts.

Walnut trees should be trained to a modified-leader system. After 4 years of training, tree should look like this. Note stubs left to shade trunk.

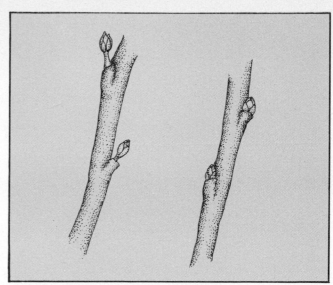

It is important to avoid scaffold development from necked-buds on walnut trees. Scaffolds should not be developed from buds shown at left. The closely attached buds on the right will produce strong scaffolds.

Wide-spreading, mature walnut tree provides shade and nuts.

leader loosely to the stake. Pinch back all shoots that compete with the leader.

After the first growing season, head the leader about three buds above the stake. Remove all side limbs. Break off buds on short stems or "necks." Removing these necked buds lets strong scaffold limbs form from secondary buds below. Limbs formed from necked buds have weak crotches and break off easily. If the leader didn't grow enough, head back the leader to last season's growth. Continue to train this leader in the second summer. Keep the leader staked up through the second summer.

In the second dormant season select four to six scaffold limbs at 5 to 7 feet above ground. Choose limbs with wide-angle crotches. Avoid limbs that are completely horizontal. Remove lateral branches below the lowest scaffold limb. Branches lower on the trunk should be cut to short stubs.

Heading of scaffolds is not necessary with tip-bearers such as 'Franquette' and 'Hartley'. Heading is important with newer varieties that bear laterally. Head scaffold limbs of 'Amigo', 'Chico', 'Payne', 'Serr' and other heavy bearers 1/4 to 1/2 during the first dormant season. Prune and head scaffolds each season.

Careful attention to this training procedure is necessary to obtain a structurally strong walnut tree.

Pruning Bearing Trees—Young, bearing walnut trees usually do not need pruning. Some new, heavy-bearing varieties stop growing or break apart if shoots aren't headed 25% to 50% annually. As trees mature and foliage becomes dense, all varieties benefit from thinning to let light into the canopy. It is difficult for the average homeowner to prune mature trees 25 to 35 feet tall. You may need to call in a professional to care for mature walnut trees.

chapter four

Pruning Roses

Roses are among the most beautiful flowering plants. Keeping roses looking lovely and healthy requires regular attention. This means attention to details such as food and water, pest and disease control, training and pruning.

Proper pruning of roses keeps plants healthy and productive, providing a continuous supply of blooms. Pruning roses is simple and easy, even for beginners. Following the guidelines presented here can result in bushes full of beautiful blooms. Detailed information on roses is available in the HPBook, *Roses: How To Select, Grow and Enjoy.*

Proper tools make pruning roses easy and enjoyable. A pair of sharp pruning shears is the most important tool you'll need. Ragged cuts made by dull tools injure rose plants and can create problems with diseases. Loppers and a small saw are useful if bushes are large. Gloves protect hands and arms from thorns.

Careful pruning of rosebushes produces beautiful blooms to brighten gardens with islands of color.

Left: The hybrid tea rose, 'Granada', is an excellent example of the degree of perfection that motivates rose growers.

BASIC PRINCIPLES

There are many kinds of roses. Special pruning methods have evolved for each kind. Use the following basic principles to keep your roses healthy and beautiful.

● Encourage new growth at the expense of old. After some roses are several years old, new basal growth virtually stops. New canes are produced high on a few older canes instead of arising from below ground. Prune away old canes just beyond where new canes start.

● Remove dead canes to the crown. Dead canes are brown and shriveled inside and out. Removing dead canes is the first step in pruning any rose. Use a saw if necessary.

● Remove portions of frost-damaged canes after buds begin to swell. Winter-damaged wood can be determined by cutting through a cane. Healthy wood is white all the way through. Any brown discoloration indicates frost damage. Frost-damaged portions of canes should be removed.

● Remove all weak, thin, spindly growth that crowds the bush's center. Spread branches out, opening the center. Remove crowding stems and twigs back to their point of origin. Leave no stubs.

● Where two branches cross, remove the one *below* the crossing point to prevent rubbing.

● Remove any suckers. Roses are *budded*, a form of grafting, onto a wild-rose rootstock. Suckers are extra-vigorous shoots that grow from rootstock below bud unions. Continued growth of suckers weakens preferred rose varieties.

Suckers are easy to identify. Suckers have a different color and character, with distinctly different leaves.

Suckers should be removed completely, not just clipped off where they emerge from soil. Remove soil from roots until you can see where the sucker is connected to the rootstock. Hold the sucker close to the trunk and pull downward to break the sucker off. Young suckers pull away easily. Removing suckers removes adjacent buds too. This does not damage the plant. If suckers are clipped off above the soil, they sprout and grow another rose bush in the middle of the existing one.

Suckers occasionally appear on the tall trunk-stem of tree roses instead of underground. Remove these suckers by close pruning.

● Always cut at an angle about 1/4 inch above an outward-facing bud. There is a bud at every leaf. The angle of the cut should slope away from the bud. A cut made at this point heals rapidly and water will drain away from the bud. Stubs will not develop if you cut close to a bud. Stubs are a point of entry for disease.

If diseases such as black spot are persistent problems, dispose of all prunings. Never leave prunings in the rose bed or in compost. Sterlize pruning tools with alcohol after each cut.

Crossed canes that touch and rub together on rose-bushes can create open wounds on canes. The lower cane should be removed by careful pruning.

Pruning cuts on rose canes should be made at a 45° angle about 1/4 inch above an outward-facing bud. Angle of cut should slope away from the bud.

ROSE LEAF TYPES

The flowering rose stem has several leaf types. Recognition of these leaf types and knowledge of general position on the stem is necessary for successful summer pruning. The illustrations on this page show the differences.

Start from the bottom of a flowering stem. Move up the stem to the first leaf. This is a *3-leaflet leaf*. Typically there is one 3-leaflet leaf. Next are two or more *5-leaflet leaves*. In the stem's middle portion are one or more *7-leaflet leaves*. Two or more *5-leaflet leaves* are above the 7-leaflet leaves. Below the flower, one or two 3-leaflet leaves can be found. On many rose stems there is a straplike simple leaf above the last 3-leaflet leaf.

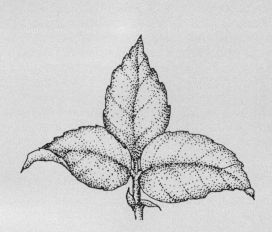

Typical 3-leaflet leaf.

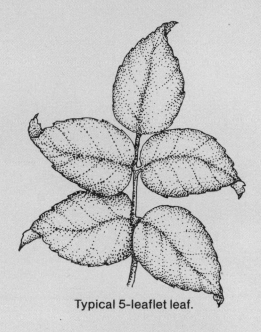

Typical 5-leaflet leaf.

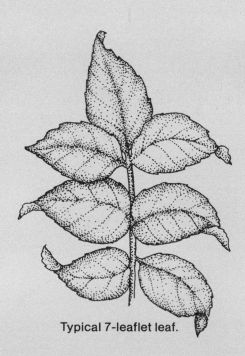

Typical 7-leaflet leaf.

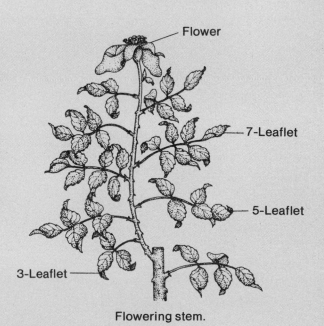

Flower

7-Leaflet

5-Leaflet

3-Leaflet

Flowering stem.

Disbudding is the removal of secondary flowering buds from a flowering rose stem. This process concentrates the plant's energy into development of one flower. This flower will be larger and stronger.

Knuckle Cuts—Knuckle cuts are used by commercial growers of rose flowers. Knuckle cutting obtains the maximum number of high-quality flowers from vigorous plants. A commercial grower cuts rose flowers immediately above the second 5-leaflet leaf, point A in the illustration below left. If a bush is getting tall or later growth is weak, the grower makes a knuckle cut. The knuckle cut is made below where the previous cut was made, at point C.

Dead Heading—This refers to removal of flowers that die on the plant. Dead flowers are cut above the highest 5-leaflet leaf if the stem is vigorous. Dead heading allows leaves to remain and continue producing energy for subsequent growth. Weak growth should be removed back to the second 5-leaflet leaf on new shoots or to the older stem.

Stop removing faded flowers in late summer. This allows seeds and the fruit of the rose, called *rose hips,* to develop and mature. Leaving faded flowers on canes in late summer ensures that no late-season, cold-susceptible growth is encouraged. This makes rose plants more winter-hardy.

Disbudding—This is done with thumb and forefinger. Disbudding directs new growth in spring and promotes development of large flowers throughout the season. As growth begins, some buds grow strongly toward the center of the plant. These buds should be removed with fingers as soon as growth begins. If three buds begin to grow from one leaf node, rub off the weaker side buds to direct the plant's energy into development of the main bud.

Roses that set flower buds in clusters are often disbudded. Removing side buds concentrates the plant's growing energy into the central flower. This causes the flower to become larger. Pinch lateral flower buds away as soon as possible.

Candelabra Canes—These are vigorous new shoots that usually appear after the first wave of blooms. These canes end in huge candelabras or branches of buds. Pinch the tips of these shoots when 6 inches tall.

These large shoots are usually less than 1/2 inch in diameter at their base. Candelabra canes are ordinary, but extra-vigorous, basal canes. If pinched, candelabra canes produce several good flowers. If not pinched, candelabra canes become unattractive and may die back if pruned when dormant.

Growth originating from a 3-leaflet bud is often weak and spindly. This growth has poor-quality flowers or no flower at all. Growth from a 7-leaflet bud is often vigorous, but it also produces a small, poor-quality flower on a large stem. In both cases stems should be pinched above a pair of 5-leaflet leaves. Pinching at this point encourages vigorous productive growth and produces high-quality flowers.

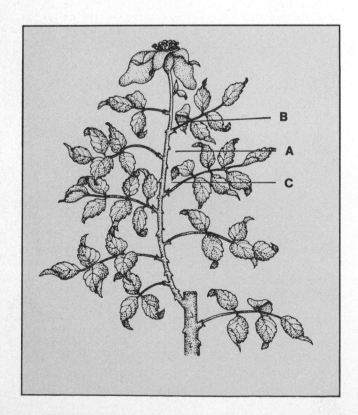

When growth is not vigorous and height is not a problem, remove faded rose flowers at point B. A cut made at point C, is called a *knuckle cut.* Knuckle cuts should be made if growth is weak or if a bush is too tall. If growth is vigorous and overall height is not excessive, remove faded rose flowers at point A, just above the second 5-leaflet leaf from the top.

Pruning New Roses

Bare-root roses from the nursery have tops shortened. In most cases additional pruning is still needed. Remove weak twigs and shorten main canes. Cut away all broken or dried roots and shorten long roots until they fit into the planting hole without bending.

Do not cut long-stem flowers from new rose plants. Cutting long stems removes food-manufacturing leaves needed by young plants.

Pruning Old Roses

Roses require annual pruning. Prune mature roses late in the dormant season. Mild-climate gardeners begin pruning in December or January. Gardeners in cold regions normally wait until March or April, just before new growth starts. Some rose species tend to die back if pruned one or two months before spring growth starts. Many varieties do tolerate midwinter pruning. If roses are pruned just before new growth starts, wounds heal quicker.

Another important reason to prune late in the dormant season has to do with winter hardiness. The earlier you prune, the earlier new growth begins. Early pruning promotes growth that might be damaged by a late frost. Conversely, pruning late in spring after growth begins wastes plant energy.

Vigorous rose plants, such as climbing hybrid teas, have several periods of rapid growth, called *flushes,* during the season. These roses bloom over a long season. They may tolerate cutting back two or three times if growing conditions are favorable. Frequent pruning encourages good blooming and maintains proper plant shape.

A few rose varieties bloom only once a year, usually in spring. Prune these roses after flowers fade to ensure growth of new wood for next spring's flowers.

Pick off faded flowers and shorten new growth after each crop of bloom. Cut back to strong side buds or laterals. The uppermost buds will form new shoots. In hybrid-tea roses and some everblooming roses, these new shoots eventually flower. After the second crop of flowers has bloomed, growth may be shortened again. This pruning system can produce three or four crops of flowers each season if conditions are favorable.

How Much To Prune—People who grow roses either professionally or as a hobby frequently differ about how hard or far back to prune roses. If winter damage has been extensive, it may be necessary to prune roses to within a foot of the soil. In general, weak-growing varieties can be pruned harder than strong-growing varieties. Hard pruning is usually practiced to produce fewer, more perfect roses. Light pruning allows a bush to grow to its natural size and shape. Lightly pruned roses produce more flowers. These flowers are slightly smaller than flowers from heavily pruned plants.

The following definitions can be used as guidelines in pruning hybrid teas and grandifloras:

Hard—Thin out all but three to five canes. Prune these canes back to leave two or three *eyes* or buds on each shoot.

Moderately Hard—Thin out all but three to five canes. Cut canes back to five to ten eyes.

Medium—Thin out all but four to seven canes. Cut canes back about 1/2 their length.

Light—Thin out all but four to seven canes. Remove cane tips.

As a general guide, remove about 1/3 to 1/2 of last year's growth. For most hybrid teas, this is five to ten eyes per cane. Remaining canes should be the thickness of a pencil.

Young hybrid-tea roses should look like this. Both canes and roots are shortened before planting.

After bloom is over, pick faded flowers and shorten new growth. Cut back to strong side buds or laterals.

PRUNING DORMANT ROSES

The best time to prune roses is during the dormant season. Begin by removing all dead, twiggy growth. Remove spindly stems that crowd the center of the bush. In general, all growth less than 1/4 inch in diameter should be removed.

Next, remove old canes at bud unions. Select canes or main stems to form the bush framework. Rose canes are old after three or four years. Old canes are grayish and have creases in the bark. New canes are a rich, reddish brown. New canes have smooth bark and brownish thorns.

Select healthy new canes to create a symmetrical plant. Use heavy loppers or a small pruning saw to remove old canes. Never leave a stump or stub. Cut canes flush with bud unions.

Shorten last season's growth by 1/3 to 1/2. Avoid cutting into old wood. Old wood is more susceptible to dieback. Thin smaller branches at the plant's top and center. Remove crossing branches and any suckers growing from rootstock.

Pruning directs growth. Roses should be directed to form an open-center, vase-shape plant. This means cutting to a bud that points up and away from the crown or center of the bush. However, some roses may tend to sprawl too widely. In such cases, prune to an inward-facing bud, directing growth in a more appropriate direction.

Prune dormant roses by removing dead, weak, twiggy growth and old canes.

Shorten last season's growth by 1/3 to 1/2. Avoid cutting into old wood because it is susceptible to dieback.

Don't leave stubs when removing canes. Cut canes flush with bud union.

Remove all other growth less than 1/4 inch in diameter. Remove stems that crowd the center of the bush.

Wound-sealers are essential for roses. Pruned rose canes can lose substantial amounts of moisture quickly, especially when days are warm. Fresh-cut canes are favorite entry sites for boring insects. Use a non-toxic sealer to coat wounds. The sealer prevents drying and protects wounds from insects and disease.

Remove all leaves from bushes in the fall. Leaves must be removed to induce full dormancy before winter. If leaves do not fall in mild-winter areas, cut them off.

Dispose of all fallen leaves, twigs and pruned stems. All these can be reservoirs of last year's disease and pest problems.

Renovating Roses

Older roses that have been untended for some time may need extensive renovation to recover their beauty and health. Older plants are quite tolerant of renovation. Most roses can be cut to the ground and recover beautifully if watered and fertilized.

The recommended renovation process is a little gentler. At the time of winter pruning, remove all canes except the youngest three or four canes. Use a saw and remove canes down to the base. Don't leave stumps. Remove all weak twigs and cover large cuts with pruning sealer.

Prune crossing canes, removing the lower one. Rootstock suckers should be removed by pulling them off.

Shorten remaining canes to balance the rose plant. Wound-sealers should be applied to all pruning cuts.

These older rosebushes have not been pruned for some time. They are in need of severe pruning and renovation to restore their former beauty.

Summer Pruning

Rosebushes are pruned during summer to increase vigor and produce high-quality flowers. Pruning is just as important during the growing season as during the dormant season. Summer pruning removes flowers for indoor bouquets and prevents seed formation.

Roses that produce seeds do not produce many flowers. Summer pruning also removes weak growth to increase plant vigor. Summer pruning of roses results in better flowers on new growth.

Exhibition Pruning

Exhibition pruning produces high-quality flowers by a specific date. Pruning basics are the same, but plant energy is concentrated into fewer flowers. Plants are pruned hard in winter and disbudded in summer. Experts rub off all but about four buds per cane.

Timing is critical. If pruning or disbudding is done too early, flowering peaks before show time. Prune too late and there won't be enough blooms to select for shows. The time between pruning and flowering varies according to climate. It usually takes about one and one-half to two months. Ask experienced exhibitors in your area about the best time to prune. Prune your bushes a few at a time, beginning one week before the best date. Continue pruning up to one week after the best date.

This exhibition-quality rose is named 'Honor'. It was judged the top 1980 All-America selection by the American Rose Society. Exhibition roses are judged on form, substance, color, size, stem and foliage, and balance and proportion.

This table of beautiful roses displays winners at the Portland Rose Society spring show. Roses are arranged by class and color.

PRUNING HYBRID TEAS AND GRANDIFLORAS

These roses produce flowers on current-season's growth. Rosebushes need moderate to heavy annual pruning to produce strong flowering canes. Prune to maintain three to six strong, healthy young canes and vigorous basal growth. Newer plants and plants of low vigor may not be able to maintain six canes. Canes should be uniformly spaced, ideally forming a vase shape.

Prune according to your purpose. Prune heavily for single long-stemmed flowers. Prune lightly for landscape display. Heavily pruned bushes produce fewer, larger flowers. Less-vigorous varieties are pruned lower. Prune these varieties to about 18 inches high and leave two or three dormant buds. Vigorous varieties are pruned to about 2 feet high. Two to four buds are left on each cane. Excessive heavy pruning of some vigorous varieties of roses encourages strong, but flowerless shoots.

Remove old, non-producing canes at the bud union. Prune overlapping interior growth to allow light penetration and good air circulation.

Remove unnecessary new shoots while still small. Remaining new shoots should be lightly pinched when about 1 foot high. Pinching encourages development of laterals. Heading back new tall shoots at regular dormant pruning time may kill the entire cane.

PRUNING FLORIBUNDAS AND POLYANTHAS

Floribundas and polyanthas are vigorous plants. Both plants produce a continuous succession of large flower clusters. Flowers are smaller and less ideally formed than hybrid tea flowers. Polyanthas and floribundas are usually grown more for landscape display than for individual long-stemmed flowers.

When cutting flowers, remove the entire *cluster* or group of flowers. Cut back to the first outward-pointing bud.

Winter-prune to retain flower-bearing laterals. Shorten them 1/4 to 1/3. Cut crowded, twiggy clusters back to a strong cane bud. Low-growing floribundas tend to produce twiggy interior growth that should be removed. Keep six to eight canes. Keep plants open, with plenty of room to develop new flower clusters.

Light pruning allows early flowering. Heavy pruning encourages new basal growth and late flowering. Prune roses harder or lighter from season to season. Pruning in this manner will balance plant response according to what the plant needs and your desires.

PRUNING MINIATURE AND PATIO ROSES

Pruning needs vary with the plant. Some micro-mini roses need no pruning. Some macro rose varieties need severe pruning in spring and touch-up trimming throughout the season.

To prune miniatures, cut at a 45° angle just above outward-facing buds. Open the plant's center by reducing the number of twigs. Covering pruning wounds with a sealer is not important because the wounds are small. But thick stems may require sealing.

Sometimes strong shoots appear and rapidly grow past all other shoots. Remove these shoots for balanced growth.

'Peace', hybrid tea.

'Simplicity', floribunda rose.

'Puppy Love', miniature rose.

'Joseph's Coat', large-flowering climber.

PRUNING CLIMBING SPORTS

Allow repeat-blooming climbing sports to become established during the first few years. Let these roses grow to the height you desire. Don't prune too hard at planting time or climbing sport roses may revert to a bush form. After initial pruning, bend canes and tie them to a fence or trellis. Flowering shoots grow from these bent canes. The same canes produce flowering shoots for many years. Each time you prune, shorten flowering shoots or laterals to 3 to 6 inches long. Prompt removal of faded flowers hastens repeat bloom.

Climbing sports do not produce vigorous basal growth as easily as bush roses. New replacement growth originates high on existing main stems. To encourage new basal growth, cut back the oldest canes to where a new stem develops.

To obtain the largest-possible flowers from hybrid-tea climbing sports, remove all lateral growth from the previous year. A series of long stems grow from horizontally trained canes. Each stem bears a magnificent bloom. Climbing sports of floribundas bear on many cluster-type laterals. Keep these laterals, but shorten them by 1/3.

Pillar roses are similar to climbing sports. Pillar roses are stiff and upright. These roses usually grow 8 to 10 feet high and are ideal for training vertically against pillars.

PRUNING LARGE-FLOWERED CLIMBERS

Flowers develop on short, 6- to 12-inch laterals. The laterals grow from 2- and 3-year-old canes.

Prune laterals in spring just before buds break. Shorten laterals to 3 to 6 inches or three or four buds. In summer, remove faded flowers to prevent seed pro-

'Centifolia' moss rose.

'Blue Moon', hybrid tea.

Climbing sports flower best when trained on horizontal supports such as this fence.

duction. Summer pruning promotes blooms from repeat-flowering varieties. Remove the oldest, dark-brown canes so new canes can replace old canes.

PRUNING SPECIES, SHRUB AND ONCE-BLOOMING ROSES

Gallicas, hybrid musks and species such as *Rosa rugosa* flower once a year. These roses need light annual pruning to maintain symmetry and remove dead and diseased canes. Remove flowers of repeat-flowering kinds. Leave flowers of once-blooming kinds so attractive hips can develop.

Old roses such as albas, centifolias, moss and damask roses produce flowers on laterals of old wood. Shorten long shoots during the dormant season. Shorten last-season's most vigorous growth by 1/3. Cut back laterals to about 6 inches long or three buds each. Cutting back harder destroys the arching habit.

Hybrid perpetual, China and bourbon roses are vigorous growers. These roses easily become a tangled mass of new laterals and sublaterals. Remove faded flowers and lightly thin dense growth. Interior twiggy growth should be removed during dormant season.

Shrub roses and once-blooming climbers include yellow and white *Rosa banksiae*, 'Belle of Portugal' and 'Mermaid'. Give these roses plenty of room to grow. Little pruning is required. Prune these roses to shape when young. When roses are mature, remove twiggy growth and old canes. In general, most of these species need little pruning. Prune old garden roses by

'Harison's Yellow', shrub rose.

removing old canes. Shorten other canes by about 1/3. These roses create more flowers if canes are arched and pegged to the ground.

PRUNING RAMBLERS

Ramblers flower in midsummer on laterals of long, flexible basal shoots that grew the previous season. Few true ramblers remain except in areas where they thrive—Nantucket, Cape Cod and the Oregon and Washington coasts. These areas usually feature at least two or three naturalized rambling roses. 'American Pillar' is the rambler often found in old gardens. 'Chevy Chase', 'Dorothy Perkins', 'Thousand Beauties' and 'Crimson Rambler' are other well-known rambling roses.

Hard winter pruning of ramblers encourages vigorous growth next summer. Hard pruning also reduces the number of flowers until the second summer. Ramblers are usually not pruned and simply become a thorny thicket. To prune ramblers for containment and appearance, remove all flowering canes to the ground immediately after flowering.

'Evangeline' rambler. This older type of rose was planted years ago. Each spring, the rosebush is covered with beautiful blooms. Ramblers are excellent for covering old buildings and trees.

PRUNING TREE ROSES

Varieties of hybrid tea, grandiflora and occasionally floribunda are grafted to trunks of selected varieties of wild, climbing roses that produce stiff trunks. Always remove any growth from tree-rose trunks below the upper bud union. Principles of pruning are the same as for respective types of roses, but tree roses are at eye level. An attractive, well-balanced tree structure is important. Lightly pruned tree roses are susceptible to toppling in strong wind. Heavy pruning is advised, depending on the variety.

Tree roses do not renew themselves with new basal canes. Canes should not be removed down to the bud union. Cut back hybrid-tea and grandiflora canes each year. Leave one or two buds from the previous season. Leave four to six buds on floribunda canes.

Remember the growth-direction effect of pruning. Cut to outside-facing buds to develop an attractively shaped head.

Check support stakes to make sure they are in good condition and do not rub or chafe plants.

Different varieties of tree roses produce different shaped trees. 'Bewitched' and 'Queen Elizabeth' produce tall, vigorous upright-growing standards. They are two of the largest tree roses, almost the size of small specimen trees. 'King's Ransom', 'Mister Lincoln' and 'Chrysler Imperial' are vigorous and upright, but not quite as tall.

'Peace', 'Chicago Peace' and 'Tropicana' are tall and vigorous. These varieties produce spreading, rounded trees.

Right: This European tree rose, 'Shreveport', makes an excellent display specimen.

'Renae', a climbing floribunda, makes a good tree rose when grafted to a trunkstock.

'Pink Peace', 'Electron' and 'Double Delight' are hybrid teas that produce dense, bushy flowering heads.

Popular grandifloras for tree roses are 'Ole', 'Pink Parfait' and 'Prominent'. These tree roses make small, dense heads that produce many flowers.

Low-growing floribundas make excellent tree roses or 2-foot-high patio standards. 'Sarabande' is compact and attractive. Others varieties are 'Angel Face', 'Cherish', 'Charisma' and 'Europeana'.

chapter five

Hedges, Vines and Espaliers

Pruning Hedges

Hedges are popular for separating spaces, giving privacy, hiding views and defining dimensions in a landscape. Hedges do require regular pruning to keep them attractive and contained.

The amount of maintenance required depends on style, either formal or informal, and the kind of plant. Informal hedges are allowed to assume a natural shape, with few changes by pruning. Occasional pruning is necessary to restrict size and keep a pleasing shape. Regular shearing is not practiced. Informal hedges require lots of space when plants are full grown.

Formal hedges generally need less space than informal hedges. Frequent shearing is required to maintain an attractive appearance. Regular maintenance is needed throughout the life of formal hedges.

Many kinds of plants are suited for use as hedges.

Two different hedge styles. On the left, Japanese boxwood is sheared to formal geometric shapes. Floribunda rose, on the right, contrasts with loose informality. Both styles require about the same amount of pruning.

Left: If your landscaping plans call for lots of hedges, choose plants that are slow-growing and easy to prune. Make shearing chores easy by using quality tools and equipment.

Some species require more maintenance than others. Slow-growing evergreens with an upright shape and small leaves make the best hedges. Slow-growing evergreens require little maintenance pruning. Wide-spreading, fast-growing shrubs with large leaves are not as desirable for hedges. Fast-growing shrubs require frequent shearings when used in formal hedges.

Conifers that sprout from old wood make excellent hedges. These plants retain lower branches well. There are many broad-leaved evergreen shrubs suitable for use in hedges in both cold and warm climates. Boxwood, holly and privet are well-suited for formal hedges. These shrubs have small leaves, dense growth and are tolerant of shearing. Deciduous broad-leaved shrubs are used for hedges in northern climates. However, these hedges must be dense to be effective screens in winter.

Flowering shrubs such as azaleas, camellias and oleanders are used for informal hedges. In most cases, flowering shrubs are pruned after blooming.

Above: This wall of green makes a private room out of the front yard. Pruning this slow-growing hedge is a big job, but it needs to be done only once or twice a year.

Deciduous, native azaleas at right create an informal hedge. Rounded shapes and colorful flowers line a woodland path at Callaway Gardens, Pine Mountain, Ga.

A rigid framework is barely visible behind this pear espalier. This pattern is difficult to achieve without strong braces.

STARTING A HEDGE

Shrubs should be trimmed from the time they are planted. Unpruned shrub on left is too dense. Foliage will soon shade out interior and lower portions, resulting in a high, open hedge with little screening. After pruning, shrub in middle will admit light to interior and lower foliage. Regrowth will come from sides and basal portions, as shown at right. Result will be a well-formed hedge with balanced foliage.

Starting Hedges—Shrubs are planted close together to form hedges. Plant shrubs 6 to 8 inches apart for small formal hedges. Plant wide-spreading species up to 2 feet apart for large informal hedges.

Do not prune conifers immediately after planting. Container-grown broad-leaved plants should be cut off 4 to 6 inches above ground after planting. Cut leggy plants short and bushy ones high.

Allow small plants, such as rooted cuttings, to establish an adequate root system before heading close to the ground. Close heading is essential to develop many strong branches down low. The lower portion of hedges look good only if healthy foliage grows from low branches.

Some shrubs naturally branch heavily close to the ground. Other shrubs branch only if they are severely headed. Hawthorn, privet, snowberry and tamarisk need severe post-planting heading. Moderate heading is needed for berberis, cotoneaster and pyracantha. Trim 25% to 35% of foliage after planting these shrubs. Don't prune evergreen conifers and slower-growing broad-leaved evergreens, except to shorten laterals.

To develop a dense hedge as a screen, trim hedge plants often the first few seasons. Shear the developing hedge two to four times each season, depending on the amount of new growth. Until plants actually grow together, shear them all the way around. Shearing this way results in dense foliage from the ground to the top. A more effective screen is grown.

Untrimmed plants fill in spaces quickly, but the resulting hedge is too loose in the bottom. The top overgrows and shades out the base. The hedge grows high, but sparse and open in lower portions. The hedge will provide little screening.

Shearing Hedges—Hedges should be sheared whenever necessary. In cold climates, the last shearing should be in late summer. Don't shear in fall. Late shearing in

It is easy to do a neat, consistent and safe pruning job from a stable scaffold. Make sure all tools are within reach and be aware of your position on the scaffold.

This dense wall of half-fencing and half-hedge assures complete privacy for the owners.

Hedge on left is poorly pruned. It has poor shape for light distribution. Light cannot reach side and lower portions of hedge. Hedge on right has good shape for admitting light to all parts of the foliage. Growth is uniform from top to bottom.

fall can cause damage to the plants if there is an early freeze.

Mature, formal hedges usually need shearing two to four times per season depending on amount of growth. Young growth is softer and cuts easier than mature growth. Frequent shearing can take less time than infrequent shearing, because work can be done faster.

One annual selective pruning is usually enough for informal hedges.

Shaping Hedges—Hedge shape can vary from rectangular to rounded or even tapered. One rule should always be followed. Shear upper parts narrower than lower parts. This is important for the vigor of lower parts, because the top soon overgrows and shades the lower parts. See illustration at left.

Be consistent in shaping hedges from the start of planting. It's easy to shear straight hedges with level tops and straight, sloping sides. Drive stakes on either end of a hedge. Stretch a stringline between the stakes as a guide for your shears.

Improving Old Hedges—Constant shearing on the same planes stimulates development of knots of twigs along hedge surfaces. Shoot vigor eventually declines. The hedge becomes less attractive. To avoid this, shear *inside* knots just before bud burst in spring. By

Old hedges can be rejuvenated. Shear inside the knots of twigs that have developed over the years.

Maintenance of these two hedges requires pruning with an eye for straight lines.

shearing inside knots, bare stubs are visible only for a short time before new foliage covers the stubs.

When only the hedge bottom has bare branches, head branches severely to stimulate new shoot growth. The top may also need extra-hard pruning.

If severe pruning combined with application of fertilizer and water doesn't improve the hedge, dehorn it. This means cutting the hedge off 4 to 6 inches above ground. After dehorning, regrow and shape the entire hedge.

Pruning Vines

Vines are pruned and tied for training purposes and containment. Vines must be pruned to maintain flowering, fruiting and appearance. Learn the growth and fruiting habits of vines so the best pruning practices can be used.

Training Vines—Many plants, star jasmine for example, can be trained as vines or free-standing shrubs. To train these plants as vines, use thinning cuts to develop several long branches. Tie branches up. To train plants as shrubs, limit the number of long branches. Stiffen branches by heading.

Vines climb on all kinds of structures, including walls, fences, pergolas, trellises and even trees. Vines climb and attach to structures by specially adapted aerial roots, tendrils, twisting leaf petioles or twining stems. Even with these methods of attachment vines need training and tying to ensure they grow as desired.

Vines bloom on previous-year's wood in spring, on current-season's wood in summer or on both old and current-season's wood.

Pruning Vines—Prune vines that bloom only on previous-season's wood *after bloom* in spring. This encourages new growth during summer and develops flower buds for next spring. If vines are pruned in winter or early spring, flower buds are lost.

Star jasmine can be developed as a shrub or a climbing vine with supports. Pruning controls the growth habit and initiates apical dominance.

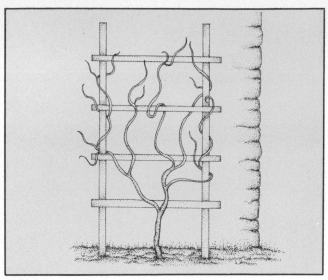

Climbing vines usually need a trellis or other structure for support. Wayward shoots should be guided and tied to the trellis.

Prune vines such as trumpet vines that bloom on current-season's growth *before growth starts* in spring. This stimulates growth later in spring and creates many flowers. Potential flowers are lost if vines are pruned in late spring or summer. Prune vines that bloom on both old and new wood, such as the Easter lily vine, during dormant season or after bloom. If possible, prune vines lightly during both seasons.

Some vines such as blue trumpet vines are vigorous, aggressive growers. They can quickly cover a tree or house. These vines must be pruned during the growing season for containment. Keep vines out of eaves and gutters, tiled roofs and shingles. Vines should be renewed if they become overgrown, tangled or full of deadwood. Renew vines by cutting to the ground or to within a foot of the ground. Some vines should be cut to the ground annually. Other vines such as grape ivy or treebine grow slowly and require little or no pruning.

Wisteria sinensis is one of the most popular, fast-growing vines. Annual pruning when vines are dormant will improve flower displays and help contain the rampant growth.

Training Espaliers

Espalier tree forms are usually two-dimensional. Espaliers are grown against a wall or as a fruiting wall or fence. Successful development of espaliers requires careful planning and patient attention to detailed training procedures for several years.

The principal objectives of espalier-training is to develop attractive small trees confined to space. The best tree designs combine limited new shoot growth with moderate fruit production. Trees are shaped for an even distribution of light and to produce good-quality fruit.

Here are general rules to follow when forming espaliers.

• Keep 20 to 24 inches between horizontal limbs for peaches and 12 inches for apples and pears.

• After outer limbs have extended 32 to 39 inches horizontally, allow inner limbs to start growing.

• Prune so outer limbs are always highest.

• Always keep limbs straight to prevent suckers. Tie or tape limbs to supports.

• Grow only three tiers of limbs for dwarf apples. Trees should not exceed 9 to 13 feet in width.

• Greater widths and more tiers of limbs can be used with more vigorous trees.

• Never allow ties to become tight and girdle limbs.

• Bend and form limbs while still flexible.

• Opposite pairs of limbs on each tier should be equidistant from the trunk. This keeps balance between fruiting limbs.

Dormant training of this apple espalier is limited to careful removal of wayward branches and tying of limbs.

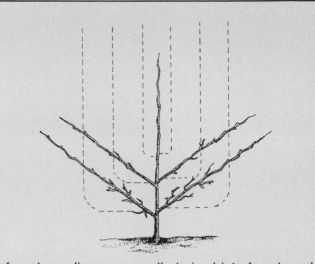

Informal espaliers are usually trained into fan-shaped frameworks.

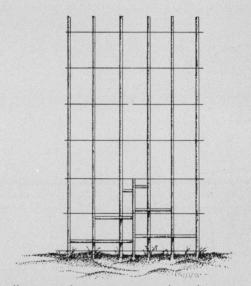

All espaliers require some support system, especially early in training.

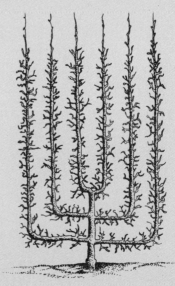

Formal espaliers are trained into rigid geometric patterns on a trellis.

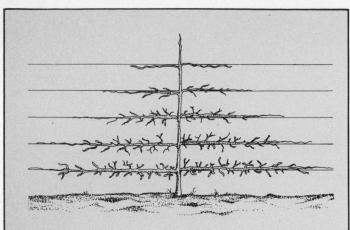

Horizontal espaliers are developed on wires stretched between posts. To develop horizontal scaffolds, head the growing leader just below each wire as it reaches that wire. Do not head secondary scaffolds. Tie scaffolds to wires.

Drapeau-Marchand system, described on page 123, requires planting trees at 40° to 60° incline from vertical. Use a wire trellis with bamboo supports.

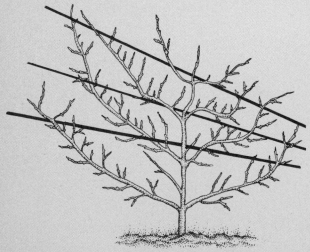

Oblique-palmette system allows four tiers of limbs to develop. Limb angles are adjusted to regulate vigor.

Horizontal Espalier is developed on a simple tight-wire trellis attached to posts, fences or walls. Shoots that grow toward or away from the wall are pinched off in summer; other shoots are tied to wires. Shoots that grow at proper heights are fastened to wires with masking tape or wire twist-ties. Tying operations must be done several times throughout the growing season. As the growing leader reaches the level of a vine, head it to develop horizontal leaders. Allow the vertical leader to grow to the next higher wire and head the leader again. Repeat the process for each horizontal wire.

The horizontal espalier's big disadvantage is uneven vigor throughout the plant. Shoots low in the tree form close to the central leader. These shoots tend to grow too strong and form water sprouts. The ends of lower limbs often lose vigor. Prune horizontal espaliers lightly. Excessive pruning upsets balance between shoot growth and fruiting.

Oblique-Palmette method increases or decreases rate of growth in different limbs by spreading or raising limbs. Balancing growth rate is easy. Spread limbs to a lower position to reduce vigor. Raise limbs to a vertical position to increase vigor

Adjusting limb position changes symmetry and affects the tree's appearance. Keeping limbs straight is difficult. Water sprouts also appear on upper sides of limbs. They are less of a problem with spur-type apple varieties than with other trees. Limbs can be kept straight by tying them to bamboo poles.

V-form Palmettes require a rigid framework or tight trellis and bamboo straighteners for each limb. Lower, outer limbs are formed first. These limbs must always be longer than higher, inner limbs. Dwarf or full-size trees can be kept in good balance with this system. Large trees are easier to train with the Baldessari-palmette method than the oblique-palmette method. See page 61.

This mature apple hedge provides easy picking at harvest time. Hedge began with semidwarf trees trained as an espalier across horizontal wires.

Candelabra Palmette forms beautiful, well-balanced trees. Candelabra palmettes require a strong, elaborate lattice framework for training and take longer to develop. Candelabra palmettes consist of horizontal arms with vertical fruiting limbs. A simple candelabra palmette can be grown from two horizontal shoots tied opposite each other on one horizontal cordon. Risers grow from horizontal limbs to form candelabra. This design is hard to balance because the risers close to the trunk grow more rapidly than risers farther from it.

Verrier Palmette was invented to avoid uneven risers. Verrier palmettes are a combination of the horizontal-palmette framework and candelabra palmette. The lower pair of limbs is grown out, tied down and then turned upward. The same procedure is followed with a second and sometimes third pair of limbs. Lower, outermost limbs are developed first.

If branches are too stiff to turn up at a sharp angle, several small saw cuts are made halfway through the limb and 1 to 2 inches apart on outer sides. Make cuts at the point where the limb will bend. These cuts allow a sharp bend to be made. Wounds usually heal in one season.

Instead of one upright at each upturned end of a tree, the upright can be headed and divided into two horizontal shoots. These shoots are tied down and allowed to grow until there is at least 12 inches between them. Shoots are then bent to a vertical position. An unusual and attractive multilevel, V-shaped candelabra palmette is formed.

Drapeau-Marchand systems, sometimes called *oblique cordons,* force trees to grow at 45° to 60° from

Pyracantha is easily trained into attractive patterns along a wall. Hand shears and loppers were used to establish branching framework.

vertical. Trees are planted at 45° to 60° and supported by bamboo supports and wires. Branches form at 90° from the angled trunks. See the illustration on page 122.

This 25-year-old sweet-cherry tree has been trained informally against a slat fence.

chapter six

Azaleas, Rhododendrons & Camellias

Azaleas, rhododendrons and camellias are popular flowering ornamental shrubs and trees. These plants are grown by gardeners throughout most of the world.

Azaleas and rhododendrons are botanically the same. Many gardeners consider them as separate species. Azaleas are primarily deciduous plants. They produce flowers of various colors and sizes. Rhododendrons are mostly evergreen, but a few varieties are deciduous. They also produce large, colorful flowers.

Camellias are popular evergreen trees and shrubs used as ornamentals. Camellias produce large, colorful flowers in different shades and shapes.

Azaleas

EVERGREEN AZALEAS
There are two groups identified by growth habit:
1. Azaleas with densely branched, compact tops.
2. Azaleas with less branching and more open tops.

Some varieties are intermediate. The open habit is more apparent in young shrubs than older shrubs. Older shrubs fill in with side branches as they grow.

Azaleas in the first group need pruning only to remove dead and shaded-out wood or for confinement.

Azaleas in the second group may be thickened by

Shearing azaleas along the edges will produce colorful flowers on the sheared edge.

Left: Brilliant azalea flowers provide pools of color in this attractive garden landscape.

heading or pinching. Lateral buds develop into shoots after pruning.

Each variety branches a little differently. Observe plants to determine the best way to prune.

All shoots need plenty of light to form terminal flower buds as growth stops later in the season. Increasing shoots by early pinching can increase flowers the following season. Pruning to increase the number of flower buds must be done after shoots have become a little woody. Prune early so a new shoot with several flower buds can develop. If pruning is done too early, when shoots are soft, a single bud breaks and becomes

dominant. Stop heading in midsummer in Northern areas and in late summer in Southern regions.

Buds below the terminal flower bud of late-blooming varieties often break and form shoots. These shoots partially hide blooms when the blooms open. For a better bloom display, rub shoots off when about 1 inch long.

DECIDUOUS AZALEAS

Some deciduous azaleas have an open, sprawling growth habit. Others are densely branched and compact. Well-established bushes of open-growing azaleas tend to produce long, unbranched shoots low on older branches.

When headed, deciduous azalea shoots branch at almost any point. To stimulate branching, pinch strong-growing shoots at various heights in early summer. Pinching develops shrubs full of blooms. Thin to remove old, twiggy growth. Watch for additional shoots low on branches in late summer. Head these shoots close to the ground to stimulate growth in lower parts of shrubs.

Renew old azaleas by increasing fertilizer and water, then prune severely. Head half or more of the old stems to the ground in spring, just before bud burst. Pinch new shoots periodically to stimulate branching.

Azalea blooms make attractive flower arrangements. Don't hesitate to cut flowers. Azaleas can easily stand extra pruning at bloom time.

'Exbury' azalea, a subgroup of the Knap Hill Hybrids, is deciduous. Large, fragrant, almost-square flowers appear before new leaves are fully developed.

These azaleas produce a living screen, offering privacy and color in this back-yard setting.

Rhododendrons

Rhododendrons generally require little pruning. Many varieties will grow more compactly and bloom more profusely with a little pruning. Flowers bloom in May or June.

Young Rhododendrons produce a large, central vegetative bud. This bud is located on top of each rosette of leaves. Smaller, less-conspicuous, leaf buds are located in axils of leaves just below the central bud. Branching will be sparse unless this large central bud is removed or disbudded. Rhododendrons continue to grow larger until flower buds are produced in the central location. Red-flowered rhododendron varieties tend to grow large and scrawny. Removing the central leaf bud produces a compact plant that flowers abundantly at an early age.

Rhododenrons can have two or more growth cycles in a single season. If plants aren't branching between growth cycles, remove central buds in summer. Always remove central leaf buds in autumn. A few varieties lack buds in leaf axils. These varieties do not benefit from disbudding. Many hybrids have a compact growth habit without disbudding.

Too much water and fertilizer can lead to excessive vegetative growth, lack of bloom and a leggy plant. Pruning can improve appearance by removing spreading branches and by making the bush more compact.

Rhododendrons have buds located in the leaf axils, but not on the bare stretches of stem between whorls of leaves. Cuts in the middle of bare portions of shoots leave stubs that do not grow. To avoid leaving such stubs, cut immediately above a whorl of leaves. Buds at that point break and form new shoots. If you wish to cut lower, it may be difficult to find latent buds on old stems. Look for a faint ring of bumps on old stems. At one time, the ring of bumps was a ring of leaves. Cut just above these leaf scars. Big, old limbs can be cut at any point. Remove stubs later, after latent buds have sprouted.

Old Rhododendrons in good vigor can be cut back to within a foot of the ground and regrown. This is called *dehorning*. At least one year of blooming is lost after dehorning. Extremely old stubs may be slow to start regrowth. It may take as long as 10 weeks before sprouting is noticeable. Prune heavily in early spring to allow regrowth to mature during the growing season. The first season after dehorning, growth of latent buds may be only a few inches. In subsequent seasons these shoots usually grow vigorously and develop a healthy, rejuvenated plant.

Flower truss of 'Nova Zembla' rhododendron at the peak of development.

Removal of the large, central vegetative bud on rhododendrons allows small, black buds to form branches. Disbudding encourages growth of more compact shrubs. Leaf buds are smaller and more pointed than flower buds.

If rhododendrons are too shaded to produce many flower buds, pruning the rhododendrons won't help blooming. Instead, prune shading trees to let more light reach rhododenrons.

Some rhododendrons do not replace cut branches with an increased number of shoots. Among these are the hybrids 'C.B. Van Ness', 'Bagshot Rub', 'Prometheus' and a few of the tender species. Rhododendrons with smooth bark, such as *R. thomsonii* and *R. barbatum,* do not respond well to pruning. These varieties seldom produce new branches from sprouts originating on older wood.

To confine a large rhododendron, train it to an espalier. Espalier rhododendrons produce good displays of blooms. Stiff wood and wide branching habit make informal rhododendron espaliers easy to maintain.

Rootstock of grafted rhododendrons may produce suckers. Remove these immediately.

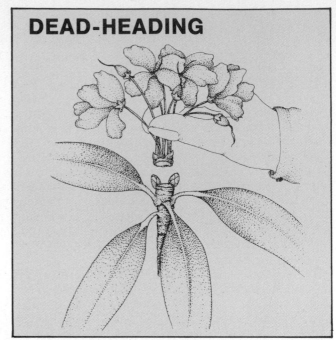

DEAD-HEADING

Remove old flowers of rhododendrons to allow new buds to develop more flowers. This is called dead-heading. Remove old flowers carefully to avoid damage to tender buds.

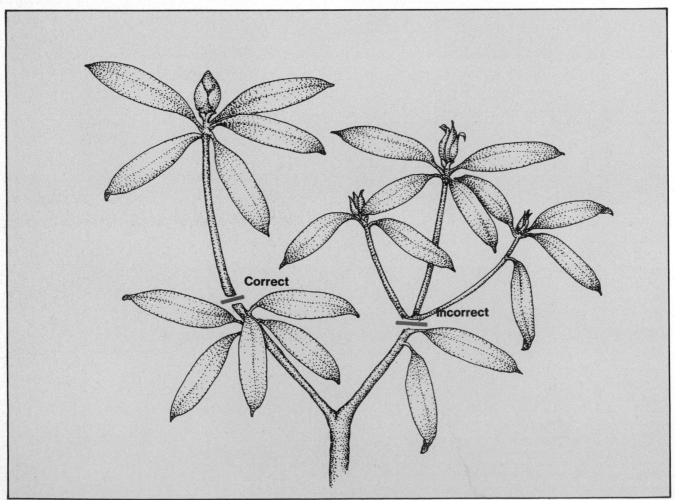

Always cut rhododendrons immediately above a whorl of leaves, as shown on the left side of this plant. Cutting at or below the whorl will leave an unattractive stub, as shown on the right side.

Camellias

Camellias require little pruning for foundation plantings. They are pruned for containment when planted close to windows and doors.

Camellias can be formally shaped with hedge clippers. Head into current- or previous-season's growth. This growth is generally a lighter color than older wood.

Varieties that produce a super-abundance of flower buds produce higher-quality blooms if some buds are removed. Camellias benefit from removal of old flowers that block seed formation.

Latent buds are located at the base of each flush of growth, where current-season's growth joins previous-season's growth. Shearing or heading *forces* or stimulates these buds, causing several shoots to grow. Thinning selectively with hand shears stimulates individual shoots to grow. The best pruning method depends on whether you want a few high-quality flowers or a large

Camellias require little pruning. Large, beautiful flowers can be produced by selective removal of excess buds.

number of smaller ones. Stimulate branching of leggy young camellias by cutting branches above where current-season's wood joins older wood.

To grow a well-shaped bush, selectively thin young camellias at planting time. Continue thinning until plants are well-established. Selective thinning produces attractive, compact shrubs.

Renewing Overgrown Camellias—Overgrown, weak or scraggy camellias can be renewed by dehorning or cutting back into old wood. However, the roots and trunk may not have sufficient food reserves to promote vigorous new growth. It is better to leave a cluster of temporary feeder shoots on top of central stems and remove lower side branches. After latent buds on old wood have grown new shoots several inches long, remove the top. This procedure produces renewed, much smaller and healthier shrubs.

Camellia japonica is a larger, more-vigorous and compact shrub than *Camellia sasanqua*. The *sasanquas* have a loose growth habit with a more natural look. *Sasanquas* can be headed to produce a more compact shrub, but with loss of naturalness.

To stimulate branching of a leggy young camellia, head just above where lighter-colored, current-season's wood joins darker-colored, previous-season's wood.

Camellias planted close to walkways, doors or windows can be trained as well-shaped bushes by selective thinning. Prune mature bushes for containment.

RENEWING OLD CAMELLIAS

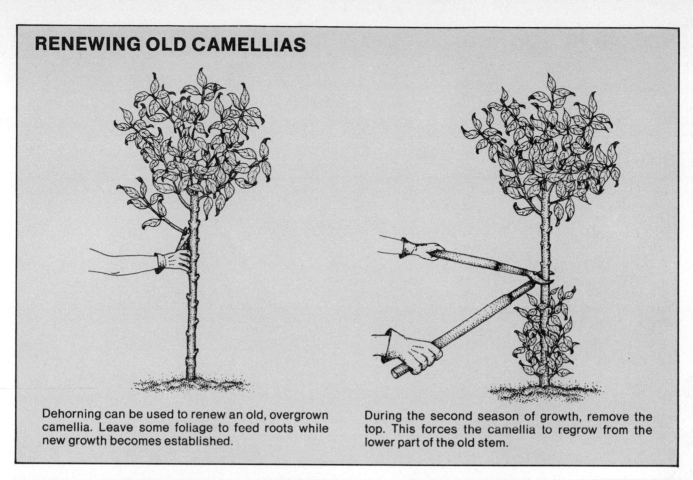

Dehorning can be used to renew an old, overgrown camellia. Leave some foliage to feed roots while new growth becomes established.

During the second season of growth, remove the top. This forces the camellia to regrow from the lower part of the old stem.

Camellias can be trained and pruned to become a large shrub or hedge, a small tree or a small bush. Careful training will produce a small tree with plenty of space underneath for gardening activities. Pruning and shaping will produce a short, rounded bush or shrub.

Encyclopedia of Pruning

This encyclopedia section is designed to provide basic pruning information for many of the most common trees and shrubs. Each listing briefly describes the plant, method and time of pruning.

More detailed information on pruning methods is provided in individual chapters that discuss specific types of plants or methods of pruning.

The plants in this encyclopedia are listed in alphabetical order according to botanical name. The plant's common name is listed directly underneath, followed by a plant description and pruning information. Pruning times are given for seasons in the Northern Hemisphere.

In several instances, plants are cross-referenced by common names to botanical listings. Instructions may also be given to refer to individual chapters for additional information.

The index on page 158 is provided to assist you in locating information on specific plants or subjects.

A

Abelia x grandiflora
Glossy abelia

Evergreen shrub that loses leaves in cold weather. Medium size, with arching branches. Blooms on first-year's and previous-season's wood. Head some old stems close to ground annually in dormant season. Prune for containment in spring.

Abies species
True firs

Conical-shaped evergreen trees and shrubs that grow to 50 feet with central leader. Prune by shearing early in the short growing season when new shoots are tender. Does not sprout from old wood. About a dozen species are used as ornamental trees.

Acacia baileyana
Golden mimosa

Evergreen shrub or small tree. Grows to 30 feet. Wide-spreading to 40 feet. Can be trained to attractive multiple trunks or single trunk. Train carefully, selecting crotches with wide angles. Stake loosely and head scaffolds to stiffen in early years. Thin mature trees and remove deadwood after flowering. Withstands heavy pruning.

Acacia melanoxylon
Blackwood acacia

Large evergreen trees that grow to 40 feet. Moderately wide-spreading to 20 feet. Trees can be trained to attractive multiple trunks or single trunk. Train carefully, selecting wide-angle crotches. Stake loosely and head scaffolds to stiffen in early years. Thin mature trees and remove deadwood after flowering. Withstands heavy pruning.

Acer species
Maples

This is a genus with many species. They vary widely in growth habit and pruning requirements. Most bleed if pruned in spring, so prune when fully dormant.

Acer buergeranum
Trident maple

Small, low-spreading deciduous tree. Can grow to 50 feet, but usually smaller. Stake and train to a central leader. Needs little corrective pruning.

Acer campestre
Hedge maple

Deciduous, slow-growing and thick. Suitable for a hedge or small tree. At-

tractive planted 3 in a clump and allowed to intertwine.

Acer circinatum
Vine maple

Small, slow-growing deciduous tree. It grows to 35 feet. Shrub valued for limbs and foliage. Train to 3 to 5 trunks or a single trunk. Let tree grow naturally.

Acer ginnala
Amur maple

Small deciduous tree or large shrub. Train to single trunk or multiple trunks. Can grow to 20 feet.

Acer macrophyllum
Bigleaf maple

Rapid-grower that quickly forms a tall, to 100 feet, spreading deciduous tree. Too big and invasive for most gardens. Head above branch whorl at 12 to 15 feet. Prune hard annually to control size. Can be pollarded.

Acer negundo
Ash-leaved maple, Box elder

Deciduous tree that grows to 50 to 75 feet. Train and prune same as *Acer saccharinum.*

Acer palmatum
Japanese maple

Small, slow-growing deciduous tree with delicate foliage texture. Grows to 30 to 50 feet. Can be grown as a shrub. Allow to take its natural shape. May be grown as single trunk or multiple trunks with little or no pruning. May be pruned for size control.

Acer platanoides
Norway maple

Deciduous, round-head tree that grows to 90 feet. Branches freely and densely along leaders. Leave small branches. Remove dead or crossing branches. Little other pruning is necessary. Thin branches of mature trees as required to reduce wind resistance.

Acer saccharinum
River maple, Silver maple, White maple

Deciduous tree, grows to 90 to 130 feet with open form. Pendulous branches. Grows extremely rapidly with weak, easily broken crotches. Train to a central leader, keeping only the well-spaced, wide-angled scaffold branches. Thin to reduce wind resistance. Remove water sprouts. Brace limbs in old trees.

Acrocarpus fraxinifolius
Shingle tree, Pink cedar, Red cedar

Deciduous tree that grows to 50 feet. Train to emphasize naturally slender shape. Needs support when young. Remove unsightly branches.

Actinidia chinensis
Kiwi

See Chapter Three, page 89.

Aesculus hippocastanum
Common horse chestnut

Large deciduous tree with heavy, pendulous branches. Grows to 100 feet. Train to a central leader as high as possible. Remove vigorous uprights growing on ends of branches to prevent breakage.

Aesculus x carnea
Red horse chestnut

Deciduous, round-head tree that grows to 40 feet. Give plenty of room and allow to branch close to ground. Avoid narrow forks. Keep central leader.

Agathis robusta
Queensland kauri

Large evergreen tree that grows to 50 feet. Train to central leader, removing all competition. Accentuate natural layered form with careful thinning.

Agonis flexuosa
Peppermint tree, Australian willow, Myrtle juniper

Evergreen tree that grows to 25 to 35 feet. Prune in spring after frost. Train as tree or espalier.

Ailanthus altissima
Tree of Heaven

Tall, to 60 feet, deciduous tree. Spreads by root suckers that must be thinned and removed in dormant season. Train to a single trunk or multiple trunks. Fast-growing with brittle wood. Train to avoid weak crotches.

Akebia quinata
Five-leaf akebia

Shrub, evergreen in mild climate. Can be cut to ground annually. Remove deadwood. Pinch to direct growth in spring or summer. Tie to trellis.

Albizia julibrissin
Silk tree, Mimosa

Fast-growing deciduous tree. Grows to 40 feet and needs staking. Train to central leader or multiple leader. Remove low limbs until crown is 6 to 10 feet high, then head leader to establish height. Head scaffold limbs to stiffen them after frost in spring.

Allamanda cathartica
Golden trumpet vine

Evergreen shrubby vine. May be trained as a shrub. Pinch during growing season to direct growth into shrub form or train as a vine.

Almond

Prunus dulcis. See Chapter Three, Page 72.

Alnus species
Alders

Fast-growing, moderately large deciduous trees. Forms central leader and grows to 80 feet. Gradually remove branches up to 6 feet high. Thin side branches if too crowded.

Aloysia triphylla
Lemon verbena

Small shrub, growing to 10 feet, or a herb plant with lemon-scented leaves and flowers. Before growth starts, lightly thin weak growth. During growing season, pinch to shape as desired. Easily trained as small tree by frequent pinching of side branches to encourage vertical growth.

Albizia julibrissin

Amelanchier species
Serviceberry, Shadbush

Large deciduous shrub or small tree. Readily sprouts from close to the ground. Lightly thin every few years for containment and appearance. Thin in late winter or spring before bloom.

Ampelopsis brevipedunculata
Blueberry climber

Deciduous vine. Head to main supports if in restricted space. Head and thin in spring for good spacing and form. Climbs with tendrils.

Andromeda polifolia
Bog rosemary

Small evergreen shrub that grows to 12 inches. Head and thin lightly after bloom.

Anemopaegma chamberlaynii
Yellow trumpet vine

Evergreen vine. Needs extensive heading. Thin wood after bloom. Remove weak shoots. Needs support for attachment.

Annona cherimola
Cherimoya

Large shrub or small tree, briefly deciduous. Can grow 15 feet tall and 15 feet wide. Good as espalier. Train to single trunk, gradually removing lower branches. Thin to let light to lower branches. Prune when dormant.

Apple
Malus species. See Chapter Three, page 73.

Apricot
Prunis armeniaca. See Chapter Three, page 76.

Aralia chinensis
Chinese angelica

Large shrub or small tree. Deciduous, grows to 15 to 20 feet. Remove suckers and water sprouts in spring and diseased or damaged stems as required.

Araucaria araucana
Monkey-puzzle tree

Evergreen, growing to 70 to 90 feet. Naturally grows as central leader. If leader is injured, select new one from shoots that develop below injury and tie it to a stake temporarily. Remove entire branches with deadwood at the trunk.

Bambusa species

Araujia sericifera
White-bladder flower

Evergreen to partially deciduous vine. Can grow to 20 to 30 feet. Little pruning necessary. Shape and prune lightly as desired.

Arbutus menziesii
Madron

Evergreen, grows from 20 to more than 100 feet. After a little early training, forms large tree. Needs little pruning.

Arbutus unedo
Strawberry tree

Evergreen, growing to 30 feet. Train to a single trunk or multiple trunks or leave untrained as dense bush.

Arctostaphylos
Manzanita

Ten evergreen species that cover the range from woody ground cover to small trees. Attractive foliage and reddish bark on branches. Little pruning required. Thin lightly anytime to show off interesting branch shapes.

Aristolochia durior
Dutchman's-pipe

Deciduous, woody, climbing vine. Little pruning required beyond removal of deadwood. Train as desired. Twines on supports.

Atriplex halimus
Saltbush, Sea orach

Salt-tolerant, medium-sized compact shrub that grows to 6 feet. Used singly or in hedges. Thin or shear annually as growth starts. This halts tendency to open out and become loose.

Aucuba japonica
Japanese aucuba

Evergreen shrub that requires little pruning. Grows to 15 feet. Not attractive as a hedge. Thin whole branches close to ground to maintain natural shape.

Avocado
Persea americana. See Chapter Three, page 76.

Azaleas
Rhododendron species. See Chapter Six, page 127.

Azara microphylla
Boxleaf azara

Evergreen shrub with fanlike, arching branches. Grows 20 feet tall, 12 feet wide. Thin moderately in spring, with cuts into center.

B

Bamboo

Arundinaria, Bambusa, Chimonobambusa, Dendrocalamus, Phyllostachys, Pseudosasa, Sasa, Semiarundinaria and *Shibataeo* species.

Bamboo are clumping-type grasses, valued for ornamental and timber uses. There are four general groups:
1. Low-growing dwarf bamboo
2. Clumping-type bamboo
3. Medium-sized bamboo
4. Giant bamboo

Dwarfs respond well to shearing. Clumping bamboo are planted in hedges and clipped or left unpruned for screens.

Prune bamboo to confine to an allocated space. Most bamboo, especially more vigorous kinds, spread by underground stems. If planted next to a fence, they may soon come up in the neighbor's lawn. If you wait too long, underground stems are too hard to cut. They must be uncovered and cut with pruning shears or a saw. A solid underground barrier of galvanized steel or concrete at least 18 inches deep is necessary to stop roots from spreading.

Thin canes, but don't remove all of them if the clump is near where people walk. New canes that emerge are tender and easily broken off. They need the protection and support of old canes.

After several growing seasons, all bamboo clumps bloom and die. Pruning does not prevent death.

Giant bamboo needs plenty of room, especially vertically. Vertical-clumping and giant bamboo are appreciated for graceful stems and fine, spreading branches. Thin clumps to show best stems rather than a crowded mass. Remove side limbs over lower 2/3 of the stem to reveal graceful lines.

Prune bamboo during period of most rapid growth. Bamboo shoots are often associated with rock or water features in gardens.

Bauhinia blakeana
Hong Kong orchid tree

Evergreen, partially deciduous for a short time. Train as a multistemmed shrub or single-stemmed tree. Grows to 40 feet. Prune during short dormant season in winter.

Bauhinia purpurea
Purple orchid tree

Partially deciduous tree that grows to 20 to 40 feet. Stake and train to a central leader or as a multistemmed shrub. Prune during short dormant period in winter.

Beaumontia grandiflora
Herald's trumpet, Easter-lily vine

Evergreen vine, growing to 20 feet or more. Blooms appear on old wood. Thin and head lightly after bloom in spring.

Beloperone guttata (Justicia brandegeana)
Shrimp plant

Round, spreading evergreen plant. Forms 3- to 4-foot mound. Pinch new growth to increase compactness. Head about one-third after bloom.

Berberis thunbergii
Japanese barberry

Medium-size, deciduous shrub with thorns. Dense, compact, red foliage and red berries in fall that persist through winter. Moderate annual thinning in dormant season is best.

More attractive natural than as a hedge. Head oldest stems about 6 inches above ground. Other species of *berberis* are evergreen.

Betula species
Birches

Contains 50 to 60 species, ranging from small bushes and shrubs to large, towering trees. Most should be trained to a single trunk. Gradually remove lower branches up to 6 feet high in late summer.

Betula occidentalis
Water birch

Grown as a large shrub or small tree, up to 40 feet. Head back lightly to train as shrub. Remove lower branches to train as tree.

Betula pendula
White birch

Deciduous weeping tree with lace-like foliage. May grow to 60 feet. Wounds don't heal quickly. Select leaders carefully and avoid large cuts. To expose white trunk, remove lower limbs when still fairly small, cutting during dormant season.

Blackberries

Rubus species. See Chapter Three, page 77.

Blueberries

Vaccinium species. See Chapter Three, page 77.

Bougainvillea
Bougainvillea

Evergreen. May be trained as a shrub or vine. Head to strong buds on heavy wood. Remove deadwood. Prune lightly in frosty climate. Head long shoots during spring and summer to contain.

Brachychiton acerifolius
Flame bottle tree

Tall shrub or tree, growing to 70 feet. Briefly deciduous. Tree is trained to a single leader, with well-spaced scaffold limbs. Needs little pruning.

Brachychiton populneus
Kurrajong

Evergreen tree that grows to 60 feet. Train similarly to *B. acerifolius*. Needs little pruning.

Brassaia actinophylla, Schefflera actinophylla
Queensland umbrella tree, Octopus tree

Evergreen house plant except in warm climates where it grows as a small tree or shrub. Can grow to 40 feet. Head as required to initiate branching. Unbranched stem can be cut to ground.

Broussonetia papyrifera
Paper mulberry

Small, spreading, deciduous tree with low branches. Wood decays quickly, so avoid large cuts or breakage. Remove suckers and prune moderately as required.

Buddleia davidii
Butterfly bush

Deciduous or semievergreen, grows to 15 feet. Requires heavy pruning after bloom. Thin to vigorous upright growth in lower half of bush, one to four times annually.

Betula species

Buxus sempervirens
Common box

Evergreen shrub or small tree, growing to 6 to 20 feet. Erect or more spreading varieties exist. Used as single shrubs or in hedges and topiary. Often hedged into formal shapes. May be dehorned and retrained. Remove deadwood.

C

Calliandra haematocephala
Red powderpuff

Evergreen shrub. Head shoots after flowering to obtain second bloom. On mature plants, thin oldest stems to ground annually.

Calliandra tweedii
Mexican flamebush

Evergreen shrub, 6 feet tall. Pinch new growth to increase bloom. Thin after bloom to enhance branch pattern. Old bush withstands dehorning. Can be espaliered.

Callistemon citrinus
Crimson bottlebrush

Slow-growing evergreen shrub or tree. Grows to 25 feet. Blooms on upper lengths of strong growth. Train as small tree, espalier or multi-trunked bush. Head a few shoots each year into wood with leaves. Prune wayward limbs.

Calluna (Erica)
Heath and Heather

See listing, page 142.

Calycanthus floridus
Allspice, Pineapple shrub, Strawberry shrub, Sweet shrub

Deciduous shrub with leaves that smell sweet when crushed. Stool-like growth habit, grows to 10 feet. Thin old branches in spring. Pinch during growing season to increase bushiness.

Camellia species
Camellias

Evergreen shrubs, small trees. See Chapter Six, page 129.

Campsis radicans
Trumpet creeper, Trumpet vine

Deciduous vine, grows to 40 feet or more. Head previous-season's growth to 2 or 3 buds in winter, leave replacement shoots long. Pinch shoots to keep lower parts full. Blooms on current-season's wood. Has aerial roots. Train to trellis.

Carissa grandiflora
Natal plum

Sprawling evergreen shrub. Grows 18 feet high and just as wide. Remove low-growing branches early. Head irregular growth to control shape. Thin lightly and remove deadwood.

Carpinus betulus
European hornbeam

50 foot tall, deciduous tree. Train to central leader with clear trunk at least 6 to 8 feet high. Needs little pruning. Outer branches of older tree may spread to ground level.

Cassia artemesioides
Wormwood senna, Feathery cassia

One of 9 species of trees or shrubs. Evergreen shrubs grow to 4 feet. Head after bloom to 2 or 3 buds on each shoot to stimulate new growth for next year's bloom. Remove 1/3 of shoots each season.

Castanopsis chrysophylla
Giant chinquapin

Large evergreen shrub or small tree. Grows to 50 feet or more. Looks good without pruning. Forms a complete canopy to ground level or can be trained to form small tree.

Cedrus species

Casuarina cunninghamiana
Beefwood, She-oak

Medium to tall evergreen trees grown in California and Florida. Train to central leader with a few well-placed scaffolds. Prune by thinning as required.

Catalpa bignonioides
Common catalpa

Rounded-form deciduous tree that grows to 30 feet or more. Train central leader to 12 feet. Older trees may need branches shortened. Withstands pollarding.

Catalpa speciosa
Western catalpa

Deciduous, pyramidal tree grows to 50 feet. Train to central leader by suppressing rival leads. Do not eliminate them. Leave a clear 6- to 8-foot stem at planting time if nursery stock permits. Prune as needed.

Ceanothus americanus
New Jersey tea, Wild snowball

Deciduous shrub. Train by light thinning to form a rigid framework up to 2 to 4 feet high.

Ceanothus sanguineus
Wild lilac

Evergreen ground cover, shrub or small tree. Blooms in spring on wood grown previous season. Thin lightly after flowering to contain. Remove suckers from base of young plants. Prune in dry weather to avoid spread of fungus.

Cedrus species
True cedars

Genus includes Atlas cedar, Deodar, Cedar-of-Lebanon and other evergreens. Maintain central leader as long as possible. Remove deadwood from under or on ends of branches. Most species won't sprout readily from old wood. Requires little pruning.

Celastrus scandens
American bittersweet

Deciduous vines grow to 20 feet. Remove fruiting branches in fall or winter. Pinch to direct growth during spring or summer. Remove long excess shoots.

Celtis species
Hackberry

Deciduous trees that are stunted

easily unless good care is given. Train central leader to 8 feet. Prune to lighten branch ends of mature trees to prevent breakage.

Cephalotaxus
Plum yew
Evergreen shrub that resembles the ycw. Responds to pruning in the same way. See *Taxus* listing, page 154.

Ceratonia siliqua
Carob, St. John's-bread
Evergreen tree. Allowed to grow naturally, it becomes a shrub with many stems close to the ground. Careful training can produce small tree to 40 feet. Train to a central leader headed at 7 feet. Lightly prune annually.

Cercidiphyllum japonicum
Katsura tree
Slow-growing deciduous tree with several ascending trunks, close crown and horizontal lower laterals. Grows to 50 feet.

Cercidium floridum
Palo verde
Deciduous tree grows 30 feet tall and wide. Minimal training is required to shape branches.

Cercis canadensis
Redbud
Round-head deciduous tree that grows to 35 feet or more. As tree ages, branches become horizontally tiered. Train as a single trunk or multiple trunks.

Cercis siliquastum
Judas tree
Deciduous tree, grows to 30 feet. Naturally grows with multiple trunks, many low branches. Thin to remove competition with leaders. Don't head leaders.

Cestrum species
Jessamine
Fast-growing, frost-sensitive, evergreen shrubs or small trees. Thin top in spring after danger of frost. Pinch growing tips for bushiness. Head severely after flowering or fruiting.

Chaenomeles species
Flowering quince
Deciduous shrubs that grow to 6 to 10 feet. Interesting, irregular growth habit. Suckers sometimes appear far from the base. Needs pruning for containment. Dormant cut branch can be

Ceratonia siliqua

forced to bloom indoors. Thin annually in dormant season to contain size. Remove suckers and water sprouts and head extra-long shoots as desired. To control vigor, head strongest shoots in summer.

Chamaecyparis lawsoniana
False cypress, Lawson cypress, Port Orford cedar
Evergreen tree that develops central leader. Rival leaders may develop later. Needs regular thinning or shearing to contain. Thinning gives most pleasing effect. Heavy pruning to reduce size exposes bare limbs that are slow to produce new shoots.

Cherry, sour
Prunus cerasus. See Chapter Three, page 80.

Cherry, sweet
Prunus avium. See Chapter Three, page 82.

Chestnut
Castanea species. See Chapter Three, page 82.

Chilopsis linearis
Desert willow
Natural habit is a large, scraggly, deciduous shrub. Needs careful training and pruning to form tree. Grows to 20 feet or more. Thin to central leader and head leaders to stiffen.

Chimonanthus praecox
Wintersweet
Deciduous shrub that grows to 10 feet. Minimize pruning for training because it delays blooming. Blooms in winter or spring on wood formed previous summer. Avoid heavy pruning because it blooms best on mature wood. Because vigorous renewal wood is produced from base, old weak wood may be removed entirely. Train into small, multiple-trunk tree.

Chionanthus virginicus
Fringe tree, Old-man's-beard
Deciduous tree that tends to have upright branches. Branch extremities are over-hanging at maturity. Train with 1 or 3 trunks. Thin scaffold limbs to desired shapes. Needs little pruning.

Chiranthodendron pentadactylon
Mexican hand plant
Evergreen tree, grows rapidly with an irregular habit. Grows to 50 feet tall. Prune to strengthen and reduce wind resistance. Head to stiffen.

Choisya ternata
Mexican orange
Dense, fast-growing evergreen shrub tolerates heavy pruning. Remove old flowers after bloom. Thin weaker growths by cutting well inside leaf canopy rather than shearing. Head old bush near ground for renewal.

Chorisia speciosa
Floss-silk tree

Deciduous, 50-foot-tall tree. Prune for shape and to remove deadwood.

Cinnamomum camphora
Camphor tree

Evergreen tree that grows to 50 feet. Heavy, upright, spreading limbs. Train to central leader, directing branches outward. Moderately slow grower. Requires removal of deadwood after initial training.

Cissus species
Grape ivy, Treebine

Medium and slow-growing evergreen vines. Remove deadwood, untangle. Climbs with tendrils.

Cistus species
Rock rose

Evergreen shrubs that grow to 4 feet. They have little tendency to sprout from heavy pruning cuts. Thin lower, outer branches down close to ground in winter. Little pruning is necessary.

Citrus

Citrus species. See Chapter Three, page 82.

Cladrastis lutea
Yellowwood

Hardy, deciduous tree that grows to 50 feet. Train as high as possible to a central leader. Suppress but do not remove side limbs. Has brittle wood, so avoid narrow crotches.

Clematis species
Virgin's bower, Leather flower, Vase vine

Includes over 200 species of herbs and woody vines, both evergreen and deciduous. Divided into three groups. The Florida group flowers on old wood in the summer. The Patens group flowers on old wood in the spring. The *Jackmanii* group flowers on new wood during summer and fall.

Clematis species, Florida and Paten groups.
C. alpina, C. balearica, C. chrysocoma, C. macropetala, C. montana

Species that flower on previous year's wood. Require little pruning. Remove deadwood and untangle. Tie to trellis after planting, remove weak ends.

Cornus species

Clematis species, Jackmanii group
C. x jackmanii, C. paniculata, C. texensis, C. viticella

Strong growers that flower on new wood in summer and fall. Head to about 1 foot annually for containment. Don't prune in natural situations.

Clethra arborea
White Alder

Small evergreen tree that grows to 25 feet. Train to central leader. If frozen, regrow by selecting a single trunk arising from the roots.

Clytostoma callistegioides
Argentine trumpet vine

Evergreen shrub that climbs with tendrils. Space main stems, tie to wires. In spring, head laterals hard, at least one-third or more. Remove weak growth in summer.

Cobaea scandens
Cup-and-saucer vine

Shrubby climber is perennial, grown as an annual. Pinch back regularly to develop bushy plant.

Coleonema and Diosma
Breath-of-Heaven

Evergreen shrubs, growing to 6 feet. Shear annually after bloom. Water and fertilize old, weak plants one month before pruning. Head all branches back about half-way a month later.

Comarostaphylis diversifolia (Erica)
Summer holly

Evergreen shrub or small tree, grows to 20 feet. Remove lower limbs to develop a tree. Otherwise prune as shrub. See Health listing, page 143.

Conifers

See following listings. *Abies, Cedrus, Cephalotaxus, Chamaecyparis, Cryptomeria, Cupressus, Juniperus, Larix, Libocedrus, Metasequoia, Picea, Pinus, Pseudolarix, Psuedotsuga, Sequoia, Sequoiadendron, Taxodium, Taxus, Thuja, Torreya and Tsuja.*

Convolvulus cneorum
Silverbush

Rapid-growing evergreen, grows 2 to 4 feet high. Tends to be leggy. Head at crown before growth starts in spring. Pinch shoots during growing season to induce bushiness.

Coprosma repens
Mirror plant

Fast-growing evergreen shrub or small tree. Needs regular pruning at any time for containment and appearance. Remove some branches entirely, thin shoots on others. Eliminate wayward branches inside canopy.

Cordyline australis
Giant dracaena

Evergreen tree that grows to 15 to 40 feet. Tall, woody palmlike stems. Grows stiff and upright, with little branching.

Cordyline indivisa
Blue dracaena
Evergreen palmlike shrub that grows to 25 feet, with 2- to 6-foot-long leaves. Remove old, dead leaves.

Cordyline stricta
Dracaena
Slender evergreen shrub that grows 6 to 12 feet high, leaves are 1 to 2 feet long. When too tall, cut long canes to ground.

Cornus controversa
Giant dogwood
Medium-size deciduous tree that grows to 50 feet. Remove lower branches if necessary.

Cornus florida
Flowering dogwood
Deciduous tree that grows to 30 feet. Train to central leader with little other attention. Remove rootstock suckers.

Cornus mas
Cornelian cherry
Small tree or shrub, grows to 20 feet. Start to a central leader in nursery, otherwise it will grow to a shrub. Develop lead up to 6 feet, but keep lower branches.

Cornus nuttalii
Mountain dogwood
Medium-size deciduous tree that grows 40 feet tall, 20 feet wide. No pruning is necessary except to ensure a natural central lead, Leave low limbs to obtain massive floral effect.

Cortaderia selloana
Pampas grass
Giant evergreen grass with sharp-edged leaves. May grow 20 feet tall when established. Remove flowers if they look messy. Burn or prune to ground periodically.

Corylus species
Hazelnut, Filbert
See Chapter Three, page 89.

Corynocarpus laevigata
New Zealand laurel
Slow-growing, evergreen shrub or small tree. Reaches 30 feet or more in height. Needs little training or pruning. Prune for containment.

Crataegus laevigata
English hawthorn
Small, dense deciduous trees. Pendu-

Cupressus species

lous, reaching 20 feet in height, 15 feet wide. Leaning is not unusual and presents no special problem. Train to a central leader, but allow tree to develop spreaders naturally at 6 to 8 feet. Leave crown moderately thick. Excessive thinning stimulates water sprouts.

Cryptocarya rubra
Evergreen. Grows as a small multi-trunked tree. May be trained to a single trunk, grows to 40 feet.

Cryptomeria japonica
Japanese cedar
Natural form is pyramidal with central trunk. Needs little pruning except for removal of wayward branches. *Cryptomeria japonica 'elegans'* is juvenile form with plumelike foliage. Central leader is weak and easily deformed or broken. Special pruning creates a tiered form with a Japanese look.

Cunninghamia lanceolata
China fir
Evergreen tree, grows to 40 feet with a 30-foot spread. Train to straight central leader with horizontal scaffolds. Responds well to heavy pruning.

Cupaniopsis anacardiodes
Carrot wood, Tuckeroo
Small evergreen tree that grows to 30 feet. Thin branches as required, but never head. Attractive as multi-stemmed tree.

Cupressus
Cypress
Evergreen trees. Grow with central leader. Stake leader if site is windy. Not well-suited for use as hedge.

Currants
Ribes species. See Chapter Three, page 83.

D

Daboecia (Erica)
Heath and Heather
See listing, page 143.

Dais cotinifolia
Pompom tree
Natural form is multitrunked and irregular. Looks best when trained to single trunk. Train for form during brief dormant period.

Daphne species
Daphne
Evergreen and deciduous shrubs are grown in ample sunlight. Little or no pruning required. Some species delay blooming for a year if pruned. Shape by cutting flower clusters or whole shoots.

Davidia involucrata
Dove tree
Deciduous tree that grows to 40 feet. Train to central leader. Gradually remove lower limbs from trunk in late summer. Remove dead or diseased wood and crossing branches.

Dendromecon
Bush poppy
Evergreen shrub or small tree that withstands heavy pruning. Thin sprawling shoots, remove deadwood and old branches periodically.

Deutzia species
Deutzia
Deciduous shrubs that need pruning for renewal of bloom. Thin oldest blooming branches at ground level immediately after blossoms have fallen. Branches of taller species are thinned to outside laterals higher up. Remove unwanted suckers from base.

Diervilla sessilifolia
Bush honeysuckle
Deciduous shrub that flowers on current-season's growth. Spreads by stolons and suckers from a central stool. As new growth starts in spring, head close to ground level.

Distictis laxiflora
Vanilla trumpet vine
Woody, spreading vine is pruned lightly for containment only.

Distictus 'Rivers'
Royal trumpet vine
Woody, spreading vine. Pinch and train to direct and contain.

Dizygotheca elegantissima (Aralia elegantissima)
False aralia
Juvenile form is a house plant. Mature form is evergreen garden shrub in subtropical regions. May grow to 10 feet. Cut tallest stem to ground periodically to ensure there are stems of various lengths. Pruning improves looks and prevents development of coarse leaves.

Dodonaea viscosa
Hopbush, Hopseed bush
Evergreen shrub, growing to 12 feet. Train to single stem or multiple stems. Suitable for hedge or espalier. Responds well to shearing. Thin as necessary.

Dolichos lignosus
Australian pea
Vine that grows to 10 feet. Cut to ground if frozen or uncontrolled. Prune to contain.

Drimys winteri
Winter's-bark
Small, multistemmed evergreen tree that can be trained to single stem. Produces strong upright growths, up to 30 feet. Little pruning is required.

Elaeagnus angustifolia
Russian olive
Deciduous spreading tree with distinctive gray foliage. Train to single leader. Select scaffolds for desired form. Limbs tend to grow long and heavy, then break in storms. Prune every few years to lighten branch ends and maintain form.

Enkianthus species
Enkianthus
Deciduous shrubs that require little pruning. Overgrown specimens break easily if dehorned. Remove dead or broken branches and unsightly growth on old branches.

Erica
Heath and Heather
See listing, page 143.

Eriobotrya japonica
Loquat
Large evergreen shrub or small tree. Train to single trunk or multiple trunks or as espalier. Naturally round and compact, growing to 30 feet. Prune in spring before growth starts. Thin branches to improve fruiting and reduce breakage. May become infected with fire blight in some areas. Cut dead parts at least a foot below start of live bark. Disinfect shears with alcohol between every cut.

Erythrina caffra
Coral tree
Briefly deciduous tree, then becomes evergreen. Grows to 40 feet or more. Has 50-foot spread at maturity. Looks best with multiple trunks or several low scaffolds. Doesn't need pruning. If pruned, it may not bloom for several years. Remove low limbs.

Escallonia species
Escallonia
Vigorous evergreen shrub that flowers in early summer on new wood. Prune by selective thinning just after bloom. Remove some old growth to ground. Vigorous varieties can be trained into trees. *E. rubra*, a low-growing type requires light thinning every other year during dormant season.

Eucalyptus species
Eucalyptus
There are three general groups among many species grown in the West:
1. Small, shrubby bushes.
2. Intermediate-sized trees.
3. Tall forest trees.

Most never need pruning, but some are messy with strips of bark, branches and leaves. All sprout from trunks if cut back. Small, multiple-trunk, shrubby types are best treated as shrubs, the medium ones as single-trunk trees and forest types as single-trunk trees.

Eucalyptus alpina
Grampian
Shrub or small tree that grows to 12 feet. Needs little pruning, except to contain.

Eucalyptus ficifolia
Red-flowering gum
Round-head evergreen tree about 25 feet tall. Tends to produce low branches that should be suppressed and removed.

Eucalyptus globulus
Blue gum
Tall evergreen tree too large for gardens. It has shaggy bark and long, sickle-shaped leaves. Tree is too big for amateurs to prune.

Euonymus alata
Winged spindle tree
Slow-growing, dense deciduous shrub valued for fall color. Needs little pruning except to control spread and shape in early spring. Grows to 8 feet.

Euonymus japonica
Japanese spindle tree
Vigorous evergreen shrub or tree that benefits from regular pruning. Grows

Eriobotrya japonica

to 10 to 15 feet. May be hedged, but unattractive when closely clipped. Older shrub may be converted to tree form by pruning to reveal trunk. Frequent light trimming of outer boundaries is better than occasional heavy pruning.

Euphorbia pulcherrima
Poinsettia

Winter-blooming evergreen or deciduous shrub used as a house plant in Christmas season. Head all stems to 2 or 3 buds in spring, usually April or May. If bloom comes too early, prune later next season. Pinch new growth to encourage bushiness.

Evodia hupehensis

Deciduous or evergreen tree that grows to 50 feet. Train to central leader with 4 to 6 feet of clear trunk. Needs sunlight, so prune other trees away from it. Branches are brittle, so avoid weak crotches. Lighten branch ends if needed to prevent breakage.

Exochorda species
Pearlbush

Deciduous shrubs that sucker extensively. Remove suckers at ground level in spring except those needed to replace older stems. Thin old wood and excess shoots after bloom.

F

Fagus sylvatica
European beech

Large deciduous tree that grows to 75 feet. Starts growing slowly, but once established grows rapidly. Heavy limbs sometimes break without warning. Train to central leader. Remove lower limbs to expose trunk.

Fatshedera lizei
Aralia ivy

Shrub or vine that grows to 8 feet or more. Cut to ground if overgrown. Pinch to control spread.

Fatsia japonica
Japanese fatsia

Evergreen that requires little pruning. Often grows to 20 feet. To control size, remove largest stems at ground level in spring. Remove suckers as desired. For bigger leaves, remove bloom.

Feijoa sellowiana
Pineapple guava

Grows multi- or single-stem, as an espalier or hedge. Natural habit is a many-stem shrub. To develop a tree, start with single-stem nursery plant. Remove all suckers at ground level and selectively pinch back to direct growth of tops. Prune in spring after danger of frost. Start as a shrub and select 2 to 5 strong stems later, removing others. Raise open area about a foot annually.

Ficus species
Fig, ornamental

Evergreens. Young growth is easily damaged by frost. Wait until danger of frost is past to remove cold-damaged wood. See Chapter Three, page 83, for edible *Ficus*.

Ficus benjamina
Weeping fig

Often grown in a container as a house plant, it may grow to be small evergreen tree. Prune as desired to contain and shape.

Ficus carica
Fig, edible

See Chapter Three, page 83.

Ficus elastica
Rubber plant

Evergreen shrub or tree that grows to 30 feet. Responds well to pruning. If a branched shrub is desired, instead of a tall, single stem, head to stimulate branching.

Ficus lyrata
Fiddle-leaf fig

Evergreen house plant, but can develop into a large shrub or small tree. Grows vertical but can be trained as a vine. Pinch tips of young plant to stimulate branching.

Ficus retusa
Indian laurel fig

Evergreen shrub or tree. Looks good trained to multiple trunks. Remove lower trailing branches to enhance tree form.

Figs

Ficus species. See Chapter Three, page 83.

Filberts

Corylus species. See Hazelnut listing, Chapter Three, page 89.

Firmiana simplex
Chinese parasol tree

Fast-grower that develops into a large deciduous tree. Train to central leader

Fagus sylvatica

and develop strong scaffold limbs. Not suitable in crowded spaces.

Forsythia species
Forsythia, Golden bells

Deciduous shrub with long, arching branches. Bears yellow flowers in early spring. Flowers only on wood from previous season. After bloom, prune branches that have bloomed last two seasons by cutting to center of bush. Prune young plants lightly; old ones severely.

Franklinia alatamaha
Franklin tree

Deciduous trees grow upright to 25 feet or more. Do not restrict natural tendency to develop multiple stems. No regular pruning is necessary.

Fraxinus species
Ash

Deciduous trees that grow to 75 feet or more. Do not head central leader. Because buds are opposite on the shoots, heading or breakage of the leader creates 2 shoots in a narrow V-shape. They develop into a weak crotch that is likely to break, so remove the upper buds at a node. This allows lower buds to produce wider crotch angles. You can also remove shoots so latent buds below can develop wider branch angles. Train central leader as high as possible, because it quickly produces a round head.

Fremontodendron californicum
Flannel bush

Fast-growing evergreen shrub or tree. Thin heavily to shape and contain immediately after bloom.

Fuchsia species
Lady's-eardrops

Evergreen and deciduous shrubs that bloom on new wood. Prune in midwinter, or in cold climates, after danger of frost. Head at 1 or 2 nodes past start of previous-season's growth. Frequently pinch tips of new growth to develop branching and more abundant bloom.

G

Gamolepis chrysanthemoides

Evergreen shrub with tendency to be leggy. Grows to 6 feet, with 8-foot spread. Pinch new growth and thin out unruly growth during bloom period to increase and prolong flowering.

Gardenia jasminoides
Common gardenia, Cape jasmine

Slow-growing evergreen shrub that requires little or no pruning. Thin weak growth during bloom period. Remove faded flower clusters. Prune to contain at about 30 inches high. Renew old, devitalized plants by dehorning.

Garrya species
Silk-tassel

Evergreen shrub that can be trained to small tree. Prune after scaly, unisexual flowers or *catkins* fade and before new growth begins. Prune to contain by making thinning cuts inside canopy.

Gaultheria shallon
Salal

Low-growing, evergreen shrub. All stems should be pruned just above a node in spring. Remove dead or unsightly growth anytime.

Geijera parviflora
Australian willow

Evergreen tree that grows to 30 feet. Needs little training or pruning.

Gelsemium sempervirens
Early trumpet flower

Evergreen vine, easy to prune and shape. Thin and head after flowering.

Ginko biloba
Maidenhair tree

Deciduous tree that grows to 50 feet. Usually develops central leader naturally, but if rival leads appear, remove them. May need staking in early years.

Gleditsia triocanthus
Honey locust

Deciduous tree that bleeds badly in spring, so prune when fully dormant. Train to central leader up to 10 to 15 feet. Head vigorous limbs on young trees to stiffen. *G. inermis* variety is thornless. Remove low thorns on thorny trees.

Gooseberry

Ribes species. See Chapter Three, page 84.

Grape

Vitis species. See Chapter Three, page 85.

Grevillea robusta
Silky oak

Wood is brittle in this evergreen tree. Tree is easily damaged in storms. Head low at planting and develop strong framework. Prune lightly after bloom each year.

Gymnocladus dioica
Kentucky coffee tree

Deciduous tree that grows to 50 feet. Train to central leader and gradually clear trunk to 6 to 8 feet or branch lower into 3 or 4 upright scaffold limbs. Young tree may require staking.

Ginko biloba

H

Hakea species
Pincushion tree

Evergreen. Train as trees or shrubs, but don't shear. Little other pruning required.

Halesia carolina
Wild olive

Deciduous tree, 25-foot spread, grows to 40 feet high. Start with single trunk and develop scaffolds at 4 or 5 feet. Little pruning required on mature tree, but can be pruned after bloom.

Hamamelis species
Witch hazel

Deciduous shrubs require little pruning. Species and varieties vary from upright to spreading. Consider this in training. Thin to strong laterals for containment after flowering and before growth begins. Because most are grafted onto seedlings of common witch hazel, all sprouts below graft union should be removed. Some types can be trained on a single trunk.

Hardenbergia violacea
Vine lilac

Evergreen vine that grows to 10 feet. Pinch to shape.

Harpephyllum caffrum
Kaffis plum

Easy to train and shape this evergreen tree into almost any form. Naturally develops dense crown but can be changed by thinning. Prune in spring after frost.

Hazelnuts

Corylus species. See filbert listing, Chapter Three, page 89.

Heath and Heather
Calluna, Daboecia and Erica species

Low-growing, fine-leaved evergreens adapted to cool, wet climates. Prune for compactness and containment. Prune after flowering and before new growth starts on winter and spring-blooming plants. Prune summer- and fall-flowering kinds in early spring as growth begins. Avoid cutting into old wood or it may not produce buds. Hide cuts by undercutting inside canopy.

Hebe species
Shrub veronica

Fast-growing evergreens suitable for

hedges. Pinch for compactness in spring or summer. If there is danger of cold injury, don't prune in fall or winter. Buds break easily from old wood if frosted or severely pruned. Remove excess fruits to avoid devitalizing plant.

Hedera helix
English ivy

Woody, evergreen vine that grows to 15 feet in length. Long juvenile period of no flowers. Pruning delays flowering. If grown on a wall or building, prune hard annually to prevent flowering. Weight of ivy can pull out boards or bricks and break out tree crowns. Prune edges to contain as ground cover.

Heteromeles arbutifolia
Christmas berry

Tall evergreen shrub that grows to 25 feet and sprouts from old wood. Versatile, can be used as hedge, bush or small tree. Thin to shape and contain in late winter or early spring. Susceptible to fire blight. Remove infected twigs, cutting well below the infection. Sterilize tools with alcohol between cuts.

Hibiscus huegelii (Alyogyne huegelii)
Blue hibiscus

Upright evergreen shrub that grows to 8 feet. Pinch for compactness after danger of frost is past.

Hibiscus moscheutos
Mallow rose

Perennial shrub that grows to 8 feet. Head 3 or 4 inches above ground annually in fall after flowering.

Hibiscus rosa-sinensis
Chinese hibiscus

Evergreen shrub that grows to 8 feet. Don't prune after September 15th. Don't prune entire shrub at one time. Head a few stems into older wood at different heights. Prune strong growing varieties severely every spring. Thin weaker shoots and head or thin stronger ones. If plant was severely damaged by winter cold, dehorn it.

Hibiscus syriacus
Rose-of-Sharon, Shrub althea

Deciduous shrub, needs only light pruning. For bigger flowers, head previous season's growth to 2 buds in midwinter.

Hydrangea species

Hibbertia scandens
Gold Guinea vine

Evergreen twining vine. If top-heavy, cut back hard. Generally needs little pruning. Remove frost-damaged shoots, untangle branches.

Holodiscus discolor
Ocean-spray

Deciduous shrub, blooms on shoots from arching, spreading branches formed the previous season. After bloom, thin part of branch system to strong young growth. Leave adequate number of older branches. Remove seed clusters.

Humulus lupulus
Common hop

Perennial vine, growing to 20 feet or more. Cut to ground in winter. Train as desired, it twines on supports.

Hydrangea species
Hydrangea

Deciduous shrubs that sprout readily from the base. Some don't lose leaves in mild climate. Flowering is terminal on 1- or 2-year-old wood. Remove old blooms by heading just above highest leaves. Keep stems that didn't flower this year to bloom next year. In winter, head stems that bloomed to 2 or 3 buds above wood of previous season.

Hydrangea anomala
Climbing hydrangea

Vine climbs by means of sporadic aerial roots that cling to any support. Prune by removing excess exterior growths in summer. As flowering

branch system extends from supporting walls, head part of spurs to a bud during spring. Don't spoil bloom by pruning it all at once.

Hydrangea arborescens
Wild hydrangea

Deciduous shrub. Needs heading to 2 or 3 buds in spring to stimulate growth.

Hydrangea macrophylla
Bigleaf hydrangea

Deciduous shrub. Head half of oldest stems to ground in early spring. Head stems that bloomed to 2 or 3 buds. Leave those that terminate in large, flat flower buds.

Hydrangea paniculata 'Grandiflora'
Peegee hydrangea

Deciduous shrub or small tree. Head year-old wood to basal 3 or 4 buds in early spring before growth starts. Head shoots of single-stemmed plants to 2 or 3 buds on well-placed branches.

Hydrangea quercifolia
Oak-leaf hydrangea

Deciduous shrub that grows to 6 feet. Can be headed to ground annually for compact shrub. Benefits from staking.

Hymenosporum flavum
Sweetshade

Small evergreen tree or large shrub. Grows to 40 feet as a tree, with a 20-foot spread. Tends to have weak crotches that split. Thin to develop strong, well-spaced branch structure. Pinch or head scaffolds to stiffen.

Hypericum species
St.-John's wort

Over 300 species include evergreen and semievergreen shrubs. Thin weak or dead branches in winter. Head all wood more than 2 or 3 seasons old to 4-inch stubs. For larger bushes, prune more severely.

I

Ilex aquifolium
English holly, Christmas holly

Many species, all evergreen, except one. Can be hedged at any time of year. Pruning is usually done during Christmas holidays, with prunings used in decorations. May be trained to a Christmas-tree shape. Prune annually to control size and to keep pyramidal shape. Thin branches for less formal shape.

Ilex crenata
Japanese holly

Slow-growing shrub that needs little pruning. Responds well to hedging. Japanese holly is frequently used for topiary.

Ipomoea species
Morning glory

Annual vines, grow to more than 20 feet. Cut to ground annually. Train to structures or use as ground cover.

J

Jacaranda acutifolia
Green ebony, Jacaranda

Deciduous or semievergreen tree, grows to 30 feet tall. Train as single- or multiple-trunked tree. At intervals of 3 or 4 feet, pinch out terminal buds to stimulate branching. Prune to contain.

Jasminum nudiflorum
Winter jasmine

Deciduous shrub. Good as a wall specimen trained to a fan-shaped trellis. Thin laterals to vigorous side shoots or buds annually after bloom.

Jasminum officinale
Poet's jessamine

Semievergreen to deciduous vine grows to 25 feet long. Needs strong support. Remove old wood after bloom if necessary.

Jasminum parkeri
Dwarf jasmine

An evergreen, just 1-foot tall, with many thin branches. Shear tops after bloom for low-spreading ground cover.

Jasminum sambac
Arabian jasmine

Evergreen shrub that tends to become bare and sprawling. Head periodically to encourage bushiness. Grows 5 feet tall.

Juglans species
Walnuts

See Chapter Three, page 98.

Juniperus species
Juniper, Red cedar

Many forms, from trees and shrubs to prostrate ground covers. All are evergreen and can be sheared or thinned. Responds poorly to dehorning. Regular pruning is not essential.

K

Kadsura japonica
Scarlet kadsura

Twining evergreen vine that grows to 12 feet. Train and prune to contain.

Kalmia latifolia
Mountain laurel, Calico bush

Slow-growing evergreen that needs little or no pruning. Poor growth is due to poor growing conditions. Pruning won't help growth. Prune lightly for containment. If required, prune after flowering. Old stems sprout if cut close to ground.

Kerria japonica
Japanese rose

Deciduous flowering shrub with open, rounded form. New canes from base may reach height of shrub and bloom the next season. Head all 2-year-old canes almost to ground level after flowers fade. New shoots from base bloom heaviest in second year. Cut off root suckers to limit spread.

Kiwi

Actinidia chinensis. See listing, Chapter Three, page 89.

Kniphofia uvaria
Red-hot-poker, Torch lily

Perennial herb, that grows up to 4 feet. Remove flower spikes after bloom. Cut off old leaves at base in fall.

Kolkwitzia amabilis
Beauty bush

Deciduous shrub that withstands, but doesn't require heavy pruning. Head some of the oldest canes at ground level each spring. Thin after bloom if necessary.

Koelreuteria paniculata
Golden-rain tree, Varnish tree

Deciduous tree that grows 30 feet tall. Stake and train when young. Little pruning required, but some thinning may improve looks.

L

Laburnum anagyroides
Golden-chain tree

Fast-growing deciduous tree. Can be

Juniperus species

trained as tree or shrub. Remove lower side branches and rub buds off trunk to train as tree. Remove seed pods because they drain tree, make a mess and are poisonous. Regularly pruning with small cuts after bloom renews wood and maintains a healthy tree. Avoid large pruning cuts because they don't heal completely. Bleeds if pruned in spring.

Lagerstroemia indica
Crape myrtle

Deciduous shrub or tree that grows to 5 to 30 feet. Blooms on current year's wood. Train to a three-leader vase similar to the peach, page 91. Thin and head to stimulate new growth and remove old growth. Remove suckers and old flower clusters.

Lagunaria patersonii
Primrose tree, Low itch tree

Evergreen tree. No pruning required except to remove deadwood and suckers. Caution: avoid contact with sap after pruning because it causes an itchy rash.

Lantana species
Shrub verbena

Evergreen and deciduous shrubs. Prune hard to remove deadwood. Remove leggy growth.

Lapageria rosea
Chilean bellflower

Evergreen vine that needs trellis. Tie main stems. Vine twines and blooms all summer. Train slender stems to desired shape. Remove weak growth in spring.

Larix species
Larch, American larch

Deciduous conifers with spreading branches. They shed leaves in winter. Central-leader trees that require little pruning. When shaded, lower limbs die and should be removed.

Laurus nobilis
Sweet bay

Evergreen. May be trained as shrub or tree with single or multiple trunks and several main scaffolds. Recovers well from heavy pruning and hedging or topiary. If pruned to expose trunk, it produces suckers.

Lavandula species
Lavender

Evergreen shrubs or large herbs that

Larix species

may need shearing to be more dense and attractive. Shear annually into young wood in early spring or, in milder climates, after bloom.

Leptospermum lanigerum
Tea tree

Evergreen shrub or small tree that generally requires little pruning. Thin in early spring to side branches that have foliage. Never prune to bare branches. Respect natural shape of bush, but don't let fine branches shade center.

Leucophyllum frutescens
Texas ranger

Evergreen shrub that grows to 10 feet. In winter, thin to shape and direct growth. Dehorn older specimens during dormant season.

Leucothoe species
Fetter bush

Evergreen shrubs that require little pruning. Remove blossoms before they set seed. If pruning is required, cut a few older growths down to ground. Thin long sprays back to side branches.

Libocedrus
Incense cedar

Grow as a specimen tree, with pyramidal crown and central leader. Tree resembles aborvitae. It can reach 80 feet or more. Requires little pruning.

Ligustrum japonicum
Evergreen Japanese privet, Wax-leaf privet

Evergreen shrub used for hedges. Shearing 3 or 4 times a year produces dense growth.

Ligustrum lucidum
Glossy privet

Evergreen tree that grows to 40 feet. Can be trained as shrub, hedge, or tree. Leave young shoots rising from spreading laterals to fill in center. Frequently used as hedge.

Liquidambar styraciflua
American sweet gum

Deciduous tree that grows to 75 feet. Train to central leader. Remove lower side branches gradually by pinching or leave lower branches. Forms good, strong central leader.

Liriodendron tulipifera
Tulip tree, Tulip poplar

Large deciduous tree. Develop central leader high so lowest limbs remain high enough to pass under. Little pruning is required.

Lithocarpus densiflorus
Tanbark oak

Evergreen. Train as small tree with central leader and a few strong scaffold branches. Mature trees need little pruning except to remove dead and broken wood.

Lonicera species
Honeysuckle

Shrubs or vines that may be evergreen or deciduous. See Chapter Five, page 119. Bush types have many variations in growth habits. Some produce a few branches from base, becoming gnarled and full of character. Others branch profusely. All grow strongly following heavy pruning. Thin all unwanted branches and head remaining branches.

Lonicera hildebrandiana
Giant Burmese honeysuckle

Evergreen vine. Remove old stems after bloom. Head to keep vine from becoming leggy at base.

Lonicera japonica
Japanese honeysuckle

Evergreen vine. Cut back hard over entire surface. Prune during dormant season or after bloom.

Lonicera nitida
Box honeysuckle

Shrubby, evergreen honeysuckle used primarily as foliage plant, often in a hedge. Branches 3 years or older lose leaves and look weak. In winter, cut old branches off near ground. To restore old hedge, cut all stems to about a foot above ground. See Chapter Five, page 115. Rapid grower, needs frequent pruning in summer.

Lyonothamnus floribundus
Catalina ironwood

Evergreen tree that requires pruning in winter to restrict size and direct growth. Remove dead flower clusters. Can be hedged.

M

Macadamia ternifolia
Queensland nut

Evergreen trees grow to 15 feet. Stake and train to central leader. Space scaffold limbs 6 to 8 inches apart vertically. Distribute evenly around the trunk.

Lonicera japonica

Macfadyena unguis-cati
Cat's-claw

Partially deciduous vine. Prune after bloom to restrict size. Head some stems low to stimulate new growth. Pinch to control.

Maclura pomifera
Osage orange

Spiny, deciduous tree that may reach 60 feet. Sometimes used as a protective hedge. Can be grown as multiple-trunked shrub or as single- or multiple-trunked tree. Remove lower limbs to shape as shade tree.

Magnolia grandiflora
Southern magnolia, Bull bay

Large evergreen tree. Train to central leader when about 8 to 10 feet high. Remove water sprouts as they form. Thin lightly in spring for more blooms. Otherwise needs little or no pruning.

Magnolia x soulangiana
Saucer magnolia

Large deciduous shrub or small tree. Can be trained to central leader, but attractive with 4 or 5 main scaffolds originating about a foot above ground. Prune mature trees by thinning. Direct growth upward or outward as required.

Mahonia aquifolium
Oregon grape, Holly grape

Evergreen with numerous sparsely branched upright stems and dark-green leaves. Resembles English holly. Head old stems to ground in late spring to encourage bushiness. Pinch new growth after bloom to encourage branching. Do not trim along top of plant.

Malus floribunda
Showy crabapple

Deciduous tree that grows 20 feet tall. Train to central leader to 10 to 12 feet, then head leader. Develop 4 to 6 well-spaced scaffold limbs. Thin lower wood to lighten branch ends each year. Prune lightly and remove suckers after bloom. Avoid severe pruning.

Maytenus boaria
Mayten

Train to a single or multiple leader as desired. Thin and trim crown when necessary. Remove suckers.

Melaleuca species
Honey myrtle, Bottle brush

Fast-growing evergreen that grows as shrub or tree. Develops mass of fine branches. Head young tree to stiffen and create branching. Thin branches on old tree to direct and control growth. Does not sucker readily from old wood. Prune by thinning to side branches after blossom season passes.

Melia azedarach
Bead tree, China tree

Deciduous tree that grows to 30 to 50 feet. Little pruning required. Remove dead wood and crossing branches.

Melianthus major
Honeybush

Evergreen shrub that produces tall canes. Can be forced to branch by heading or leave tall. For spreading foliage, head about 1 foot above base of each cane. Season is not important. For tall plant, stake 2 or 3 canes and do not head them. Responds well to heavy pruning.

Metasequoia glyptostroboides
Dawn redwood

Deciduous conifer resembles a redwood when in leaf. It is a tall columnar, central-leader tree, growing to 80 feet. Regenerates leads from heavily pruned wood. Use as specimen tree.

Metrosideros species
Iron tree

Small evergreen trees that reach to 30 feet. Require support when young. Looks best with 3 to 5 trunks. Remove side branches up to about 6 feet in spring, after growth has begun.

Murraya paniculata
Orange jasmine, Mock orange

Large evergreen shrub that reacts well to most pruning. Can be trained to tree or sheared as bush or hedge.

Myrica pensylvanica
Bayberry

Deciduous or partly evergreen shrub. Needs little pruning. Prune for containment or renewal during dormant period.

Myrsine africana
African boxwood, Cape myrtle

Compact evergreen shrub. Useful for hedges. May be clipped in formal shapes. Old specimens may develop long, woody, bare stems terminated by bunches of bushy foliage. Prune severely in spring for appearance.

Myrtus communis
Myrtle

Evergreen shrub commonly used for hedges. Can be sheared, but more attractive if thinned. Cut longest shoots well inside canopy.

N

Nandina domestica
Sacred bamboo,
Heavenly bamboo

A slow-growing evergreen or semideciduous shrub. Gradually becomes too tall, with little or no foliage on lower portions. Head about half of stems at 6 to 12 inches to refurbish lower portions. Head to ground when older leaves have turned from red to green in spring. Head remainder of stems the following year.

Neopanax arboreus
Five-fingers

Forms a small evergreen tree without training. Train as multistemmed tree, head to height of 6 to 8 feet.

Nerium oleander
Common oleander

Vigorous evergreen grown as a bush, hedge or small tree. *Warn children that all parts of the plant are poisonous!* Don't burn prunings or use in compost. Won't bloom when sheared. In spring remove wood that has bloomed by cutting to ground. Thin to restrict size. Pull, don't cut, suckers from base. To train as a tree, stake the trunk or trunks. Pinch off buds along the trunk, except at the end, until height of 6 feet has been reached.

Nyssa sylvatica
Sour gum, Tupelo, Pepperidge

Forms large deciduous tree. Train to central leader and gradually remove branches in dormant season to height of 6 to 10 feet. Remaining branches are semipendulous and will descend to eye-level. Crooked branches and twiggy growth are natural. Don't ruin

Nerium oleander

shape by pruning. Control height by topping at about 20 feet.

O

Olea europaea
Common olive

See Chapter Three, page 90.

Olive

Olea europaea. See Chapter Three, page 90.

Olmediella betschlerana
Costa Rican holly, Manzanote

Evergreen shrub. Prune as small tree. For single trunk, pinch back side limbs on strongest stem. Remove competing stems.

Osmanthus species
Devil weed

Slow-growing evergreen shrubs or small trees. Pinch branch tips in spring and early summer to direct and control growth. Hedge can be sheared in early spring. Thin long growth of shrub to inside laterals in May. Heavy pruning of overgrown specimens should be done a month earlier.

Ostrya virginiana
American hornbeam

Deciduous tree that grows to 40 feet. Train with a central leader. Develop a clear trunk to height of 6 to 8 feet. Not tolerant of shade from other trees. Mature trees require little pruning.

Oxera pulchella
Royal climber

Evergreen vine or shrub. Train by

tying to supports. Prune lightly to direct growth after flowering. Remove dead and broken branches.

Oxydendrum arboreum
Sourwood, Sorrel tree

Deciduous tree, reaches 50 feet. Encourage natural tendency to form central leader. Remove weak crotches. Keep branches close to ground to strengthen trunk.

P

Parkinsonia aculeata
Jerusalem thorn,
Mexican palo verde

Deciduous. Stake young trees and train to central leader with branching either high or low. Mature trees require little pruning beyond removal of deadwood.

Parthenocissus quinquefolia
American ivy, Virginia creeper, Woodbine

Vigorous, climbing, deciduous vine with aerial roots. Keep out of tiles, shingles, eaves and gutters. Restrict size and spread. Pergolas may be used as support.

Passiflora species
Passion flower

Semievergreen or deciduous vines. If out of control, cut to ground. Prune regularly to control. Head laterals to basal bud in spring. Climbs with tendrils.

Paulownia tomentosa
Princess tree

Fast-growing deciduous tree. Develop central leader up to 6 feet and thin weak wood to shape. May be headed about 6 inches above ground in spring. This stimulates extremely rapid growth and huge leaves, creating a tropical foliage effect. Resulting shoots are thinned to one. Remove any frost-damaged wood in spring.

Peach and Nectarine

Prunus persica. See Chapter Three, page 91.

Pear

Pyrus communis. See Chapter Three, page 99.

Pecans

Carya illinoinensis.
See Chapter Three, page 94.

Pernettya mucronata
Pernettya
Evergreen shrub with invasive underground stolons. Contain by root pruning or with physical barrier. Head and thin to contain and shape as desired.

Persea americana
Avocado
See Chapter Three, page 76.

Persimmon
Diospyros species. See Chapter Three, page 96.

Phellodendron amurense
American cork tree
Deciduous tree that grows to 50 feet. Maintain central leader to 6 to 8 feet. Strong scaffolds usually take over above that height. Easy to train. Little pruning required.

Philadelphus species
Mock orange
Deciduous shrubs that flower on laterals of growth produced previous season. Encourage strong growth by thinning after bloom, removing some of the flower-bearing wood. After a branch is 4 or 5 year's old, head to ground level. On more vigorous specimens, half of stems may be cut to ground.

Philodendron species
Philodendron
Evergreen shrubs and vines that tend to become too tall. Allow to cascade downward from a high pot or gradually weight down the end. This forces the plant to bend over and grow down or horizontally. Can be cut back to base.

Phormium tenax
New Zealand flax
Clumping evergreen perennial. Cut off dead or sunburned leaves close to ground periodically. Clumps may be thinned by removing some leaves or by division in the spring.

Photonia species
Photinia
Evergreen or deciduous, grown as shrubs or small trees. Valued for bright-red young foliage. Fast grower that sprouts from old wood if pruned hard for containment or renewal. Useful in hedges and screens, or as small, single-stemmed trees. Attractive when sheared several times a season because they continue to produce new, bright-red foliage.

Picea species
The spruces
Evergreens. Grow as individual specimen trees with a central leader and little or no pruning. Must receive plenty of sunlight.

Pinus species
Pines
Most are trees, many are centuries old. Some pines are large shrubs. Others are small and slow-growing. Most pines look best if trained to a central leader. Don't prune into old wood because there are no latent buds to sprout. By exposing the trunk and inner portions of limbs and by bending limbs to give an uneven form, a young pine can be made to look old and weathered.

Pistacia vera
Pistachio
Deciduous tree that grows to 60 feet. Train to modified central leader with well-spaced, lateral branches. Stake tree for first 2 or 3 years. Develop 3 to 5 main leaders with first one about 4 feet above ground. Develop others at about 1-foot intervals. Pinch off undesired growth first few years. Avoid large wounds, because they heal slowly. Tree bears on wood formed the previous year. Slow-growing, so little pruning is required to contain. Male tree is vigorous and may need more pruning. Male trees are necessary to pollinize female tree. See Chapter Three, page 96.

Pittosporum species
Pittosporum
Evergreen trees and shrubs. Train and prune as hedges or as single- or multiple-trunked trees. Hedge several times annually or train into less formal tree. Direct growth by thinning and cutting underneath overlapping laterals.

Platanus x acerifolia
London plane tree
Deciduous tree, can be pollarded. Train with 8 to 12 feet of clear trunk on leader. Retain larger scaffold limbs for display of attractive bark.

Plantanus occidentalis
Eastern sycamore
Deciduous tree. Train with 8 to 12 feet of clear trunk. Keep large scaffold branches to display bark. Can be pollarded.

Pinus species

Platanus racemosa
California sycamore
Deciduous. Can be trained single- or multiple-trunked. Easily trained to interesting trunk forms. Withstands, but does not require heavy pruning.

Plumbago auriculata
Cape leadwort
Semievergreen, can be trained as shrub or vine. For shrub, head to stimulate branching. Thin all side branches to develop a vine. Because most bloom is on younger wood, thin out old wood deep into center of bush to stimulate new growth. Removal of oldest 1/3 of all wood results in more and larger blooms.

Plums, Prunes
Prunus domestica, Prunus salicina. See Chapter Three, page 97.

Podocarpus gracilior
African fern pine
Evergreen shrub or shrubby tree. Train as hedge, small shrub, or tree. Tree may be single- or multistemmed. Needs careful staking. Grows slowly. Hedges can be cut to ground and regrown. Direct growth by pinching.

Polygonum aubertii
Silver lace vine
Deciduous vine. May freeze in cold regions. Head main shoots to 3 or 4 buds on last year's growth. In spring, thin side shoots.

Pomegranate
Punica granatum. See Chapter Three, page 98.

Populus species
Poplars, Cottonwoods
Tall, columnar trees used as windbreaks. Easily trained to a central leader, but keeping water sprouts off trunk is futile with some species. Train to develop a few strong scaffold limbs. Contain mature trees by pruning with small cuts. Trees bleed if pruned in spring. Spreads by root suckers.

Potentilla fruticosa
Shrubby cinquefoil
Deciduous shrub. Thin weakest growth in spring, cutting to side branch inside shrub. Remove branches that tend to form a mat underneath. Head any strong vertical risers from center to maintain overall shape.

Pittosporum species

Prunus avium
Cherry, sweet
See Chapter Three, page 82.

Prunus caroliniana
Cherry laurel
Large deciduous shrub or small tree. Train to single leader at 8 to 10 feet. Develop several strong scaffold limbs.

Prunus cerasifera
Cherry plum, Flowering plum, Myrobalan plum
Deciduous tree. Train to 3 leaders as described for plums in Chapter Three, page 97. Remove suckers and water sprouts annually.

Prunus cerasus
Cherry, sour
See Chapter Three, page 80.

Prunus domestica, Prunus salicina
Plums, Prunes
See Chapter Three, page 97.

Prunus dulcis
Almond
See Chapter Three, page 72.

Prunus ilicifolia
Holly-leaved cherry
Evergreen. Forms a small tree or can be used as hedge or screen. Prune anytime.

Prunus laurocerasus
English laurel, Cherry laurel
Fast-growing, dense, large-leafed evergreen shrub. Produces black berries that are spread by birds. Used as screen or hedge between properties or sections of garden. Large, overgrown specimens regenerate if pruned to old wood. Prune during growing season.

Prunus mume
Japanese apricot
Deciduous tree that grows to 20 feet. Train to 3 leaders. Prune by extensive heading after flowering. Every year, head 1/2 the shoots to 6-inch stubs. Head other shoots the following year. Regular renewal of flowering wood is essential.

Podocarpus gracilior

Prunus species

Prunus persica
Peach and Nectarine

Deciduous tree. Train with 3 leaders. Thin shoots lightly every year, especially in tree tops. This keeps tree flowering abundantly. See Chapter Three, page 91.

Prunus salicina
Japanese plum

See Chapter Three, page 73.

Prunus serrulata
Japanese flowering cherry

Small deciduous tree. Head erect types 1-1/2 to 2 feet above ground. Let numerous scaffold limbs develop. Develop a few strong scaffolds on spreading types. Remove lower branches for canopy effect. Little pruning is required in mature trees except for containment or to remove diseased limbs and deadwood.

Pseudolarix
Golden larch

Deciduous tree with wide-spreading branches. Grows to 50 feet or more. Train to central leader. Requires little other pruning.

Psuedotsuga menzieii
Douglas fir

Large timber species of the Pacific Northwest. It may grow 75 feet tall, but it is also grown as a Christmas tree with a pyramidal form. Prune by shearing shoots during growing season. Maintain a central leader. Entire limbs may be removed for thinning purposes.

Psidium cattleianum
Yellow strawberry

Small evergreen effective as a single- or multiple-stemmed small tree. The shrub form may be used as informal hedge or screen. Stems that are too tall can be cut to ground or headed to stimulate bushiness. Thin branches to irregular pattern to develop pleasing, informal effect.

Punica granatum
Pomegranate

See Chapter Three, page 98.

Pyracantha species
Firethorn

Evergreen shrubs that are prized for red berries displayed against deep green foliage in fall and winter. Berries grow on wood formed previous season. Some species are prostrate ground covers and require pruning to confine them. Remove occasional upright shoots.

Because they are compact and fairly slow-growing, pyracantha make attractive espaliers. They are also effective when grown as specimen shrubs in more natural landscapes. They require little pruning.

Pyracantha may be sheared, but this can greatly reduce production of berries. For maximum berry production, remove wood that has fruited by thinning to well-placed shoots. Pinch shoots just outside the outermost flower clusters to control growth.

Pyrostegia venusta
Flame vine

Evergreen vine that climbs by tendrils, reaching 20 feet in length. Prune to contain.

Pyrus communis
Pear

Central-leader training is best for this deciduous tree. Training to 3 leaders is also appropriate. Prune to lighten branch ends as needed to counteract floppyness of young trees. See Chapter Three, page 99.

Pyrus kawakamii
Evergreen pear

Evergreen that can be pruned as a shrub or a tree; easily grown as an espalier. It requires staking when trained as tree. Develop a central leader to 3 or 4 feet, then 3 leaders. Head leaders to upright shoots to counteract floppyness. Head shoots hard after bloom to stiffen young tree. Prune in summer to remove shoots killed by fire blight. Cut a foot below lowest diseased part. Dispose of prunings. Sterilize tools with alcohol.

Q

Quercus species
Oaks

This large genus has many species, both evergreen and deciduous. They are known for strong wood that is resistant to breakage. Most require minimal training and little pruning.

Quercus agrifolia
California live oak

Round-head evergreen that spreads wide and grows to 70 feet or more. Pinch back extra twigs on young tree to increase growth. Select wide-angled scaffold branches 10 to 12 feet above ground. If mildew appears, prune and dispose of mildewed branches.

Quercus palustris
Pin oak, Spanish oak

Tall, deciduous tree. Carefully train central leader, selecting scaffold limbs at 8 to 12 feet.

Quillaja saponaria
Soap-bark tree

Evergreen tree, train to multiple trunk. Thin to reduce bushiness.

Pyracantha species

Quercus species

Quince

Cydonia oblonga. See Chapter Three, page 98.

R——————————————————————

Raphiolepis indica
Indian hawthorn

Slow-growing, leathery-leaved evergreen shrub. Requires little pruning. Pinch lightly to direct growth. Occasional removal of rootstock suckers may be required.

Raspberries, Blackberries

Rubus species. See Chapter Three, page 77.

Rhamnus alaternus
Italian buckthorn

Evergreen shrub, maintained with little pruning. Useful as hedge or small tree.

Rhamnus californica
Coffeeberry

Evergreen shrub. Requires little pruning. Head or thin uprights.

Rhamnus crocea
Redberry

Small evergreen shrub that withstands heavy shearing.

Rhamnus frangula
Alder buckthorn

Deciduous shrub or small tree. Train as desired during dormant period. Suitable for use as a hedge. Prune to improve appearance or for containment at any time.

Rhododendron species
Rhododendrons

See Chapter Six, page 127.

Rhus typhina
Staghorn sumac

Deciduous shrub or small tree that grows to 25 feet. Train with short, clear stem when young. Prune in spring to remove weak, crossing or unattractive branches.

Ribes species
Currants, Gooseberries

This large genus of deciduous shrubs includes currants and gooseberries. They grow as bushes with many stems originating from below ground. *Ribes* flower on wood formed previous season. If desired, whole shoots may be cut to ground for regrowth. See Chapter Three, pages 83 and 84.

Ribes sanguineum
Pink winter currant

Large, vigorous-growing deciduous bush. Prune for bouquets or flowers. Blooms on wood produced previous season.

Ribes viburnifolium
Catalina perfume

Evergreen currant. Usually a low-spreading border plant, ground cover or trailing shrub. Preserve spreading habit by moderate pruning to contain or remove uprights.

Robinia pseudoacacia
Black locust

There are numerous deciduous varieties with different growth habits. Grows rapidly with brittle wood. Train to central leader. Select wide-angled scaffold limbs. Remove suckers and broken limbs in established trees.

Romneya coulteri
California tree poppy

Perennial. Top dies back and should be cut nearly to ground each year. Prune roots to contain.

Rosa species
Roses
See Chapter Four, page 101.

Rosmarinus officinalis
Rosemary
Evergreen shrub or herb that regrows strongly after pruning. Head shoots after bloom to stimulate new growth. Pinch young plants to control growth. Thin older plants. Use as hedge.

Rubus species
Blackberry, Black raspberry, Red raspberry
See Chapter Three, page 77.

S

Salix species
Willows
Deciduous trees and shrubs that have two basic types, weeping and erect. Weeping species are used as ornamentals. Some species form central leaders. Others form a spreading head with wide-angled branching. It is difficult to maintain dominance of the leader. Certain species require careful leader selection, staking and training. Most should have scaffold limbs developed 12 to 15 feet up, with gradual removal of all lower limbs on leader.

Salix babylonica 'Aurea'
Golden weeping willow
Stake main stem to 15 to 18 feet. Gradually remove side branches and direct growth into scaffold limbs originating up high. Prune older trees as required to balance top and prevent breakage of over-extended limbs.

Sambucus species
Elderberry
Fast-growing, small, deciduous trees. Train with multiple trunks. Remove lower limbs to create an attractive clump. Thin as required to improve appearance.

Santolina chamaecyparissus
Lavender cotton
Small evergreen hedge or ground cover. Shear in early spring and late summer.

Sapium sebiferum
Chinese tallow tree
Deciduous tree. Train to single trunk and remove suckers. Prune as required to improve shape.

Salix species

Sarcococca species
Sweet box
Small, compact, evergreen shrubs that require little pruning. Remove dead limbs at the ground or strong side limbs. Sprouts from roots.

Sassafras albidum
Sassafras
Deciduous tree that is trained to central leader. Retain the leader through crown as long as possible. Remove branches up to 6 or 8 feet to display furrowed bark. Roots tend to sucker.

Schinus molle
California pepper tree
Evergreen tree that grows to 40 feet. Train central lead high enough to accommodate people or traffic under it. Prune in spring, but avoid cuts of over 4 inches in diameter because it bleeds and the wood rots easily. Lightly thin branches annually.

Sciadopitys verticillata
Umbrella pine
Evergreen tree that can be trained to many forms, including bonsai. Thin branches to create impression of old, withered tree.

Semele androgyna
Climbing butcher's-broom
Vine that grows to 50 feet in length. Remove deadwood and thin.

Senecio cineraria
Dusty-miller
Small, shrubby perennial. Old wood tends to become leggy and brittle. Head close to ground level in spring to stimulate production of abundant new foliage.

Sequoia sempervirens
Coast redwood
Rapid-growing, gigantic evergreen tree that grows to 100 feet or more. Remove suckers around base, but otherwise don't prune. Suckers regenerate if cut back to ground.

Sequoiadendron giganteum
Giant redwood, Big tree
Gigantic evergreen tree that grows to 250 feet or more. Extremely large trunk. Pyramidal trees are sometimes used for hedges or screens when young, but they soon become too big.

Simmondsia chinensis
Jojoba, Goat nut
Slow-growing evergreen shrub adapted to arid areas. It grows to 6 feet. Requires little pruning or training, but withstands shearing. Makes attractive 4- to 6-foot hedge.

Skimmia japonica
Japanese skimmia
Slow-growing evergreen. Plants are male or female. Groups of shrubs are valued for beautiful leaves, flowers and fruit. Prune to remove deadwood in summer.

Solandra guttata
Cup-of-gold plant
Evergreen shrub. Head to promote branching and flowering.

Sequoia sempervirens

Solanum rantonnetii
Blue potato bush

Evergreen or deciduous shrub that can be staked and trained as tree. It is rangy and sprawling, requiring annual heading and pinching to keep compact outline. Head to ground level in early spring for strong growth and large flowers.

Sollya fusiformis
Australian bluebell creeper

Evergreen grown as a ground cover because of low, vine-like growth habit. With support, it can climb to 8 feet. Regular pinching is required if grown as shrub.

Sophora japonica
Japanese pagoda tree, Chinese scholar tree

Deciduous tree, grows to 20 feet. Retain leader as long as possible or until it reaches 6 to 8 feet. This reduces competition from lower laterals. Bleeds heavily, so prune in late summer. Lower limbs weep extensively. Best used as specimen.

Sorbus aucuparia
European mountain ash

Deciduous tree. Train with a central leader. Fast growing, it benefits from staking. Can also be grown with multiple trunks without staking. Avoid narrow crotches for scaffolds.

Sparmannia africana
African hemp

Evergreen shrub or tree that tends to grow wild and rangy unless thinned and headed.

Spiraea japonica
Japanese spirea

Spreading, deciduous shrub that produces blooms in spring. Blooms best on young wood formed previous season. Some types bloom on current-season's wood and spread by suckers. Improve by severe pruning in spring. Head old stems back to ground or strong side branch just after flowers have dropped.

Stauntonia hexaphylla

Evergreen vine, woody climber. Train to trellis and thin after bloom in spring.

Sophora japonica

Stenocarpus sinuatus
Firewheel tree

Evergreen tree that grows to 30 feet tall, 15 feet wide. Training required, but no pruning

Stephanandra species

Deciduous shrubs prized for brilliant color of bare young shoots in winter. Thin old growth to vigorous side branches or remove after flowering. Shrubs push up vigorous new shoots from below ground annually.

Stewartia species

Slow-growing, deciduous species. May be shrubs or trees. Should not be pruned for training. Small branches close to ground may be removed in spring after danger of frost. Do not prune for containment because this ruins shape.

Stigmaphyllon ciliatum
Orchid vine

Woody vines are evergreen. Prune to contain.

Strawberries
Fragaria x Ananassa

Strawberries don't require pruning. It is helpful to remove some or all runners unless wanted for new plants. In Pacific Northwest, they are cropped once a year. Disease control may be aided by pruning all leaves immediately after harvest. Healthy new foliage regenerates by late summer.

Strelitzia reginae
Bird-of-paradise

Evergreen perennial. Remove dead and injured leaves. If main stalk becomes excessively tall, remove it and allow replacement by suckers from base.

Styrax japonica
Japanese snowbell

Deciduous tree. Train to single leader by pinching side limbs. Do little pruning afterward.

Styrax obassia
Fragrant snowbell

Deciduous tree that grows to 30 feet. Train to single leader. Some thinning may be required to protect against strong winds.

Symphoricarpos species
Snowberry

Deciduous shrubs that spread by underground stems, forming an invasive thicket. Prune to remove deadwood or confine. Prune underground stems with sharp shovel.

Syringa vulgaris
Common lilac

Large deciduous shrub that may reach to 15 to 20 feet. Blooms in spring on wood produced previous summer. Remove flowers after bloom by heading just above small developing shoots. These shoots form next year's flower buds. Remove suckers arising from below ground. Rejuvenate old plants by removing up to 1/3 of oldest wood. Cut to vigorous side branches where possible. To shape and stimulate new growth, plants may be thinned or headed, or both, in early spring. This results in some loss of flowers.

Syringa vulgaris

Syzygium paniculatum
Australian brush cherry

Evergreen tree. Regrows well following severe pruning. Responds well to shearing. Can be trained as small tree or as an espalier. Needs sturdy stake in early years to train as tree.

T

Tabebuia chrysotricha
Golden trumpet tree

Evergreen tree, briefly deciduous. Rounded, spreading, growth habit. Stake and develop central leader at 6 to 8 feet. Annual pruning after bloom is required for shaping, removal of wayward branches.

Taxodium distichum
Bald cypress

Tall evergreen tree, generally grown with central leader. Often reaches 100 feet or more with buttressed trunk. Train to central leader. Remove low limbs when required. Usually needs no other pruning.

Taxus species
Common yew

Includes 8 species of evergreen trees and shrubs, some growing to 50 feet. Use as individual shrubs or hedge. With shearing, yews quickly form tight hedges or shrubs with precise geometric shapes. Less formal look can be obtained by cutting at various distances from base of the plant. Whole branches may be removed from center.

Badly overgrown specimens may be pruned severely in spring. The best time to trim yew hedges is in late summer. Varieties with erect, clustered limbs can be held to a tight form by tying limbs together. Subsequent growth covers ties.

Tecomaria capensis
Cape honeysuckle

Evergreen vine or shrub that needs support. To develop as shrub, head frequently during growing season. Otherwise, let sprawl.

Teucrium chamaedrys
Germander

Evergreen vine often used as ground cover. Regrows well following spring pruning. Large specimens may be sheared.

Teucrium fruticans
Germander tree

Evergreen shrub or small tree. Produces large purple flowers on branches. Framework tends to be bare and leggy. Train young plants to be more bushy by pinching during summer. Head lightly after each bloom cycle and thin or head as required after spring frost has passed.

Thuja species
Arborvitae

There are many varieties of evergreen arborvitae, including dwarf shrubs and trees over 150 feet high. Frequently used as individual specimen shrubs or in hedges. For hedges, keep leader and allow to grow 6 to 12 inches above intended height of hedge. Then cut back to about 6 inches below this height. Shear laterals when they reach intended height.

Thunbergia grandiflora
Blue trumpet vine

Large, evergreen, climbing vine. Regrows quickly after freeze. Train to trellis or building. Prune to contain this vigorous vine to allotted space.

Tilia americana
American linden, Basswood
See Tilia cordata, below.

Tilia cordata
Small-leaved European linden

T. americana grows more rapidly than *T. cordata*. Train both to central leader as high as necessary to clear people. Select widely spaced scaffolds. Older trees may need occasional pruning to remove deadwood.

Torreya californica
California nutmeg

Small evergreen tree resembles the yew. It has a pyramidal growth habit and grows to 45 feet. Sprouts from stumps. Carefully stake and train leader to avoid losing the leader to laterals, a development that would spoil symmetry. Prune to contain.

Trachelospermum jasminoides
Star jasmine

Evergreen vine that must be headed 1/3 annually. Renew by heading into old framework. Train to support.

Tristania conferta
Brisbane box

Head branches of this evergreen tree to reduce weight of leaves that concentrate terminally and to stimulate branching. Thin to develop picturesque branch pattern.

Tsuga species
Hemlock

Small to medium-sized evergreen trees that often reach to 75 feet. Not suited for shrubs. Require little pruning.

U

Ulmus americana
American elm

Dutch elm disease is slowly destroying this large deciduous tree species. Remove and burn deadwood or dying wood. Root pruning may be required to protect pavement.

Ulmus parvifolia
Chinese elm

Train to central leader at 12 feet. In winter frequently thin out branches in crown to reduce wind resistance. Shorten excessively long or weeping branches.

Ulmus pumila
Siberian elm

Deciduous tree that reaches 50 feet. Train to central leader and select wide-angled crotches. Lighten branch ends through annual pruning. Remove diseased and deadwood.

Umbellularia californica
California bay, Oregon myrtle

Evergreen tree best trained to central leader. Remove low limbs and thin to reduce shading of ground level plants.

V

Vaccinium species
Blueberries

See Chapter Three, page 77.

Viburnum species
Arrowwood

Deciduous or evergreen shrubs that have characteristic stool-like growth habit. Often produces strong shoots from low on base or from lower, older branches. Healthy specimens rarely need pruning. Old or crowded plants may be thinned and shortened to bring flowers to eye level.

Vitex lucens
Pururi, New Zealand chaste tree

Evergreen tree. Train to a central leader up to 10 feet, then develop well-spaced scaffold limbs. Little pruning required other than removal of weak or damaged wood.

Vitis species
Grapes

See Chapter Three, page 85.

W

Walnuts
Juglans species

See Chapter Three, page 98.

Wisteria floribunda
Japanese wisteria

See *Wisteria sinensis*, below.

Wisteria sinensis
Chinese wisteria

Deciduous wisteria may be trained as vine or a small tree. Wisteria climbs by twisting around supports. Grow over a trellis, against a wall, or on a building. Long side arms require supports to hold weight. May be slow to bloom unless grown on special dwarfing rootstock.

When training leaders on wall or trellis, try to keep them separated. Otherwise, they twist around each other. It is almost impossible to separate them later. Head laterals that arise from scaffolds to about 6 inches in

Wisteria sinensis

midsummer. Shorten to 2 buds in midwinter.

When trained as a small tree, side branches need permanent props for support. They have an attractive, gnarled, twisted appearance. Prune in summer and winter.

Japanese and Chinese wisteria are pruned the same way, except pruning helps to increase flower-cluster size of Chinese wisteria.

X

Xylosma congestum
Xylosma

Evergreen or partly deciduous shrub or small tree. Quickly sprouts new growth after heavy pruning. Training and pruning methods depend on objective—compact shrub, small tree or clump with interesting-shaped framework and bushy crown. Thin weak branches, examining effect as you proceed, until branch structure is revealed. Stake and train to central leader to develop tree.

Z

Zauschneria californica
California fuchsia

Rangy perennial herb or shrub with invasive root system that grows to 6 feet. Head to about 5 inches above ground in fall to contain. Remove deadwood in spring.

Zelkova serrata
Japanese zelkova

Large, deciduous shade tree. Train central lead to at least 6 to 8 feet. Select scaffold limbs with wide-angle crotches, well-spaced along leader. Thin during dormant season to favor strongest laterals. Head long scaffolds to stiffen.

Ziziphus jujuba
Common jujube, Chinese date

Deciduous tree that grows to 30 feet. Train to multiple leader with 3 or 4 scaffold limbs. Prune during dormant season for containment. Remove suckers.

Glossary of Terms

A

Acclimation—The ability of a perennial plant to become accustomed to changes in climate or seasonal temperature. Involves complex physical and chemical changes.

Adventitious Buds—Growth buds that appear in locations where they are not ordinarily expected. Adventitious buds usually appear after an injury or pruning. Suckers and the shoots that arise from pollarding trees are examples.

Apical Bud—The tip of a growing shoot. Sometimes called the *terminal bud.*

Apical Dominance—The inhibiting by the apical bud of the development of dormant buds below the apical bud. Initiated by the hormone *auxin.*

Auxin—A hormonal chemical produced by plants. Auxin plays an important role in apical dominance.

Axil—The angle between the leaf stalk and the stem.

Axillary Bud—The bud located between the leaf and the stem.

Axillary Shoot—A shoot that grows from the bud located between the leaf and the stem.

B

Bark—The outside covering of the stems and roots of trees and woody plants.

Basal—The part of the trunk or branch nearest the base, as in basal shoots, basal growth or basal leaves.

Bench Cutting—To spread a tree by heading the leaders to outward growing shoots. It creates a benchlike appearance.

Bonsai—The art and science of dwarfing and shaping trees and shrubs in shallow pots by pruning and controlled fertilization.

Bract—A modified leaf, growing at the base of a flower or on the stalk. Bracts can be large and attractive. Examples are poinsettia and dogwood.

Branch Point—The point on a tree or shrub where a secondary limb grows out from a primary limb.

Break—Pruning back to an *axillary bud.* The subsequent development of lateral shoots.

Bud—A small swelling or projection on a plant. The shoots, leaf clusters or flowers that develop from the buds.

C

Callus—The protective layer of tree cells that form over a wound.

Cambium—A layer of living cells beneath the bark on woody plants.

Candle—The new terminal growth on a pine. Needles emerge from these candlelike projections.

Cane—A vigorous stem on a rose, raspberry or similar plant.

Central Leader—The trunk or central stem of a plant.

Compound Bud—A bud that contains both leaf and flower primordia. Under ordinary conditions, a leaf *or* a flower will develop.

Conifer, Coniferous—Any of the cone-bearing trees and shrubs, mostly evergreens. Bearing cones.

Crotch—The angle between the trunk or large branch and secondary branch.

Current Growth—The shoots that grow from this year's buds.

Cutting—A stem section that forms adventitious roots for propagation or for insertion at a graft point. Sometimes called a *slip.*

D

Dead Head—Removing the spent flower or unripe seed pods from a plant such as a rhododendron.

Deciduous—Refers to the shedding of all or nearly all foliage each year; not evergreen.

Dehorn—In pruning, this means the removal of large branches in the top of a tree or shrub. Considered a rejuvenating process. Usually reserved for trees that have been neglected.

Dieback—A disease of vascular plants. Characterized by the tips of twigs and branches dying backwards towards the main part of the tree. Caused by parasites and low moisture.

Disbud—The removal of surplus buds or shoots before they develop, usually by pinching.

Dog-Leg—Sharp curve or bend in a branch. Usually considered unattractive and should be removed.

Dormant—The period of little or no growth in a plant. Usually during the coldest seasons or winter months.

Drop-Crotching—A method of pruning large trees. The main branch or leader is removed by cutting it back to a lower crotch. This lowers the height of the tree.

Dwarf—A plant that is much smaller than normal plants of the same species. Pruning creates a dwarfing effect in plants. This is because the amount of regrowth that occurs after pruning never equals the amount of plant material removed and the growth that would have been produced by the removed material.

E

Espalier—To train a tree to grow flat against a fence or wall, usually in a regular pattern.

Everbearing—Produces flowers, fruit or leaves throughout the year, or every season.

Evergreen—A plant that has green, functioning leaves throughout the year. Opposite of deciduous plants. Examples include conifers, rhododendrons and holly.

F

Feeder Roots—Extensive network of subterranean roots that absorb and store nutrients and water from the soil.

Flower Bud—The plant bud that produces one or more flowers.

Force—To cause the branches or shoots of a plant to develop or grow faster or change direction. Forcing is done by selective pruning of other buds or branches.

Formal—An orderly or regular arrangement of plants in a garden. Includes smooth, precise shearing and pruning of shrubs and hedges to achieve symmetry and balance.

G

Girdle—The process of completely removing bark from around a trunk or branch. Used in grape production to produce bigger, sweeter fruit.

Grafting—A means of propagating where the stem or bud of one plant is induced to grow and become part of another plant.

Growth Habit—Refers to the genetic commitment of a plant to grow tall or short, wide or narrow, weeping or upright.

H

Hardiness—The ability of a plant to withstand temperature extremes of cold. A tolerance of frost or freezes.

Head Back, Heading—Cutting back of limbs, branches or buds to reduce the size of a tree.

Head Height—The maximum height where a young tree should be headed to produce the primary scaffold limbs.

Heartwood—The oldest, non-living wood at the center of the trunk. Part of the xylem.

Hedge, Hedgerow—A planted row of trees or shrubs of the same species. Hedges can grow naturally or be sheared to produce a solid screen.

Hill—The small pile or mound of soil that is piled around the roots and base of plants. Also refers to plants rooted in that pile. Term used in planting of fruiting vines.

Hormone—A chemical substance produced by plants and distributed throughout plants.

I

Inclusion—A wounded area of a plant that has been covered by callus growth.

Informal—Growing in a natural shape or form. Pruning emphasizes and helps plants assume flowing, uneven forms. Opposite of formal.

Inhibitor—A chemical substance that slows or prevents growth in plants.

Inner Bark—Generally referred to as the *phloem.* This is the live tissue next to the bark that carries food and nutrients throughout plants.

Internode—The space on a stem between two nodes.

L

Latent Bud—A bud that does not develop in the season it was formed.

Lateral—A branch that is attached to, and smaller than, a larger branch or trunk. Sometimes refers to branches, buds or shoots on the side.

Lateral Bud—A side bud as distinguished from an apical bud.

Leader—A growing stem that is longer and more vigorous than any other.

Leaf—Any of the flat, thin, expanded organs that grow from the stem or twig of a plant. Leaves collect sunlight, and through photosynthesis, produce starches and sugars as food for plants.

Leaf Scar—Point on a twig where a leaf was attached. Usually visible as a thin line or thick area on nodes just under buds.

Leaf Stalks—The stalk of a leaf; the *petiole.*

Limb—Any of the larger branches on a shrub or tree.

Linear Row—Plantings in a straight row. Plant rows are uniform in width and length. Refers to fruiting vines and bushes.

M

Modified Central Leader—A pruning system used for fruiting trees. During the first years of growth, the central leader is supported and encouraged. Then the leader is suppressed to allow development of well-spaced scaffolds and wide crotch angles. Allows easy harvesting of fruits.

Modified Leader—See Modified Central Leader.

N

Node—The point on a stem where leaves branch out.

O

Open Center—A pruning technique for fruit trees. The center is left open and free of main branches. Makes treatment with chemical sprays and harvesting easier. Called *vase pruning.*

P

Perennial—A plant that lives for three or more growing seasons.

Petiole—The stalk of a leaf.

Phloem—The vascular tissue that serves as a path for the distribution of food materials in a plant. Sometimes called the *inner bark*. The phloem lies between the exterior bark and the cambium.

Photosynthesis—The formation of carbohydrates, starches and sugars, from carbon dioxide and water. Photosynthesis occurs in the leaves of green plants that are exposed to sunlight.

Phototropic—Movement of part of a plant toward or away from light sources.

Pinch Back, Pinching—Pruning by cutting back the growing tip of a shoot using thumb and forefinger.

Pleach—A method of intertwining branches so they grow together to form an arbor.

Pollard—To cut back drastically to the same main branches every year. Pollarding leaves many stubs and is tolerated by only a few trees, such as sycamore and cherry.

Primary—Refers to the first occurrence or first in importance and value. In botany, the first main branches that support secondary branches and limbs. The first shoots or buds to appear. See primordial.

Primocane—A biennial shoot or cane, particularly of a bramble, during the first year of growth and before flowering.

Primordial—The earliest structures formed in the development of a plant. Examples are primordial buds or flowers.

Prune, Pruning—The removal of dead or living parts from a plant to increase fruit or flower production or to improve the plant's form

R

Root—The part of a plant below ground that lacks nodes, shoots and leaves. Roots hold plants in position, absorb water and nutrients and store food.

Root Cap—The loose cells at the tip of growing roots. Root caps are rubbed off by the movement of roots through the soil. Root caps are constantly replaced.

Root Hairs—The tiny, thin-walled, hairlike tubular outgrowths from a growing root. Root hairs absorb water and minerals from the soil.

Rootstock—In grafting, the stems and roots of the plant to which scions are grafted.

S

Sapwood—The soft, living wood between the inner bark of a tree and the heartwood. Sapwood conducts water throughout the tree. Sapwood is part of the xylem.

Scaffold, Scaffold Branches—The basic supporting structure or branches of a tree. Scaffold branches provide a strong base for secondary branches and tertiary limbs. Usually grow from the main trunk or large branches.

Scale—A small, modified leaf that protects a bud.

Scion—The bud or stem of the desired plant that is grafted on rootstock.

Screen—A row of trees or shrubs used for privacy or concealment.

Secondary Branches—Branches that form and grow from primary branches. Usually appear during the second growing season.

Shear, Shearing—Pruning method used to remove excess growth from shrubs and hedges. Shearing produces a smooth, straight surface.

Shoot—A terminal stem and its leaves.

Skeletonize—Severe pruning operation that removes all extra limbs and branches from a tree or shrub. It leaves nothing but a basic skeleton.

Spur—The system of short, slow-growing branches that carries flower buds and fruit.

Spreaders—Mechanical devices, usually boards with notched ends, used to force or spread primary scaffold limbs away from the trunk. Used to produce wider, stronger crotch angles.

Stake—Long wooden or metal poles used to support young trees, shrubs and vines.

Stamen, Staminate—The pollen-bearing organ of a flower.

Stem—The trunk or main support of a plant or tree. Also refers to the small branches that bear flowers and fruit.

Stub, Stubbing—The stump of a limb or branch that remains between a pruning cut and a node on a tree or plant. Also means to cut off a limb, leaving only a short stump.

Suberin—A waxy or fatty substance contained in cork.

Sucker—Usually refers to the unwanted shoots arising from adventitious buds or the rootstock in grafted plants.

T

Terminal, Terminally—The end or apex of a branch, shoot or bud. Positioned at the end of a branch or shoot.

Tertiary—Referring to the third or final stage of occurrence. In plants, the third level of branching. Usually means the terminal branches or limbs, as opposed to the primary or secondary branches.

Thinning—Reducing the number of shoots on a branch system to eliminate the effects of overcrowding, improving air circulation and light penetration to inner leaves.

Tip-Prune—Cutting or pinching back the growing tips to promote bushier side growth.

Topiary—Shaping a tree or bush into a dense unnatural form, usually an animal or geometric shape.

Topping—A drastic pruning procedure that removes the top of a tree.

Trellis—A structure made of thin strips of wood crossing each other. Used to support climbing vines.

Trunk—The main stem or supporting structure of a tree.

Truss—A cluster of flowers or fruit.

U

Underwriters' Laboratories, Inc.—The Underwriters' Laboratories, Inc., referred to as UL, is an independent non-profit organization. Its purpose is "to establish, maintain and operate laboratories for the investigation of materials, devices, products, equipment, construction methods and systems with regard to hazards affecting life and property." The Underwriters' Laboratories tests a product under extreme conditions. If the product passes minimum safety requirements, the product is "Listed by UL."

V

Vascular—Refers to the specialized conducting tissue of plants—the xylem and phloem. The xylem moves water and mineral salts. The phloem moves sugar and other organic substances.

Viable—Able to take root and grow. Living and growing.

W

Water Sprout—Vigorous, soft shoots that arise from buds as a result of pruning or damage to trees.

Whorl—Circular growth of branches around the growing tip.

Wind-Rocking—The loosening of a plant's root system as a result of the plant being rocked or moved by wind.

X

Xylem—The tissue of plants that conducts water and minerals.

Index